REFORM AND POLITICAL
CRISIS IN BRAZIL

Studies in Critical Social Sciences Book Series

Haymarket Books is proud to be working with Brill Academic Publishers (www.brill.nl) to republish the *Studies in Critical Social Sciences* book series in paperback editions. This peer-reviewed book series offers insights into our current reality by exploring the content and consequences of power relationships under capitalism, and by considering the spaces of opposition and resistance to these changes that have been defining our new age. Our full catalog of *SCSS* volumes can be viewed at https://www.haymarketbooks.org/series_collections/4-studies-in-critical-social-sciences.

REFORM AND POLITICAL CRISIS IN BRAZIL

Class Conflicts in Workers' Party Governments
and the Rise of Bolsonaro Neo-fascism

ARMANDO BOITO

TRANSLATED BY
ANGELA TESHEINER
LENITA M. R. PISETTA

Haymarket Books
Chicago, IL

First published in 2022 by Brill Academic Publishers, The Netherlands
© 2022 Koninklijke Brill NV, Leiden, The Netherlands

Published in paperback in 2023 by
Haymarket Books
P.O. Box 180165
Chicago, IL 60618
773-583-7884
www.haymarketbooks.org

ISBN: 978-1-64259-807-0

Distributed to the trade in the US through Consortium Book Sales and
Distribution (www.cbsd.com) and internationally through Ingram Publisher
Services International (www.ingramcontent.com).

This book was published with the generous support of Lannan Foundation and
Wallace Action Fund.

Special discounts are available for bulk purchases by organizations and
institutions. Please call 773-583-7884 or email info@haymarketbooks.org for more
information.

Cover design by Jamie Kerry and Ragina Johnson.

Printed in the United States.

10 9 8 7 6 5 4 3 2 1

Library of Congress Cataloging-in-Publication data is available.

This book is dedicated to my grandson Leonardo, who will live his youth in the challenging 21st century

⁖

Contents

PART 2
The Nature and Dynamics of the Crisis that Led to the
Impeachment

Preface to the English Edition

In this preface, I intend to offer the reader who is not closely acquainted with Brazilian politics some factual information to facilitate reading this book; I present its themes, clarify the theoretical approach adopted, and, finally, explain the conditions of production of the research from which this book originates. This is a revised and expanded version of my work published in Brazil in 2018, *Reforma e crise política no Brasil – os conflitos de classe nos governos do PT*. Campinas and São Paulo: Editora Unicamp and Editora Unesp.

I

A serious political crisis shook Brazil in 2015–2016 and, since then, the country plunged into a deep economic crisis, has been facing an accelerated deterioration of the popular classes' living standards, and sees its democracy threatened. That political crisis triggered a dynamic that, first, caused the deposition of the president elected in 2014 – Dilma Rousseff of the Workers' Party (PT) – through a fraudulent impeachment process, and then led the country to an extreme right-wing government, headed by President Jair Bolsonaro. As we will see in this book, this government combines a new type of fascism with the economic and social policy of neoliberalism. This crisis should be analyzed in light of the more general context of contemporary events in Latin America, but before we do so, let us try to see it more closely.

Dilma Rousseff had been elected for a second presidential term in October 2014, and her election campaign was based on a discourse that criticized neoliberalism and, particularly, financial capital and its demands for a restrictive fiscal policy that was contrary to economic growth. The Brazilian Social Democracy Party (PSDB) – which, despite its name, never had anything to do with social democracy and was, in fact, the vanguard of neoliberalism in Brazil – did not accept the result of the polls. This was the fourth consecutive time the PSDB was beaten in the presidential elections. It had been defeated by the PT of Lula da Silva and Dilma Rousseff in 2002, 2006, 2010, and again in 2014. This seemed to be too much for the party, which decided to break with the democratic game. The PSDB went to court trying to prevent Dilma from taking office, to no avail (see Table 1 for a history of the political parties in government).

That would have been the end of it, had it not been for the fact that, stimulated by the behavior of the PSDB and the mainstream press, the upper fraction of the Brazilian middle class started to promote in 2015 massive street

TABLE 1   Brazilian governments – 1995–2021*

Governments	Political characterization	Social, economic, foreign, and citizenship policy
1995–2002 – President Fernando Henrique Cardoso (Brazilian Social Democracy Party – PSDB) Fernando Henrique is a well-known intellectual who, in the distant past, had defended left ideologies. His party, the PSDB, was the vanguard of neoliberalism in Brazil.	Two presidential terms – each of four years, as determined by law. Dismantling of the developmentalist state and installation of the neoliberal capitalist model.	Minimal state, privatizations, trade liberalization, denationalization, curtailment of social rights. Foreign policy of subordination to the United States. Sale to private capital of dozens of large state-owned companies. Reduction by half of the average customs tariff. End of the legislation that required the general readjustment of wages according to the inflation accumulated in the previous year.
2003–2010 – President Lula da Silva (Workers' Party – PT) Lula da Silva was a metalworker and trade unionist. His party was created in 1980 by the workers' union movement and the progressive fraction of the middle class. Since the late 1990s, it has become a center-left party which the right and the far-right consider their main enemy.	Two presidential terms – each of four years, as determined by law. Moderate changes in social, economic, foreign, and citizenship policy. Maintenance of the neoliberal capitalist economic model.	Neodevelopmentalism: State intervention in the economy to stimulate growth and reduce poverty. Foreign policy in conflict with the U.S. policy. Political recognition of the black, feminist, indigenous, and LGBT movements. Government strongly opposed by the mainstream press, as well as by the neoliberal right and far-right. Lula da Silva concludes his second term with record popular approval.

TABLE 1   Brazilian governments – 1995–2021 *(cont.)*

Governments	Political characterization	Social, economic, foreign, and citizenship policy
2011–2016 – President Dilma Rousseff (Workers' Party – PT) Economist belonging to the ECLAC's developmentalist tradition. First woman to become president of Brazil.	Two presidential terms – the second having been cut short when she was impeached. Her policy was a kind of "neodevelopmentalism of crisis," with successive advances and retreats in the socioeconomic policy.	Maintenance of the main points of Lula's government policy, but with concessions to neoliberal fiscal policy. Strong defense of and initiative for the formation of the BRICS. Extension of labor rights to domestic workers, breaking with the tradition of wealthy Brazilian families to treat them as servants. Measures in favor of the black, feminist, indigenous, and LGBT movements.
2016–2018 – President Michel Temer (Brazilian Democratic Movement – MDB) Notoriously corrupt politician belonging to a large conservative party with cronyist practices. He was Vice-President to Dilma Rousseff.	Government created by the impeachment coup. Completed the remaining time of Dilma Rousseff's second term. Return to neoliberal politics, now in even more extreme terms.	New privatizations, denationalization of companies, radical neoliberal reform of labor law and the public budget – actual freeze on public spending for a period of twenty years.
2019–2022 – President Jair Bolsonaro (Liberal Social Party – PSL – currently unaffiliated to any party) A far-right politician, he is a retired Army captain. He publicly	In office since January 1, 2019. Neoliberalism in economic and social policy, and neo-fascist stance towards democratic rights. Bolsonaro has militarized his	Neoliberal Social Security reform, new measures against labor law, measures against indigenous peoples, suspension of environmental protection initiatives, passive subordination to the United

TABLE 1   Brazilian governments – 1995–2021 (*cont.*)

Governments	Political characterization	Social, economic, foreign, and citizenship policy
defends the return of Brazil's military dictatorship, the use of torture against left-wing politicians, and the relaxation of legal regulations to allow big landowners the use of firearms against peasants and indigenous people.	government: he has appointed about nine thousand Armed Forces officers to his cabinet and other senior public positions traditionally held by civilians.	States' foreign policy, and aggressive stances against China and the Arab world in the international arena. Anti-communist and anti-democratic discourse, also hostile to the black, feminist, indigenous, and LGBT movements. During the first half of 2020, Jair Bolsonaro spoke at several street demonstrations calling for the closure of the National Congress and the Supreme Federal Court.

* *Observation.* Brazil is a presidential democracy. The President of the Republic accumulates the positions of head of state and head of government, and has a fixed term of office of four years, maintained even if the government does not have or comes to lose the majority in the National Congress. Furthermore, Brazilian presidentialism has authoritarian characteristics. The National Congress is of minor importance. The presidents tend to abuse their prerogative to issue the so-called Provisional Measures, which do not require the approval of the Legislative Branch to come into force. In theory, the National Congress can later revoke such measures, but it is very difficult to achieve that in practice.

demonstrations whose manifest objective was the fight "against corruption," and whose latent objective, although initially surreptitious, was the deposition of the elected president. The protesters were actively instigated by a large, highly politicized judicial operation, called "Operation Car Wash" (*Operação Lava-Jato*), which had uncovered corrupt practices among politicians from several parties, including the PT, and businessmen who provided equipment and services to the Brazilian oil giant – Petrobras. The prosecutors and the judge who worked on Operation Car Wash disrespected elementary rules of the criminal procedure and passed privileged and confidential information to the mainstream press, which started a relentless campaign to stir up the people "against corruption" and against the PT government, practically calling for street demonstrations. The movement quickly changed from the alleged struggle "against corruption" to the explicit struggle for the impeachment of Dilma Rousseff.

The Brazilian bourgeoisie was divided. A substantial part of it had been opposing the PT governments since Lula da Silva's presidency (2003–2010), but another part had shown them its support. In the political crisis of 2015 and 2016, the part of the bourgeoisie that had been backing the PT governments started gradually to defect. The segments that left the government felt dissatisfied with the fall in economic growth and uncomfortable with what they considered to be the growing interventionism of the PT governments in the economy, and that is why they welcomed the PSDB's promises that, with the deposition of Dilma Rousseff, it would be possible to carry out the neoliberal reforms in the Social Welfare System and the Consolidation of Labor Laws (CLT). Rousseff's government was severely weakened and, for reasons that we will analyze in this book, the labor and popular movements did not mobilize significantly in her defense.

The forces that ousted Dilma Rousseff in August 2016 intended to carry out, shall we say, a "one-off surgical intervention." In their view, they were merely correcting a "transient shortcoming in democracy." In the 2018 presidential election, everything should have returned to normal, preferably with the PSDB assuming the Presidency of the Republic. That is not what happened, though. The events of 2018, the result of a very particular set of circumstances that we will examine in the Afterword, written especially for this English edition, caught observers and analysts of Brazilian politics by surprise. The candidacy of Jair Bolsonaro – a retired military man, an unimpressive federal representative in Congress, and a defender of the military dictatorship – proved to be much stronger than initially expected. Conversely, the candidates of the traditional big bourgeois parties, such as the PSDB, showed weak numbers in the polls. To defeat the PT candidate Fernando Haddad – Lula da Silva had been arrested and prevented from running as a result of the lawfare that victimized him – the bourgeoisie then decided to embark on the risky political move of supporting Jair Bolsonaro. The "market," as the reports in the mainstream press showed, endorsed the candidacy of the extreme right, even though the candidate was not under its control. Bolsonaro's approval rates in the polls grew sharply and steadily as the income and formal education levels of the sample subjects increased. In the middle of 2018, mainly thanks to the support of Pentecostal and Neopentecostal Christian churches, he managed to obtain electoral support among the popular classes as well and won the October election.

During the PT administrations (2003–2016), Brazil was one of the countries included in the "pink wave" of reformist governments that took over South America in the 2000s and part of the 2010s –Argentina, with Nestor and Cristina Kirchner, both of the Peronist Justicialist Party; Uruguay, with Tabaré Vázquez and José Mujica, of the Broad Front; Paraguay, with Fernando Lugo; Bolivia, with Evo Morales, of the Movement for Socialism (MAS); Ecuador, with Rafael Correa, of the PAIS Alliance; and Venezuela, with Chaves and Maduro. Since 2012, with Fernando Lugo's deposition, these governments have been thrown, one by one, into a crisis. It is inevitable to draw the connection between these political crises and the economic crisis of capitalism that began in 2008. Some of these governments were overthrown by coups d'état of a new type; others were defeated in the polls.

To understand Brazilian politics, there is something important the reader should know right from the start. Although the PT governments, as center-left governments, were included in the "pink wave" of South America, they presented a serious weakness when compared to their counterparts in the subcontinent. Brazil, like all other South American countries, is a presidential democracy. The PT's government, due to the weakness of the parliamentary representation of the left and center-left, depended on conservative parties to build a precarious support base in the National Congress. Their support base both within the party and in Congress was fragile and unstable, severely hindering the progressive reach of their policies, thus facilitating the August 2016 coup d'état. Suffice it to remember that, in the Brazilian case, it was a party belonging to the government's own allied base – in fact, its largest and most important party, since it even held the vice-presidency of the Republic – that coordinated, to the surprise of some, the fraudulent impeachment process against Dilma Rousseff. In Latin American countries whose left and center-left governments and parties hold the majority in the National Congress, the path of the coup d'état through impeachment is blocked. This is the case, for example, of Argentina, Uruguay Bolivia and Venezuela. These progressive governments had a parliamentary majority – or close to it – constituted by their own parties or, in the Uruguayan case, by an alliance of progressive parties. In fact, and contrary to the current perception that persists among Brazilian politicians and observers, the Brazilian left and center-left, including the PT, have a rather weak party organization when compared to their counterparts in the countries aforementioned. In addition, the Brazilian left and center-left have their eyes excessively focused on executive positions, and their candidates emphasize their own figure at the expense of the image of the party to which they belong, thus demonstrating the powerful influence of the populist, presidentialist, authoritarian, tradition of Brazilian politics in the bosom of the country's left and center-left.

In the early 2020s, the left and center-left have already returned to power in Argentina and Bolivia and are about to do so in Ecuador. The Brazilian situation, as we have indicated, is quite different. A new 'pink wave' is taking shape in Latin America and Brazil, this time, may be left out.

II

This book is divided into two parts, both of which analyze, over twelve texts, the Brazilian politics of the recent period. In the first part, we analyze the governments headed by the Workers' Party (PT) between 2003 and 2016. They were governments that we call neodevelopmentalists, given that they sought to stimulate economic growth and reduce poverty through state intervention in the economy, moving away from the neoliberal program and ideology of the so-called minimal state. These are the themes examined in this part: the social, economic, and foreign policies advanced by these administrations; the heterogeneous political forces that, as leading or subordinate forces, either backed the PT governments or challenged them; the clashing interests, ideologies, and political programs; the political phenomenon of "Lulism" – an expression derived from the name of former President Lula da Silva – and the insertion of different social movements, rooted in different popular segments, in the political process at the time.

In its second part, the book analyzes the various dimensions and consequences of the political crisis that resulted in the ousting of President Dilma Rousseff in August 2016 and, subsequently, the rise to power of the extreme right candidate Jair Bolsonaro in January 2019. We maintain that the dynamics of the crisis were determined, fundamentally, by the distributive conflict among classes and class fractions, and that it resulted, above all, from an offensive by the political camp that aspired to restore the neoliberal policy that had prevailed in Brazil in the 1990s. These are the topics examined in this part: the interests and objectives of the different political forces that mobilized to depose the Rousseff government; the destabilization of Brazilian democracy as a result of an impeachment process without a crime of responsibility that could justify it – a real coup d'état; the fragile resistance of the democratic and popular camp to this coup d'état; the institutional conflicts

and the politicization of the judiciary as an integral part of the political crisis; the abrupt change, immediately after the deposition of Dilma Rousseff, of
the content of the social, economic, foreign, and environmental policies of the
Brazilian state; and the circumstances that allowed the victory of candidate
Jair Bolsonaro in the 2018 presidential election. We seek to demonstrate, as we
have already indicated, that the Bolsonaro government engenders the combination, never before witnessed in the Brazilian political history, of extreme
neoliberalism and a new type of fascism.

III

The theoretical approach we have adopted, which is grounded on Marxist
political theory, seeks to detect, on the one hand, the relations among the
institutions, the political process, and the clash among parties and ideologies;
and, on the other hand, the conflicts among the different classes and class fractions present in the economy and society. Some clarifications are in order here.
First: I use the word *conflicts* and not class *struggle* because what we have in
Brazil is a dispute over the distribution of the wealth produced and not over
the organization – capitalist or socialist – of the economy and society. The
class struggle itself, the one whose main goal is to overcome capitalism, does
not exist in Brazil today. Second, it is true that distributive class conflicts are
not the only conflicts that determine the conduction of Brazilian politics. The
struggles of women, blacks, and the LGBT movements had a significant presence in political disputes during the PT governments, in the dynamics of the
political crisis of 2015–2016, and, as we will see, even more so in the rise of Jair
Bolsonaro to the Presidency of the Republic. What we understand, however, is
that distributive class conflicts have occupied the main position throughout
this period. Third: our theoretical approach, which consists of establishing the
link of politics with the economy and society, differs from the hegemonic insti-
tutionalist approach in contemporary Political Science, given that the latter
separates the action and the political institutions from society as a whole. Our
analysis does not ignore the importance of the values and norms that govern
the different political institutions, but it does not treat them the same way that
Institutionalism does. To illustrate this, Chapters 8 and 9 of this book deal specifically with different institutions of the Brazilian state and consider, simulta-
neously, institutional determination and class determination in the action of
the persons in these institutions.
    Fourthly, it is worth clarifying that we conceive of the distributive conflicts
among classes and class fractions not in a bipolar but in a multipolar way, and

that is precisely the reason why we refuse to operate with the simple conceptual opposition between capital and labor, or between bourgeoisie and working class. Capital, that is, the bourgeoisie, is not a homogeneous bloc without
fissures, as we can ascertain from the classic Marxist texts since the *Manifesto
of the Communist Party* and from the theoretical developments carried out
in this field by Nicos Poulantzas. As a rule, the bourgeoisie is divided – albeit
in a flexible and, to some extent, unstable way – into fractions that can intervene, and did intervene in the case we analyzed, as autonomous social forces
in the political process, that is, social forces endowed with a political program
of their own. We had a fraction of the Brazilian bourgeoisie interested in the
neodevelopmentalist policy of the PT governments, and another fraction that
embraced the neoliberal policy. Another reason why we refuse the simple
opposition capital/labor is that it dismisses the diversity that exists among
the dominated classes, especially in an economy of dependent capitalism
as the one we find in Brazil. Our approach aims precisely at contemplating
this diversity: it analyzes the middle class and its different fractions, which
actively, massively intervened in various political camps during the crisis of
2015–2016; it analyzes the position of the peasantry and its various layers, not
least because each layer received a different treatment from the PT governments; it addresses the matter of the marginal mass of workers, who played a
fundamental role as a support-class – politically disorganized, but electorally
decisive – for the governments and candidates of the PT; and, of course, our
approach also considers the working class in the strict sense – the manual
wage workers – whose union movement was politically divided in the period
in question.

  Finally, it is worth mentioning that yet another reason why our analysis
would not go very far if we were satisfied with the simple capital/labor opposition is that, during most of this period, it was not the conflict between the
bourgeoisie and a unified bloc of the popular classes that was at the center of
the political process. The popular movements were limited to a demanding and
very segmented struggle, which is why they ended up accommodated in either
of the two political camps into which the Brazilian bourgeoisie was divided: the
neodevelopmentalist camp and the neoliberal camp. Consequently, the main
contradiction around which the whole Brazilian political process revolved was
that between the bourgeois fractions.

IV

The chapters that make up this book were written between 2007 and 2020. They are the result of the research I have been conducting on Brazilian politics. Throughout this period, and as my studies progressed, my analysis underwent some rectifications. However, the basic ideas with which I explained the success of the PT governments also proved to be very useful later on to explain why these governments plunged into crisis. My first chapters already made it very clear that the PT governments were facing powerful interests and, moreover, that the political front that supported these governments was riddled with internal contradictions that could become exacerbated, opening the gates to the advance of enemy forces as soon as the political climate looked propitious.

As it happens with collections, like the one I am publishing now, the reader will find some repetitive content in the chapters. I tried to reduce these repetitions, but to make each chapter of the book readable and understandable on its own, I could not avoid them entirely. This occurs mainly on the subject of the characterization of the bloc in power during the studied period. However, they are repetitions only in part. From one chapter to the next, some conclusions change and, even when I return to ideas from previous texts, I do it with a new formulation, seeking to improve the presentation and clarification of the theses.

Most of this book is the result of research that I carried out when coordinating a collective research project titled "Politics and Social Classes in Neoliberal Capitalism," which was funded by the São Paulo Research Foundation (Fapesp). Each researcher had a specific object to investigate within the general theme expressed in the project title. My task was to study the organization of the state power and the political process in Brazil in the period under consideration, in order to characterize the general political context of the other more specific topics of the research. Of the twelve texts gathered here, three were written in coauthorship with colleagues who worked with me – Alfredo Saad-Filho, Andréia Galvão, Paula Marcelino, and Tatiana Berringer. I thank them for allowing such texts to be published here. In addition to these colleagues, teachers and students from the University of Campinas (Unicamp), the University of São Paulo (USP), and São Paulo State University (Unesp) also took part in the project. In total, we were about 30 active researchers. I would like to thank all of them for the rich exchange of information and ideas they provided me. I would also like to thank the researchers at the Center for Marxist Studies (Cemarx) at Unicamp, where the project was based. Whether they participated or not in this project, they have shared the ambitious task of renewing Marxism and producing knowledge about Brazil.

It does not hurt to add: the theses and arguments presented here are my responsibility.

São Paulo, February 2021

Tables and Charts

Tables

Charts

PART 1

Reform and Social Classes in the PT Governments

∵

State, Bourgeoisie, and Neoliberalism in the Lula Government

Before getting into the main theme, it will be necessary to make a little digression to present the theoretical background of our work.[1] There is in Brazil a rich tradition of studies on proprietary classes; this field of research is diverse in its theoretical orientations and have in recent years undergone important changes.

The most traditional topic of these studies is large-scale export agriculture. Restricting ourselves to 20th century authors, the study of this theme goes back to the works of Octavio Brandão, Caio Prado Jr., Nelson Werneck Sodré, Pierre Monbeig, Celso Furtado, Florestan Fernandes, and other precursors of social sciences, political economy and the modern intellectual debate about Brazil. The most important themes in this field are economy and society that were based, in the Northeast region, on sugar cane, and in the Southeast on coffee. Studies on industrialists are more recent, but far from new. Nelson Werneck Sodré, Florestan Fernandes, Octavio Ianni, Hélio Jaguaribe, Fernando Henrique Cardoso, Warren Dean, Boris Fausto, Luciano Martins, and many others focused on the industrial bourgeoisie as the industrialization process in Brazil in the post-1930s started and developed. Some of these authors were the first to analyze industrialists using the concept of bourgeoisie, with the aim of thinking about the complex political relations that social sector maintained with the hegemonic centers of capitalism, with the state and the workers. Though some of these studies lack empirical support, they are very sophisticated and have fostered lively discussions, being linked, either openly or implicitly, to the political discussion about the future of Brazilian economy and society. The debate concerned whether or not there was a national bourgeoisie in Brazil interested in forming a broad class front for an autonomous national development.

The theoretical bases of these studies varied. For instance, we can think about the difference between, on the one hand, the Soviet-type of Marxism practiced by Nelson Werneck Sodré, to whom the bourgeoisie was the leading social agent of a "capitalist-type" of development process; and, on the

---

1 This chapter was written in 2007, the first year of the second mandate of the Lula government.

other hand, the political economy of Celso Furtado, who merged Keynes's economic theory with the sociology of Karl Mannheim, attributing to the intelligentsia the role of driving development, which Furtado conceived simply an "economic development" (Monteiro, 2006). Despite this variety of theoretical trends, most of these studies were, to a greater or lesser extent, either carried out by Marxist authors or influenced by Marxist theory. These authors worked with the concept of social class and thought of the bourgeoisie in a complex way that comprised a subdivision of that class into fractions (national, associated, agrarian, industrial, etc.), whose specific interests would have relevant effects on the national political process. The concepts of bourgeoisie, capitalist state, imperialism, capitalist development, and others were at the core of the study of the state formed in the post-1930s, of the national-developmentalist ideology, of the industrialization policy, and of important events in the political history of Brazil, like the Revolution of 1930 and the military coup of 1964. However, this type of analysis has lost ground in the social sciences and almost fell into disuse in the academic environment.[2]

This is one of the factors that have contributed to Marxism losing its high regard in Brazilian university circles, though that was not observed everywhere in the academic world. Suffice it to say that Marxism began its upward trajectory in the United States academia around the same time. Notions such as social class, class fraction, ideology, and class state have disappeared, in Brazil, from research on activities connected to industry, banking and agribusiness. In most cases, such sectors are studied as groups competing among themselves to influence the policy of the state – an entity that is presented, implicitly, as a neutral arena where multiple interests compete on equal terms. More recent studies tend as well to isolate the bourgeois sector being studied from other sectors or fractions and even from the rest of society. It may seem preposterous today to discuss the possibility of alliances between this or that bourgeois fraction and other classes or social sectors. These more recent studies have better empirical grounds and systematic data collection; they also present more sophisticated analyses of the relationship between industrialists and the state's decision-making process. They therefore constitute an important contribution to research on the Brazilian state and Brazilian capitalists. Examples are the works of Ary Minella on bankers, Eli Diniz and Renato Boschi on industrialists, Adriano Nervo Codato, and Paulo Neves Costa, as their high quality makes

---

2   This type of research has never completely disappeared. See the works of Perissinotto (1994) and Farias (2017).

them essential references in the study of the Brazilian bourgeoisie. (Diniz and Boschi, 2004; Minella, 1997; Codato, 1997; Costa, 1998).

Our research work on the Brazilian bourgeoisie resumes the Marxist tradition that today is almost forgotten in this area of study. We conceive of the business community – bankers, industrialists, big landowners, traders – as members of the capitalist class, and the Brazilian state as an entity shaped to serve the fundamental interests of that social class – by means of its institutions and the people who work for them. Furthermore, within the field of Marxist theory of class and state, we employ the specific concept of bloc in power, developed by Nicos Poulantzas, to reflect upon the bourgeois class as a unity (social class) that is diversified (class fractions) in their relations with the state and the rest of society (Poulantzas 1968).

In using the concept of bloc in power[3] the researcher has to identify the fractions of the ruling class that act as a distinctive social force in a given situation: s/he must detect the economic interests of different fractions of the bourgeoisie that give rise to the formation of distinctive groups that pursue their own goals in the political process. It is also necessary to clarify which fraction's interests are being prioritized by the state economic policy and which have been relegated to a lower level. The identification of the interests effectively prioritized by state policy indicates which hegemonic fraction is within the bloc in power. Poulantzas suggests that, as a general rule, the bloc in power in the capitalist state has a more or less stable hierarchy, revealing the existence of a hegemonic fraction within it. However, the author also contemplates the possibility of a crisis of hegemony, identified by a situation in which none of the bourgeois fractions in a bloc in power is able to impose its specific interests as a priority for state policy. The concept of bloc in power, which covers classes and class fractions, also allows Poulantzas to take a new and sophisticated approach to political regimes in democratic states, relating forms of government (Presidentialism or Parliamentarism), disputes between branches of the state apparatus (Executive and Legislative), and the political party game (the various types of multi-party or two-party systems) to the hegemony within the bloc in power (Poulantzas, 1968).The main idea is that the organization of the state and the party system can be largely explained by the conflicts among the fractions of the ruling class, and between the ruling and working classes.

---

3 We prefer to translate the original French "*bloc au pouvoir*" as "bloc in power" and not as "power bloc," and this for two reasons. The expression "bloc in power" translates more accurately the original French expression and is also more theoretically appropriate because it indicates, as was Nicos Poulantzas' intention, that political power has an institutional place that is the state.

There is a strong prejudice against Althusserian Marxism in Brazilian circles. However, resorting to Poulantzas, we are not so distant from the Brazilian tradition referred to above as it might seem at first sight. Brazilian scholars used to operate with notions and theses that brought their analyzes close to the ones we could obtain by using, explicitly and consciously, the Poulantzian concept of bloc in power and the treatment it suggests for the political regime. Didn't Boris Fausto's controversy with Nelson Werneck Sodré about the Revolution of 1930 concern the conflict between different fractions within the capitalist class? Sodré, in a brief passage, perhaps overemphasized by Fausto, described the 1930 Revolution as a coup by the rising bourgeoisie against the decadent class of landowners, while Fausto, in order to refute him, tried to present the Revolution as the result of an oligarchic crisis caused by disputes among the regional fractions of the ruling class. There is much common ground in these two works, which was in fact what allowed the type of discussion they engendered. The political process expresses, in the two works, class actions and class interests; in both, the state is, before and after 1930, the state of the ruling class. What is the difference then? In Sodré's work, it was a different ruling class or class fraction whose interest predominated – decadence of the great landowners, political rise of the bourgeoisie. In Fausto's work, the conflicts among the regional sectors of the ruling class, the so-called oligarchic dissidences, would have generated a crisis of hegemony, a notion expressly employed by Fausto, and that had been already used by Francisco Weffort in his studies on post-1930 populism. When Antonio Carlos Meirelles, in an excellent but little-known text, intervened in the debate to criticize Fausto's criticism, the link between the political regime and the bloc in power was what served as reference (Meirelles, 1973). Meirelles argued that although Fausto had demonstrated the absence of the industrial bourgeoisie from the movement that ousted Washington Luís, as well as the importance of the oligarchic crisis for triggering the political-military movement, there still remained the fact that the centralization of the political regime had altered the balance of forces within the bloc in power, which paved the way for the industrialization policy that would become evident in the late 1930s. With this purpose, Meirelles used the Gramscian notion of passive (bourgeois) revolution to characterize the 1930 movement.

Something similar happened with the discussions about the national bourgeoisie. Fernando Henrique Cardoso, in his studies about the business community and dependency, endeavored to refute the thesis, which he generically attributed to communist intellectuals and the Brazilian Communist Party (PCB), which proposed that there would be in Brazil a national bourgeoisie liable to assume an anti-imperialist stance (Cardoso, 1966). In the debates about the meaning of the 1954 and 1964 coups d'état, issues related to the existence of an autonomous project of capitalist development and a national bourgeoisie marked Brazilian political science (Ianni, 1972).

The declining regard for Marxist theory among Brazilian academic circles, the abandonment of research on the bourgeoisie as a social class and the last wave of internationalization of the capitalist economy – the so-called globalization process – might suggest that this approach and the debates it entails would have been surpassed. We believe this is not the case. In addition to working with the concept of bloc in power, we have employed another specific concept also elaborated by Nicos Poulantzas – that of internal bourgeoisie – to understand what happens with the Brazilian bourgeoisie in its relations with the state and with international capitalism.[4] In our opinion, the so-called globalization process has failed to fully absorb the bourgeoisie of a dependent and semiperipheral country such as Brazil. This means that conflicts between an associated bourgeoisie, which is the local representative of the current form of dependence, and an internal bourgeoisie, with its own base of accumulation and specific interests, explain an important part of the Brazilian political process. We have elaborated two main working hypotheses based on these concepts. The first propounds that in the neoliberal period initiated during the Collor government and extending to the present there is the prevalent hegemony of big international financial capital, for which the big Brazilian banks function as an associated bourgeoisie. The second hypothesis is that the Lula government represents a novelty: without breaking with the hegemony of big international financial capital, Lula promoted the political rise of Brazil's big internal bourgeoisie within the bloc in power. Therefore, at least in the theme that concerns us here – the business community and its relationship with the state – the Lula government would not be a mere continuity of the Fernando Henrique Cardoso (FHC) government, despite the maintenance of the neoliberal capitalist model.

1   The Bloc in Power in the Neoliberal Period

The economic and social policy of the Brazilian state throughout the 1990s and the first half of the 2000s gave Brazilian capitalism certain minimally stable

---

4 The concept of internal bourgeoisie indicates the fraction of the bourgeoisie that occupies an "intermediate position" between the associated bourgeoisie, which is a mere extension of imperialist interests within colonial and dependent countries, and the national bourgeoisie, which in some national liberation movements of the 20th century assumed anti-imperialist positions. See Poulantzas, 1976.

characteristics that allow us to speak of a new model of capitalist development. This model, which has been called neoliberal, can be defined by its contrast to the preceding one: the developmentalist model – both in its national reformist phase (1930–1964) and in the pro-monopoly phase of the military dictatorship (1964–1985). Many elements highlight the contrast between the developmental and the neoliberal models: in the latter, the pace of economic growth slows down, the role of the state as entrepreneur and service provider declines, the priority accorded to industrial growth and development disappears, the denationalization of domestic economy expands, social and labor rights are reduced to levels even lower than those of the military dictatorship phase of the developmentalist model. Such elements provide us clues to identify the hegemonic bourgeois fraction in this neoliberal period. To do so, we must detect which bourgeois fraction is primarily benefited by the characteristics of the new model.

In the period of the developmentalist model, there was in Brazil an expansion of labor and social rights, albeit limited and non-linear. The neoliberal model of capitalism has reversed this trend. From this well-known element, new conclusions can be drawn. Insofar as this reduction of rights contemplates the interests of the entire Brazilian bourgeoisie and of the international capital invested in the country, we must consider it as an element that has ensured a minimum political unity of the bourgeoisie around the neoliberal model. Many analysts, including the Economic Commission for Latin America and the Caribbean, ECLAC's critical economists, have not realized this fact. Considering that the neoliberal model promotes the deindustrialization of the country, understood here as the reduction of the industrial product in the total GDP and the technological downgrading of the installed industry, they show their perplexity in face of the industrial bourgeoisie's support or, at most, very limited criticism of neoliberalism. They dismiss the fact that the industrial sector is part of the capitalist class and that the neoliberal model also brings advantages to it. Even big companies, which are believed to respect labor legislation, are benefited by the deregulation of the labor market and the consequential reduction in costs – although indirectly, through their suppliers and the practice of subcontracting. The commodification of rights and services such as health, education and social security also serves, in various ways, the interests of different sectors of the bourgeoisie. First, it stimulates the business expansion of a new bourgeois fraction that we call the new service bourgeoisie, a direct beneficiary of the state withdrawal from the provision of basic services. As we will see later, the growth of the new service bourgeoisie is just one of the changes promoted by the neoliberal model in the composition of the Brazilian bourgeoisie. Second, commodification reduces traditional social spending by the state, responding to pressures from big capital to appropriate the public budget. The Lula government maintained deregulation and commodification, and preserved the reforms promoted by FHC, in addition to preparing new reforms – social security reform, civil service reform (generalization of hiring under the CLT regime), labor and union reform, privatization of hospitals and universities, and others. This element of the neoliberal model recovers – partially and in a new historical situation – a characteristic of the capitalist model in force before 1930: the deregulated labor market and the absence of social rights.

While the dismantling of labor and social rights has guaranteed the political unity of the bourgeoisie around the neoliberal program, other neoliberalist elements have divided the bourgeois class into several fractions according to specific interests. Most works that rely on the concept of social class to analyze the bourgeoisie ignore this division, imagining a bourgeois class with homogeneous interests in face of a neoliberal model that would be entirely favorable to it. By pursuing this idea, these works fail to explain the conflicts that this model has been creating among entrepreneurs themselves. The mistake in this approach is symmetrically opposite to the one previously mentioned, which consisted in separating the industrial sector from the whole of the capitalist class. It is exactly by examining such separation that we can detect which bourgeois interests are prioritized and which are neglected or disregarded by neoliberal politics.

The second element of the model to be considered is the privatization policy that greatly reduced the state capitalist sector in Brazil, which had been one of the driving forces behind capitalist industrialization in the post-1930s. Again, the break with the developmentalist model is evident, although its political consequences are not evident for many who write on the subject. Privatization, in this new phase of Brazilian capitalism, directly serves the interests of the big private economic groups, i.e., the group of big capital – national or foreign, industrial or financial. However, the middle bourgeoisie, due to rules established by the Brazilian state for the privatization process, remained excluded from the great deal provided by the auctions of state-owned companies. Fewer than a hundred big private economic groups have taken over almost all of the state-owned companies as they were auctioned off, counting on all kinds of favors – underestimation of the companies' value, possibility of using so-called "rotten currencies," financing subsidized by the Brazilian Development Bank (BNDES), privileged information, preference and help from government authorities, etc. Big industrial Brazilian companies, such as the Votorantim, Gerdau, and Vicunha groups; big banks, such as Itaú, Bradesco, Unibanco, and Bozano Simonsen; and big foreign companies, such as Portuguese and Spanish telephone companies – in short, Brazilian big capital (be it industrial or financial) and foreign big capital have appropriated sectors as the steel industry, petrochemicals, fertilizers, tele-communication companies, road administration, public banks, railways, etc. As a result, the participation of state-owned companies in Brazilian GDP has fallen sharply over the past two decades.[5] Privatized companies are today among the most profitable of Brazilian capitalism. The Lula government inherited and maintained the privatization project (which included the dra-conian contracts that ensure high profitability for the new private monop-olies), and did not even consider investigating the most rumored cases of corruption involving privatization policy. In addition, privatized companies that claimed to be facing difficulties, such as Ferronorte, have received priv-ileged financial assistance from the government, in a move that goes against the stated objectives of the privatization policy. The legislation on Public-Private Partnerships (PPPs) for public services and infrastructure, created by the Lula government, was his most ambitious proposal in the area of privat-ization. These same big economic groups monopolize access to the exploita-tion of infrastructure services, with the privilege of having, as established by the PPP legislation, their profitability ensured by law – the supplementa-tion of public money is guaranteed for the enterprises that do not reach the "expected profitability."

The privatization policy is an element of the neoliberal model that affects different sectors of the bourgeoisie unequally. As we have indicated, it has increased the assets and profits of big capital – to the detriment of medium capital – and has been harmful to the interests of the bureaucratic layer that controlled these big state companies. In terms of class structure, the reduction of state-owned companies means the reduction of a sector of the Brazilian bourgeoisie, since the top management of these companies acted as a national state bourgeoisie. Along with the expansion of the new service bourgeoisie, this is another important change that occurred in the composition of the Brazilian bourgeoisie. As mentioned earlier, this change entails a political consequence that has been overlooked in studies on the subject: it restricts the social base and the political influence of bourgeois national-reformism in Brazil (Boito Jr., 2002a).

The third element we consider important in neoliberal policy is trade lib-eralization and financial deregulation. In this case, even the industrial sector

---

5   From 1989 to 1999, among the 40 biggest companies operating in Brazil, the number of state-owned companies dropped from 14 to just seven. (Diniz & Boschi, 2004).

– an important sector of big private capital – had its interests neglected or passed over in favor of national and international financial capital.

For the analysis of financial capital and the current accumulation model, we rely on François Chesnais, for whom the dominant form of capital today is financial capital, understood as "[...] the fraction of capital that is valued in keeping the money form" (Chesnais, 1997). Big financial capital in Brazil is diversified in terms of origin, type of insertion in the Brazilian market, and area of operation. Brazil has, above all, big commercial banks – national and foreign –with a network of offices in the country – Bradesco, Itaú, Unibanco, Santander, HSBC, and others. Data from the late 1990s indicated that, of the 200 banks then operating in Brazil, 25 alone held more than 80% of the total assets. The balance of bank profits in the first quarter of 2005 showed that the country's five biggest banks accounted for 69% of all banking system profits; when considering the top ten, this share rose to 83% of total profits.[6] In Brazil, big banks and big industrial groups remain relatively separate, and a Brazilian peculiarity in the context of Latin America is the importance of big national banks, a sector that until the mid-1990s, by the way, did not have foreign investors worthy of note (See Minella, 1997). The other companies and institutions that make up financial capital are foreign commercial and investment banks (which, since they lack an office network in Brazil, have short and long term investments in the country), and national and foreign investment funds and pension funds. In Brazil and other dependent countries, this financial capital functions, to a large extent, as usurious and predatory capital – interest-bearing monetary capital at very high rates that does not finance capitalist production (ownership of public debt securities, provision of consumer loans at rates of up to 8% per month, payroll-linked loans at "popular" rates directed at low-wage earners and retirees, etc.).[7]

For big financial capital to be appreciated quickly and at high rates, some aspects of state policy are fundamental, such as: a) the integration of the national financial market with international markets, i. e., the financial

---

6 The survey was carried out by the Central Bank of Brazil and encompassed 106 banking institutions. See "Lucro dos Bancos Cresce 52% no 10 Trimestre," (*Folha de São Paulo*, Jun 4, 2005, B-9).

7 Although monetary capital always remains external to production, it may function as capital that we could call indirectly productive when it is lent to the active capitalist who will, in fact, convert it into means of production and labor force for the generation of surplus value, which does not happen with usurious capital. See recent texts by François Chesnais, Gérard Duménil, Dominique Lévy, Isaac Johsua and Suzanne Brunhoff that served as the basis for the "Séminaire d'Études Marxistes" of the first semester of 2005 at the *École des Hautes Études* in Paris. See <www.jourdan.ens.fr/levy/semo5.htm>.

deregulation that ensures free conversion of currencies and free circulation of investments in public securities and in stock exchanges; b) a relatively stable and free exchange rate that allows the conversion and reconversion of currencies in a smooth and cost-effective manner; c) payment of external and internal public debt with a high basic real interest rate to ensure high remuneration for public securities owned, mainly, by the companies that have more liquidity, i.e., by financial capital itself. The balance sheets of the big Brazilian private banks show that the revenue from interest on public debt securities over the past few years represents about 40% of their total revenue; d) freedom for financial capital to charge as much as possible for capital borrowed from capitalists and consumers – free banking spread; e) fiscal adjustment that guarantees the payment of interest on public debt securities – in European countries, limited public deficits; in Latin American countries, primary surpluses. It is certain that all of these five elements were maintained or increased during the Lula government.

Financial deregulation is linked both to the recent advance in denationalization of dependent economies such as Brazil and also to the trade liberalization that was promoted in these countries. On the one hand, the purchase and sale of shares or even the acquisition of public and private companies is one of the mechanisms for appreciation of international financial capital; on the other hand, the big industrial-financial groups of the ruling countries demanded that Latin America should liberate trade in order to increase their exports to that region (Chesnais, 1997). We all know that neoliberal policy suppressed protectionism in Latin American domestic markets; we also know that protectionism had been the hallmark of the developmentalist model. This liberalization, besides serving the interests of international capital, had the objective of inhibiting – by cornering the internal bourgeoisie with competing imported products at a lower price – the increase in prices of industrial products, hence containing the domestic inflation and contributing to the internal stability of the currency and a relative stability of the exchange rate. During the first FHC term, such policy generated successive deficits in trade balance, a situation that was "compensated" in the way that best suited the interests of financial capital: a very high basic interest rate to attract volatile foreign financial capital aiming at fast and high appreciation. The entry of this short-term risk capital would make up for the instability in trade balance and external accounts. Of course this policy had every chance to produce in the future, as it in fact produced, a continuous increase of public debt and external imbalance.

Trade liberalization and financial deregulation serve, therefore, the interests of big financial capital, national and international, even to the detriment of the big internal industry. The latter lost the captive market for its products, started to pay much more for the capital it borrows for investments, and suffered a reduction in the part of the state revenue destined for infrastructure and the promotion of production. Some authors emphasize that big industrial groups do reserve part of their capital to invest in the financial market. Our understanding, however, is that this fact does not write off the losses that monetary and trade liberalization policies entail for the industry or, at least, it does not stop the industrial groups from pressing against these losses.

In conclusion, we can say that big national and international financial capital is the hegemonic bourgeois fraction in the neoliberal model because all aspects of neoliberal policy – dismantling of labor and social law, privatization, trade liberalization and financial deregulation – fully meet the interests of that fraction of the bourgeoisie. Except for the first element, all the others contradict, to a greater or lesser extent, the interests of the other fractions that make up the bloc in power – medium capital, state bourgeoisie, big industrial capital. The practical result of the objective correspondence between the neoliberal capitalist model and financial interests is the higher rate of profit that the financial system has obtained over the last few years as compared to the rate of the productive sector. According to a survey by ABM Consulting, from 1994 to 2003, the profit of the ten biggest Brazilian banks grew no less than 1,039%.[8] During the first year of the Lula government, banks once again set profitability records. Some surveys carried out by investment platform Economática and the Brazilian Institute of Tax Planning (IBPT) showed that investment in funds yielded, in the same period, four times more than investment in productive sectors, and these investments were subject to less taxes.[9] During the first quarter of 2005, the banks' profit maintained its upward trend – growing 52% compared with the same period in 2004.[10]

In addition to the objective concurrence between the interests of big financial capital and the neoliberal model, there is also the matter of national and international financial capital displaying a political and ideological identification with the successive neoliberal governments in Brazil. The policy of these governments, from FHC to Lula, has been approved by the IMF, the World Bank, and the Brazilian Federation of Banks (Febraban). A meaningful evidence of this situation is the symbiosis between the management staff of the successive governments of that period, mainly the staff of the Ministry of Finance and the Central Bank, and the management staff of the national

---

8   Lucros dos Bancos Sobem Mais de 1.000%. *Folha de São Paulo*, Jun 21, 2004, B-3.
9   Fundos Rendem 4 Vezes Mais que Produção. *Folha de São Paulo*, Jun 11, 2004, *Caderno Dinheiro*, B-1, B-3 e B-4.
10 Lucro dos Bancos Cresce 52% no 1º. Trimestre. *Folha de São Paulo*, Jun 04, 2005, B-9.

and international financial sector. Starting one's career as a director of the Central Bank and continuing it as a private bank executive or vice-versa has been a common situation in the Brazilian political scene for years. As we will see next, the Lula government presented some minor changes in this configuration.

2   The Political Ascension of the Industrial Bourgeoisie and Agribusiness under the Lula Government

The political hegemony of big national and international financial capital was not exerted without resistance or under the same conditions throughout the neoliberal period. Perhaps due to the great mismatch between the PT's public image and the real course followed by the Lula government, some intellectuals were led in their criticism to emphasize an element of continuity between FHC and Lula.[11] We believe this emphasis to be unilateral and erroneous, so our analysis is different. As previously stated, the novelty of the Lula government lay in how it promoted a complex political operation that consisted of enabling the political ascension of the big industrial bourgeoisie and agribusiness, mainly the sectors oriented to export trade, without breaking the hegemony of the financial sector, and still maintaining the subordinate position of medium capital in the bloc in power.

During his first term, FHC increased trade liberalization, by promoting another round of suspension of tariff and non-tariff barriers to imports, deepening the deregulation of capital inflows and outflows, keeping the exchange rate up, and increasing the interest rate and public debt. He accumulated growing deficits in the trade balance and made a tough fiscal adjustment – though at present it may seem a mild adjustment, in view of the extremely high level of primary surplus imposed by the Lula government on the country. According to data from the Central Bank of Brazil, FHC obtained, as a percentage of GDP, 0.27%, 0.08%, and 0.01% of primary surplus, respectively, in 1995, 1996 and 1998; in 1997, there was a small primary deficit of 0.95% of GDP. Two aspects of this policy were particularly criticized by the big internal industrial bourgeoisie: the trade liberalization and the level of interest rates. During the first FHC government, the Federation of Industries of the State of São Paulo

---

11   We refer to the work of left-wing critics of the Lula government such as Francisco de Oliveira (F. Oliveira, 2010) e Leda Paulani (2008).

(Fiesp), seconded by the National Confederation of Industry (CNI), voiced the dissatisfaction of this sector.

At this point in our analysis, we must consider the political presence of the working classes. In methodological terms, we can distinguish the business community from the rest of society and select it as an object of study. However, what happens within the capitalist class correlates with the rest of the political and social world. Depending on its characteristics and its insertion in the set of political relations, a certain industry may be able to establish alliances or fronts with sectors of the popular classes, which are excluded from the bloc in power. In the case under examination here, it is important to remember that the big industrial sector had the support of the Unified Workers' Central (CUT) and the majority of the Workers' Party (PT), mainly its São Paulo section, in their protest against the liberalization of trade and high interest policies. CUT was led by a new labor aristocracy represented by skilled workers from the automotive industry, the oil industry, and banks; despite protests by its leftist minority, it aspired to the resurrection of the old developmentalism, which union leaders expected to regain through the reduction of interest rates and other measures to encourage investment. The proposal of sectorial chambers presented by CUT in the early 1990s was conceived as the privileged space for this alliance, where entrepreneurs and workers from each industry would discuss, together with the government, the factors considered to be the bottlenecks in production and employment – financing, taxes, hiring policy, etc. These chambers were basically planned for the industrial sector, and the only one that succeeded was the Automotive Sector Chamber, which was later closed by the FHC government. In addition to the sectorial chambers, on several occasions Fiesp and CUT worked together to devise proposals and economic policy projects – as in the tax reform proposal, prepared by Fiesp and CUT with the participation of the Economic Research Institute Foundation (Fipe-USP), a proposal that aimed at "reducing the tax burden on productive capital."

The apex of this alliance was in June 1996, when the Fiesp board of directors declared its public support, including through a text signed by its president and published in the mainstream press, of a national strike against unemployment that was being organized by CUT and Força Sindical. During May and June of that year, Fiesp was organizing, with the collaboration of the National Confederation of Industry (CNI), a demonstration in Brasilia of industrialists from all over the country against the "fast pace" of trade liberalization, against the "slow pace" of privatizations, and against the current interest policy. The FHC government felt the pressure and, without changing its general policy, took a step backwards: it relied on WTO rules – safeguard, countervailing duties, and anti-dumping agreement – to create barriers to the import of fabrics from China,

South Korea, and Formosa, and also to the import of toys.[12] In the 2002 electoral campaign, the PT struggled to attract support from Fiesp; Lula da Silva stated in a speech that they would lead a government of production against speculation. They seemed to rekindle the traditional illusions of the Brazilian left wing about the supposed political role of the "national bourgeoisie."

Besides this political pressure, an economic factor must be considered. Although Brazil's growing trade deficit served the interests of international capital, this situation could also create problems in the medium and long term for both national and international capital. The imbalance in the external accounts – caused by the payment of the debt, by the growing remittance of profits resulting from the advance of the internationalization of the economy, and by trade liberalization itself – could jeopardize the Brazilian state's ability to pay and, in an extreme situation, even preclude international financial capital to enter and leave the country freely due to shortage of reserves. The Brazilian economy neared this critical situation as it faced the 1999 currency crisis during the transition between Cardoso's first and second term. The specter of what United Nations Economic Commission for Latin America and the Caribbean (ECLAC) developmentalists called "foreign exchange bottleneck" haunted Brazilian external accounts. The situation required some course correction and FHC realized that. He dismissed Gustavo Franco – the ideologist of the exchange rate appreciation – from the presidency of the Central Bank, devalued the Brazilian currency (Real), and replaced the trade deficit with a policy of trade surplus. The positive balance trade, together with an emergency agreement that had been reached with the IMF, became the assets that the second FHC government (1999–2002) used to regain international financial capital's confidence in the Brazilian economy. This was the "seed" of the export policy to be implemented later by the Lula government.[13]

As can be seen, there were several factors responsible for the new international trade policy and the corresponding political rise of the big internal industrial bourgeoisie and agribusiness. Given the economism that dominates the analysis of Brazilian economic policy, it is important to highlight the political factors that led to this change: the pressure from the big industrial bourgeoisie

---

12   The issues of Fiesp's magazine published from April to July 1996 provided ample coverage of these events and highlighted the action and objectives of the industrialists – in June, Fiesp's publication changed the sober title *Notícias* (News) for the assertive *Revista da Indústria* (Magazine of the Industrial Sector).

13   The export-oriented industrial sectors increased their influence within Fiesp throughout the 1990s, which makes the entity's position during the second term of the Lula government understandable. See Bianchi, 2004.

throughout the 1990s, the converging pressure from the unions and the very election of Lula da Silva as president in 2002. National and international economic factors also counted: the threat of a foreign exchange bottleneck in the 1999 currency crisis, the growth of international trade in raw materials and natural resources, the increase in prices of these products, the diminishing flow of dollars from the investment funds of dominant nations to dependent countries in the 2000s, and finally, the great exchange rate devaluation caused involuntarily by Lula's imminent victory in 2002.[14] When he took office, Lula decided to intensify the course correction started by the second FHC term. He implemented an aggressive export policy centered on agribusiness, natural resources, and low-tech industrial products, and also took the exchange and credit measures necessary to maintain such policy. The very profile of Brazilian industry had changed, with the decline of more sophisticated sectors and the rise of sectors linked to the processing of natural resources such as ores, paper and cellulose, food products, etc.[15] The flagship of exports was agribusiness, the industrial sector responsible for about 40% of all of the country's sales abroad: the soybean complex stood out as the top-exporting segment, followed by meat, wood, sugar and alcohol, paper and cellulose, leather, coffee, cotton and fibers, tobacco, and fruit juice.[16]

It was a victory – though partial – for the big internal industrial bourgeoisie and agribusiness. Although this bourgeois fraction remained a secondary force within the bloc in power, since the state continued to prioritize the interests of financial capital, the Lula government granted it a much more comfortable

---

14   The continuation of this research will define a more precise profile of the big internal bourgeoisie, specifically of its exporting branch. The profit of different segments of the big internal bourgeoisie is differently affected by the exchange rate according to at least two variables: whether a company's or a segment's goods are priced in strong currency (as happens with agricultural products) or in national currency (as happens with industrial products); and whether the company or segment has a high or low openness index. Companies and segments that have a low openness index (import little raw material, inputs and equipment) and whose products are fixed in Brazilian reais are the most harmed by the exchange rate appreciation; at the other extreme, companies or segments whose goods are priced in strong currencies and which have a high openness index are the least hampered by exchange rate appreciation. Much of the agribusiness sector is halfway between these two extremes. (See Pimentel Puga, 2006).

15   Taking stock of the period 1992–2000, Ricardo Carneiro states: "What can be concluded from the set of data is that the structure of Brazilian foreign trade has faithfully reflected the changes occurred in the production structure, with exports concentrated in sectors with less technological content, and the reverse occurring with imports." (See Carneiro, 2002).

16   Exportação do agronegócio chega à marca dos US$ 39 bi. *Folha de São Paulo*, 7 de janeiro de 2005, p. B-3.

position in the Brazilian economy. This result is reflected in Fiesp's behavior. During the 1990s, this entity used to criticize the more finance-related aspects of economic policy and trade liberalization; however, during the Lula mandate and with the support of the federal government, Fiesp came to be chaired by an ally of the Brazilian executive power. The Lula government multiplied the institutional channels to consult with industrialists and exporters, in stark contrast with the conduct of the FHC government, according to reports of the businesspeople themselves (see Diniz, 2006).

As for the size of the exporting companies, big capital predominated. According to data from the Brazilian Foreign Trade Association, Brazil had 19,000 exporting companies in February 2005. Of this total, only 800 companies were responsible for 85% of the country's total exports. As for the origin of capital, of the 40 biggest Brazilian export companies responsible for 41% of total exports, 22 were foreign.[17] The government claimed to be encouraging the participation of small and medium-sized national companies in such a great business opportunity but, according to the Brazilian Micro and Small Enterprises' Support Service (Sebrae), the thousands of micro and small exporting companies of the industrial sector accounted for only 2% of its exports.[18] Therefore, this "dollar chasing" attitude represented a policy that served the interests of big national and foreign capital linked to agribusiness, mineral extraction, and low-tech industrial products. Once again medium capital occupied a subordinate position.

3   Political Rise, but No Hegemony Established

Why then, despite the governmental stimulus to the export sector and its consequential high profitability, do we insist that big internal and international financial capital remained hegemonic within the bloc in power during the Lula government? The answer is: because this government stimulated production, but only within the limits allowed by the fundamental interests of big financial capital.

First, it primarily stimulated export-oriented production. From the financial point of view, it was not important to prioritize production aimed at the domestic market. Big financial capital needed to reduce the imbalance of external accounts, without which its free circulation and high remuneration would

---

17   Múltis usam país como base exportadora. *Folha de São Paulo*, October 17, 2004, p. B-1.
18   Real valorizado já reduz base exportadora. *Folha de São Paulo*, May 27, 2005, p. B-1.

be compromised. The main objective of stimulating production was, therefore, exportation, i.e., chasing dollars and other strong currencies – and it was not in popular domestic consumption that these currencies could be obtained. For this reason, production for exports was specifically encouraged instead of production in general. Second, even under this export promotion policy, everything should be done in a way that did not exceed the measure of what mattered to financial capital. Chasing dollars was fine, but just as long as the dollars obtained were used to pay the interest of the debt. Thus, the primary surplus and interest rates remained high even if this limited the growth of exports. In fact, there was a lack of infrastructure and human resources – roads, silos, ports, personnel for health surveillance and the like – for the Brazilian capitalism to grow at least within the average rate of the main Latin American economies and, even so, still as a mere platform for exports. However, from the point of view of financial capital, it was not desirable to divert to infrastructure the money that should be directed to remunerate the banks. The bottlenecks could perhaps be overcome by the PPP s, designed by the Lula government precisely to circumvent infrastructure problems without threatening the policy of high primary surpluses. The same reasoning applies to the policy of high basic interest rates, which strengthened the usurious profile of financial capital, diverting it from production financing and making investments more expensive, thus limiting the growth of exports. From what we can see, the high primary surplus and the high interest rate during Lula's government were not a financial deviation embedded in a globally developmentalist policy. In fact, they were consistent with this new and modest export-oriented economic growth. The increase in exports was accompanied by an increase in the primary surplus, which jumped from an average of 1% of GDP in FHC's first term to 3.5% in his second term, and was around 4.5% during the Lula government.

Lula's foreign policy also illustrated the new situation in the bloc in power: it was not disconnected from domestic policy, as suggested by those who considered it to be the "healthy part" of the government. President Lula claimed to be fighting for a new "commercial geography," and here lies the secret link between his foreign policy and his economic policy. Brazil's foreign policy was both subaltern (to imperialism) and dominant (over the small and medium-sized economies in the periphery). On the one hand, Brazilian capitalism's subordinate position in the international division of labor was reaffirmed by the policy of regressive specialization in foreign trade; on the other hand, the government really wanted to take its due place in the agricultural, natural resources, and low-tech industrial sectors, even though Brazilian capitalism had to expand at the expense of other Latin American bourgeoisies, and even in spite of specific commercial tensions with some dominant countries. The fight against agricultural protectionism in Europe and the United States as well as the deterioration of relations with Argentina highlight our argument.

The Brazilian state's effort to build an alliance of peripheral countries, established in the so-called G-20 at the Cancun WTO meeting in October 2003, aimed precisely at suspending agricultural protectionism in the dominant countries. The discourse that the Lula government used to legitimize G-20's claim was neoliberal and called for a "real liberalization" of markets, focusing its endeavors on the trade of agricultural products. New concessions in the trade liberalization policy for industrial products and services remained a possibility, in exchange for the dominant countries' withdrawing their agricultural protectionism. In doing so, the government forfeited the fight for a regulation of international trade that favored dependent countries. The hegemonic face of this policy undermined the alliance with Argentinian capitalism in Mercosur, because the Brazilian big internal bourgeoisie, as a subordinate ally of big financial capital, aspired to have access to growing portions of the Latin American market.

4   The Political Regime and the Hegemony of Financial Capital

Let us now say a word about the political regime that corresponded to that bloc in power. As we have already indicated, from our theoretical perspective, the preponderance of one branch of the state over another, the conflict between the Executive and the Legislative powers, the party system in place, and the several conflicts within state and government, considered together with other intervening factors, must be seen under the light of disputes among the bourgeois fractions that constitute the bloc in power. Brazilian hyperpresidentialism – which essentially consisted of the appropriation of legislative functions by the Federal Executive – served the interests of the hegemonic fraction within the bloc in power. Everything related to this political and institutional arrangement necessarily referred to the dispute of interests among the bourgeois fractions. A fortuitous strengthening of the National Congress and of the states' and municipalities' executive powers could pose a threat to the hegemony of financial capital. Given its nature as a political regime centered on the bureaucracy's decision-making capacity and on bureaucratic legitimacy to the detriment of representative legitimacy, hyperpresidentialism also leads to the decline of the governing and representative functions of the political parties.

We do not mean that the top of the federal government bureaucracy and the leaders of state governments acted in unison to defend the interests of big financial capital. It was the Ministry of Finance and the Central Bank that held privileged positions in this scheme of concentration of power for the benefit of the hegemonic fraction. They were, therefore, the main centers of power defining economic policy – the Ministry of Finance was responsible for controlling macroeconomic variables and determining the budget allocation for all the other ministries. However, in other sectors of the top bureaucracy and in other government decision-making centers, both in the FHC period and even more so in the Lula period, big industrial capital and agribusiness also held important positions from which they sought to resist measures of economic policy that were contrary to their interests. During Lula's two terms, these frictions were renewed: the old conflict between José Dirceu (Chief of Staff) and Antonio Palocci (minister of Finance); Carlos Lessa (BNDES) and Henrique Meirelles (Central Bank); Dilma Rousseff (Chief of Staff) and again Henrique Meirelles; etc. During the FHC period, the prominence of extreme neoliberals, such as Pedro Malan, Gustavo Franco and Armínio Fraga – over moderate neoliberals such as José Serra, Dorothea Werneck, and others – was more evident. In the Lula government, the dynamics of these conflicts within the government was one of the main signs of the growing strength of the big internal industrial bourgeoisie and agribusiness. At the beginning of his second term, in January 2007, Lula launched the Growth Acceleration Plan (PAC), which seemed to be entirely geared to the interests of the big internal bourgeoisie, mainly the industrial fraction. The Ministry of Finance was entrusted to a heterodox economist, Guido Mantega, and the Ministry of Development to a monetarist economist. This constituted an inversion in relation to the whole FHC period, when the most important ministry remained under the control of an orthodox economist, which left the secondary Ministry of Development to the neodevelopmentalists.

The subordinate fractions of the bloc in power, unequally contemplated by the federal government policy, had greater access to the National Congress and to the subordinate branches of the state – municipality and state governments – in the political regime in place. Recent political history indicates that many characteristics of that economic model and many economy policy decisions, if dependent upon the National Congress's decisions, would face difficulties due to the publicity they would attract and the heterogeneous character of the parliamentary representation – big financial capital was not able to homogenize the National Congress as it used to do within the Federal Executive. Whenever neoliberal reforms demanded constitutional reform and, therefore, had to pass through the National Congress, the difficulties were immense and many of them never got off the ground.

The party system was consistent with the preponderant role of the Executive branch, beginning with the Federal Executive. In Brazilian neoliberalism, there was no party government, but government parties. Congress members of the President of the Republic's party acted as a mere support base for the government in Congress, having to conform to political decisions about which they were not even consulted. It was like that with PSDB during both FHC terms and also with PT during both Lula terms, differently from what many people would expect. As a drastic result of weakening the Legislative branch and the political parties' governing functions the Brazilian political regime produced a great number of parties, some of medium or large size like the PTB, whose only function was to serve as a parliamentary base for the current government in exchange for favors. The other parties were divided between the interests of big financial capital and the internal bourgeoisie. The majority wing of the PSDB, the electoral vanguard of neoliberalism in Brazil, represented big international financial capital and the interests of Brazilian entrepreneurs and bankers closely linked to that capital. The PT, born as a left-wing social-democratic party and linked to the union movement, had been moving closer to the big internal bourgeoisie since the mid-1990s, when the so-called *Majority Sector* (Campo Majoritário) started the process of programmatic and organizational reformulation of the party. In line with this bourgeois fraction, the PT sought to contain or reverse only the economic policy measures that harmed it, such as high interest rates and trade liberalization, maintaining those that favored it even at the expense of workers' welfare, such as social security reform, flexibilization of employment contract in the public sector, labor reform, etc. The former PFL, renamed Democrats (Democratas), also represented international financial interests, but among all the major parties it seemed most aligned with the new service bourgeoisie. PMDB had basically three wings: the governing wing, one closer to international financial interests, and a third still linked to the middle bourgeoisie and the old state bourgeoisie. It is important to remember that as the political regime greatly reduced the governing function of the parties, their representative function had also been undermined. The different social sectors did not perceive the parties as an important instrument of power and directed their struggle and pressure right towards the state bureaucracy. As a result, the representative link between the parties and society was weakened.

This approach may open new perspectives for the analysis of party struggles during both terms of Lula's presidency. How should we interpret, in this context, the PSDB's opposition to the government in episodes such as the "*Mensalão*" corruption crisis or the "*Cansei*" movement?[19] Was it an attitude

---

19   "*Cansei*" (I'm tired) was a protest-movement organized by high-profile society in Brazil about lack of ethics in politics and government in the *Mensalão* scandal and the 2006–2007 Brazilian aviation crisis.

of the financial capital party against a government that promoted the interests of the big industrial internal bourgeoisie and agribusiness? Initially, during the *"Mensalão* crisis," we believed that this was not the case. It seemed that PSDB, in turning against the government, was withdrawing from its own base, since at the time the main employers' entities made a point of providing public support for the Lula government at the height of the crisis. PSDB's persistent position, however, seemed to indicate an organic phenomenon. The struggle for hegemony in the bloc in power appeared to have spilled over to the partisan political dimension (Nucci Júnior, 2007). The PSDB acted as a representative of financial capital and garnered support from the upper middle class, which seemed uncomfortable with the expansion of compensatory policies during the Lula government – its so-called "social-liberalism." The upper middle class was attracted by the moralistic discourse that attributed corruption to the rulers' evil nature and believed it was possible to establish or restore the neutrality and impersonality from which the institutions of the capitalist state had supposedly deviated.

Let us return to the concentration of power in the Federal Executive. Behind it, there was a whole political ideology that was systematized and disseminated, either consciously or unconsciously, by the representatives of big financial capital. Its main elements were: the concept of monetary policy as a technical matter; the defense of provisional measures as an equally technical consequence of the need for speed in governmental actions; the unilateral accusation of parochialism, cronyism, and patronage leveled at the National Congress, at budget amendments proposed by representatives and senators, etc. All these ideas legitimized the concentration of the decision-making power in the Executive branch and promoted the political marginalization of the Legislative. Some of them, such as the supposedly technical character of monetary policy, an idea invariably defended by all presidents and directors of the Central Bank since the early 1990s, were pure mystification; others, such as the accusations of cronyism, patronage and parochialism against the National Congress, pointed to existing aspects of the institution, but did so in a way that produced more mystifications. The depreciation of the National Congress suggested an alleged efficiency and political grandeur of the Executive; the discourse regarding parochialism of amendments by representatives and senators hid the fact that small and medium-sized companies, precisely those that economic policy aimed to marginalize, were located in the parish. The executive budget proposal, which designated one third of the Federal Government's revenues to pay interest on the public debt – i.e., to only about 20,000 families, according to economists' calculations – was supposed to be technical and rational, while an amendment proposed by a state or federal representative or senator seeking to pave the streets of a small town or finance small businesses was said to be motivated by parochialism and cronyism. This kind of discourse also hides the fact that it is the function that makes the politician: it seems clear that a belittled congress attracts politicians willing to support successive governments in exchange for favors. We find an extreme facet of this situation in the increasing number of fugitives from justice running for office in search of parliamentary immunity. In other words, the discourse in defense of the Executive and financial capital reverses the terms of the problem: the effect of the Legislative's political weakening is presented as if it were its cause. Therefore, the portion of truth that such ideological discourse contains is no more than the necessary quantity for its effectiveness as a mystifying discourse.

5   Final Considerations

The logic underlying the hierarchy of the bloc in power has its roots in Brazilian neoliberal capitalism. Such logic is synthesized by the economic policy of the state and results from the insertion of Brazilian capitalism in the changes occurred in the international division of labor and from the political correlation of forces within the country.

The economic policy defines a hierarchy of fractions of the capitalist class, favoring certain dimensions of capital over others. As to function, it favors the financial function; as to size, it favors big capital; as to the destination of production, it is the foreign market and the high-income share of the domestic market. These priorities correspond, one by one, to the dimensions that have been overlooked. As to the capital function, it overlooks production, i.e. the active capital; as to size, it overlooks the small and medium capital; and as to the destination of production, it is the internal market for popular consumer goods. We could add that big private companies were favored at the expense of big state companies, especially during the privatization auctions of the 1990s.

Such priorities establish a hierarchy of bourgeois power that comprises two extreme positions. At the top, we have big international financial capital and big national banks, while at the bottom of the pyramid we have medium capital, invested in the productive sector and focused on the domestic market for popular consumer goods. The former concentrates all the cumulative advantages in terms of economic policy and acts as a distinct class fraction; the latter carries all the cumulative disadvantages with regard to the economic policy and does not even constitute an autonomous fraction of the bourgeois class. Between the two extremes we find the big industrial internal bourgeoisie and agribusiness, mainly the big export-oriented companies. We are then left with three positions: the hegemonic fraction, whose interests have been prioritized by economic policy both in the 1990s and in the 2000s; the intermediate fraction, which started an upward political trajectory during the Lula government and whose conversion into a hegemonic fraction is a real possibility – as we have already indicated, "globalization" has not absorbed the whole of the Brazilian bourgeoisie; and finally, we have the fraction marginalized by state policy, the small and medium-sized companies in the productive sector focused on the domestic market for popular goods, whose interests are always ignored when confronted to the interests of big capital, be it financial or productive, either for export or the domestic market. This is a general picture that considers typical situations. There are more complex situations, of sectors that are at the same time favored and neglected by the state economic policy, as is the case of medium-sized banks and small export-oriented companies. Over the past few years, many small and medium-sized banks have gone bankrupt and many small export-oriented businesses have prospered.

This chapter focused solely on the theme of the bloc in power in the neoliberal period in Brazil, particularly on the relations between the bourgeoisie and the Lula government. We did not investigate the relations of this bourgeoisie and the government with the working classes, although it is impossible to completely separate these two sides of Brazilian politics – so much so that we have resorted to the political presence of the working class in order to analyze the political rise of the big internal bourgeoisie. There are other issues related to the working class that would deserve examination. For example, can the growth of compensatory policies such as the "Family Grant" program have a significant impact on the economic policy and the bourgeois fractions' relative positions within the bloc in power? Could it go so far as to considerably promote the businesses of medium-sized companies focused on the market for popular consumer goods? Do policies to encourage industrial production and agribusiness, mainly aimed at exports, represent, in contrast to the strictly financial policies, any improvement for Brazilian wage earners and peasants? Our analysis suggested that such policies have constituted a very limited change. We could add that they neglected the development of the internal market because, in a model that favors export, wages count first as a cost and a disadvantage in international competitiveness – which makes the agrarian reform unfeasible, due to the strategic role attributed to agribusiness. But such a discussion would require much more reflection. We indicate these themes only to show that, by treating entrepreneurs as a ruling class, and not just as any social sector, our work necessarily suggests broader political and social issues for contemporary Brazil.

The Lula Governments

The New "National Bourgeoisie" in Power

The new wave of internationalization of the capitalist economy, characteristic of the last quarter of the 20th century, has induced some authors to affirm or suggest that any nationally based bourgeois fraction has purely and simply disappeared.[1] Contrary to this expectation, what we saw in the 2000s was the political rise of a new national bourgeoisie within the Brazilian state's bloc in power.[2]

We do not refer here to the old national bourgeoisie, which, according to Marxist authors and to analyses proposed by 20th century communist parties, might supposedly join the working class in an anti-imperialist front. We refer to a new national bourgeoisie, a fraction of the bourgeois class to which the concept of *internal bourgeoisie* coined by Nicos Poulantzas fits perfectly (Poulantzas, 1974). Writing in the first years of the 1970s, just when the notion of globalization was being disseminated by Anglo-Saxon writers, Poulantzas warned us that, at the national level, lingered an internal bourgeoisie that was not going to disappear with the new wave of internationalization of the capitalist economy. In dependent countries, this bourgeois fraction would have occupied an intermediate position between the old national bourgeoisie, which might adopt anti-imperialist practices, and the old associated bourgeoisie – a mere extension of imperialism within those countries. The new internal bourgeoisie would therefore find a middle ground between two extremes, having its own accumulation base and being able, at the same time, to associate with imperialist capital, thus limiting its expansion within the country.

In Brazil today, it was the Lula government that promoted the political rise of this fraction of the Brazilian bourgeoisie (Boito Jr., 2005b). A warning is required at this point, so that the synthetic expression in the title – the new national bourgeoisie in power – does not mislead the reader. The big internal Brazilian bourgeoisie has never been excluded from power. As a fraction of the bourgeoisie, it has shared state power with the other fractions of this social class, i.e., it has integrated the bloc in power (Poulantzas, 1968). What

---

1 This idea is supported by Miglioli (1998), and Pijl (1998). The latter believes in the formation of a single bourgeois class at the world level.

2 This chapter was written in 2010.

happened is that its relative position has improved. Would it have become hegemonic in the bloc in power, i.e., would this specific fraction's interests have turned into the main priority of the Lula government's economic policy? At this point, we prefer to leave this question open. We claim merely that, under Lula's economic policy, the interests of the big internal bourgeoisie have been increasingly prioritized among the initiatives and measures of the Brazilian state. The first milestone in this process was the transition, in 2002, from the "Fernando Henrique Cardoso (FHC) era" to the "Lula era." The political rise of the big internal bourgeoisie within the bloc in power became more evident in 2006, as the Lula government moved from its first to its second term. The economic project that expresses this relationship between the Lula governments and the big internal bourgeoisie will be called here "neodevelopmentalism."

We shall shortly offer a brief characterization of neodevelopmentalism as an economic policy proposal representing the class interests of the big internal bourgeoisie. But first, let us make a methodological observation. Characterizing projects and models of the capitalist development is a complex task. The first difficulty is theoretical and relates to the choice of relevant criteria to identify the stages of capitalist development and characterize their respective models; the second difficulty is empirical and refers to the issue of detecting what does or does not fit in a previously defined capitalist model in the face of a historical reality that always eludes the purity of models. The third type of difficulty involves situations in which the well-known, already characterized models begin to change, as in the case with which we are dealing: the neoliberalism of the 1990s is not the same as that of the 2000s. Such situations give rise to the question of whether we are facing a change *of* model or a change *within* a model. Despite these three types of difficulty, we believe it is possible to define, even if provisionally, neodevelopmentalism as *the developmentalism that is possible in the peripheral neoliberal capitalist model.*

In the 2000s, Brazilian capitalism grew, on average, twice as much as in the 1990s. However, we insist on the prefix "neo" to indicate the existence of important differences in relation to the developmentalism of the 1930–1980 period. Three differences deserve particular mention. All of them cater to the interests of the big Brazilian internal bourgeoisie and also represent its commitment to international financial capital. The first characteristic is that the new developmentalism produces more modest rates of economic growth because it is limited by the financial accumulation still in force – a fundamental aspect of the neoliberal capitalist model. Investments and economic growth are inhibited by the rollover of the public debt and by the high interests on state revenue and on profits of companies in the productive sector.

The second distinguishing feature of the new developmentalism is that it embraces regressive specialization, which is a step back imposed by the neoliberal capitalist model on dependent countries, such as Brazil, that have managed to develop a more complex industrial park. The new developmentalism is therefore focused on sectors that process agricultural products, livestock, or natural resources, and that favors low technological density segments when it comes to the processing industry. The old developmentalism, in contrast, forced the opening of loopholes in the international capitalist division of labor: firstly, through the industrialization policy itself, and then through constant attempts – occasionally successful – to internalize more sophisticated productive sectors such as basic industry, consumer durables, capital goods, aviation industry, informatics, defense industry, and others. In the neodevelopmentalist model, the big national companies ranked among the strongest in their respective segments on a global scale (except for Embraer) are: Friboi, Brazil Foods, Vale, Gerdau, Votorantim Celulose, and others that process low added-value products.

Later, in the 2000s, we faced a version of developmentalism that was much more oriented than its predecessor to the foreign market, i.e., to exports. This also resulted from the maintenance of the neoliberal capitalist model. Exports were stimulated by the income reconcentration process that had occurred during the neoliberal decades and the liberalization of Brazilian economy. Furthermore, since other dependent countries have also gone through a liberalization process, a dependent but stronger capitalist economy such as Brazil was able to take advantage of this superiority to occupy markets hitherto inaccessible due to more or less widespread protectionism. In this regard, the political behavior of the big internal bourgeoisie was exemplary. In the 1990s, industries oriented to the domestic market had a predominantly defensive and timid attitude in the face of trade liberalization: industrialists complained about the fast pace of trade opening and the lack of a state policy to prepare Brazilian industry for open competition. In the 2000s, the internal bourgeoisie abandoned its defensive position and, settling into the neoliberal model, gave up the protectionism inherited from the old developmentalism and started to conquer neighboring markets that had also been opened up. In consonance with this stance of the big internal bourgeoisie, the Brazilian state under Lula adopted a foreign policy that focused on the countries of the Southern Hemisphere, as well as an aggressive financing policy through the Brazilian Development Bank (BNDES) – both policies aimed at promoting Brazilian companies and investments abroad. (We shall not discuss here whether or not the Brazilian state and capitalism have established an imperialistic relationship with other Latin American countries, but we will highlight the complexity of the situation. The big Brazilian companies that had been investing heavily in Venezuela supported the Chavez government. For example, Marcelo Odebrecht, president of the construction company that bears his surname and had started several projects in that country, spoke in favor of the Chavez administration and criticized the mainstream Brazilian press which, in Odebrecht's opinion, created a negative and deformed image of the Venezuelan president).

Although the Lula governments represented the big internal bourgeoisie, it would be a mistake to affirm – as did several analysts and critics of the administration – that the Brazilian bourgeoisie supported Lula fundamentally because his would have been the government that best managed to maintain the labor and popular movements within the limits of moderation. However, one of the problems of this thesis is that a large part of the bourgeoisie did not support Lula at all. This fact can be verified by the political and parliamentary attitude of parties such as the Brazilian Social Democracy Party (PSDB), Democrats (DEM), and other minor parties, as well as by the conservative political opposition promoted by organs of the mainstream press. This begs the question: why was there an opposition bourgeoisie? To understand this fact, it is necessary to consider that, in addition to the big internal bourgeoisie, there was also in Brazil a big bourgeoisie perfectly integrated and subordinated to foreign capital. This bourgeois fraction, which defended an extreme neoliberal economic policy, had its interests dismissed by the Lula government in many ways. This is why this *associated bourgeoisie*, a subordinate ally of big international financial capital, wanted the PSDB's return to power. The bourgeois fraction that supported the Lula administration did so fundamentally due to this dispute within the bloc in power, and not because it felt that Lula's would be the best government to contain the labor and popular movement.

In order to overcome the big associated bourgeoisie and international financial capital – the most economically powerful and influential bourgeois forces among private institutions exerting hegemony (Gramsci) – the big internal bourgeoisie was led to form a front in association with the trade union and popular movements.[3] This front, however, suffered from an original sin: it had

---

3   Front and alliance are not the same. In an alliance, different classes or class fractions, each acting independently and based on its own political program, are brought together in an organized way, establishing a minimum common agenda. In a front, classes and class fractions, not necessarily organized independently, are articulated around converging goals, but this convergence is not always clear to the social forces involved. A social force that is involved in a front without realizing it is unable to direct it. Even if the unaware force resorts to radical action, it may function as an instrument of the driving force.

not stemmed from an initiative of its hegemonic force, the big internal bourgeoisie. It was first and foremost the indirect and, to some extent, unexpected
result of the trade union and popular movements' struggle. And why is it so?
Because throughout the 1980s and 1990s, the trade union and popular struggle
was the main factor in building and affirming the Workers' Party and an electorally viable reformist field led by the PT. The big bourgeoisie cannot take full
credit for the victory of Lula's candidacy in the 2002 presidential election. Both
the labor and popular movement's political limitations and ability to exert
pressure pushed the big internal bourgeoisie into a political front that the popular movement itself was unable to conduct. The front was unified, though
precariously, around the neodevelopmentalism of the big internal bourgeoisie,
whose success depended to a great extent on the labor and popular movement
that, however, was not satisfied with the limits of this development project.
Thus, the labor and popular movement was not the hegemonic force of the
front that defined the *objectives* of the struggle, but its main force, on which
depended the *success* of the struggle. This mismatch between the hegemonic
(bourgeois) and the main (labor and popular) forces has generated conflicts
and instabilities within the neodevelopmentalist political front.

This was the front that the Lula government, maneuvering in the midst of
difficulties, sought to maintain and consolidate. The president had his own
political asset: thanks to cash transfer programs, he could rely on impoverished
and disorganized workers, with whom he managed to establish a populist
political relationship. The government's economic policy also brought some
gain to unionism – by increasing employment in the public and private sectors, improving wages for civil servants, and promoting a small restoration of
the minimum wage – in addition to offering a lure to the union movement: the
officialization of union centrals. As a result, Lula gained the support of most of
the union movement (Galvão, 2012). The government also implemented public
policies addressing organized popular demands. The greatest example is the
housing program called "My House, My Life" (*Minha casa, Minha vida*), which
meets the demands of the active homeless movements throughout Brazil,
albeit in a limited way (Hirata & Oliveira, 2012). These concessions to some
popular demands displeased the bourgeoisie, including the big internal bourgeoisie that the government represented. The publications of the Federation
of Industries of the State of São Paulo (Fiesp), for example, criticized what
industrialists considered to be the state's excessive spending on personnel. But
the government preserved the strategic interests of the internal bourgeoisie: it
made sure not to trigger any broad process to regulate the labor market or to
restore public services and social rights. Instead, the government imposed
lesser sacrifices on the big internal bourgeoisie in order to promote it, through

the formation of a political front, to a position within the bloc in power that this fraction would not have the strength to conquer by itself. Moreover, the fact that a significant part of the administration came from the union movement rendered unnecessary any disciplinary action by the government against the class it represented.

We therefore witnessed something similar to what the communists of the 1950s imagined as a solution to Brazil's political and social problems: a front or alliance uniting part of the Brazilian bourgeoisie with the organized labor movement. However, in addition to the similarities indicated, the differences between what the communists wanted and the political situation under Lula were equally important.

In the following sections we will present some analytical and empirical elements to support these ideas.

1   FHC, Lula, and Disputes within the Bourgeoisie

A rigorous analysis of the bloc in power in Brazilian neoliberal capitalism would require, on the one hand, a precise indication of which economic segments were organized as fractions of the bourgeois class and, on the other hand, a comparison between the strategic and secondary demands of the different bourgeois fractions and the government measures that constituted the state's economic policy. Such a procedure might give us a clear profile of the bloc in power and its hegemonic fraction. That would require a greater research effort than what we have endeavored so far. We will, however introduce a few elements.

Both the big associated bourgeoisie and the big internal bourgeoisie are part of the world of big capital. These are represented by big businesses that wield economic power and, in most cases, act as monopolistic – or oligopolistic – companies in their fields of activity. Therefore, a shift of monopoly power from one of these fractions to the other would not represent a political change of major importance (Saes, 2001). The big associated bourgeoisie and the big internal bourgeoisie may take turns in the bloc in power's central position without promoting fundamental changes in economic and social policy and without causing institutional ruptures in the state or in the political regime. This is quite different from what happened in scenarios of relevant political change, such as in 1930, when the big coffee-based capital was ousted from the state hegemonic position, or in 1964, when the old national bourgeoisie and the populist front were defeated. Whether it was the big associated bourgeoisie or the big internal bourgeoisie occupying the hegemonic fraction within the bloc in power, the development policy favored big monopoly capital to the detriment of small and medium-sized companies and also of the workers' interests. What then distinguishes these two fractions of the big bourgeoisie? We believe that it is their position in the face of imperialism. The big associated bourgeoisie aims at an almost limitless expansion of imperialism, while the big internal bourgeoisie, though linked to imperialism and relying on its action to boost Brazilian capitalism, seeks to impose limits on that expansion.

At the origin of the Latin American neoliberal capitalist model, there was a pressure from international financial capital – conglomerates that unified industries, banks, and services under the command of the financial system – to open Latin American domestic markets and privatize well-run state companies in the region – which is a push towards dismantling the developmentalist capitalist model inherited from the Vargas period. We mean openness in a broad sense: commercial openness to facilitate the import of industrial products from central economies, and openness to foreign investments in areas hitherto controlled by state-owned companies or by private national companies. Such pressure was directed at various economic segments: industrial, banking, agricultural, insurance, health, education, and others. There was also pressure for Latin American economies to enter the international financial valuation circuit through a new legislation that would facilitate volatile investment in these countries' public debt securities and stock exchanges, and guarantee the safe and rapid repatriation of these investments at favorable exchange rates. A broad, heterogeneous and powerful segment of the Brazilian bourgeoisie had thrived on this policy adopted by Collor and, afterwards, by FHC. National financial groups had benefited from high interest and freedom of entry and exit of capital. This included national companies that had associated with foreign groups to participate in the auctions of state-owned companies, commercial companies linked to imports, business groups in the areas of health and education, part of the internationalized sectors of the local industry, and others that perceived, and indeed enjoyed, new business opportunities and the possibility of association with foreign capital due to the policy of privatization and openness. Research is yet to be done to give us a true picture of such groups, but from what we know we can affirm that it was a powerful sector of the Brazilian bourgeoisie that, from within the country, was also putting pressure on governments to open the gates to trade liberalization and foreign investment.

However, another sector of the Brazilian bourgeoisie was reluctant to accept the neoliberal openness. This sector, which eventually formed the fraction that we call big internal bourgeoisie, took considerable time to support Collor's candidacy and did so more to prevent Lula's victory than to join Collor's program.

This explains why, as soon as he faced his first political crisis, Collor was abandoned by the big internal bourgeoisie. It is worth remembering that Fiesp and other associations of Brazilian industrialists joined the national campaign for Collor's impeachment, having even sent representatives to motivate the masses at the "Collor Out" (*Fora Collor*) protests (Martuscelli, 2012). The big industrialists, together with agribusiness, formed the most important segment of the big internal bourgeoisie, maintaining a contradictory relationship with the neoliberal program. They supported, as did the whole bourgeoisie, the *social policy of neoliberalism*: wage deindexation, deregulation of labor relations, reduction and cuts in social rights – in the areas of public health, public welfare, and education. However, they were reluctant to accept – or even opposed – important aspects of the neoliberal economic policy: they rejected the policy of trade liberalization, which threatened the captive market created by developmentalism for local industry and sought to maintain the positions of strength they had conquered in Brazilian capitalism, since these positions were being threatened by the neoliberal reforms.

The big internal bourgeoisie had brought together various sectors: industrial groups, banks, agribusiness, construction and others. What united these heterogeneous sectors of the Brazilian capitalist class in the same bourgeois fraction was their dispute with international financial capital, both within the country and increasingly in the international arena, especially in the Southern Hemisphere. There were contentions between the productive and banking sectors, and between exporting companies and those mainly oriented to the domestic market. In short, the big internal bourgeoisie treated such contentions as secondary issues in comparison to their dispute with big international capital. The big internal bourgeoisie feared to be dominated or destroyed by big foreign economic groups. For instance: industrialists wanted customs protectionism for their products; bankers requested state intervention to limit the entry of foreign capital in their sector; sugar mill owners in São Paulo state's countryside demanded the association of Petrobras with sugar mills for the production of ethanol. According to one of their representatives, the mill owners feared that the balance between national and foreign capital would be disrupted in favor of the latter if Petrobras did not exert its economic power to the advantage of national plant owners; the shipbuilding industry wanted that the state gave preference to purchasing from national shipyards; large export businesses and companies interested in investing in and developing heavy construction works in other countries required the government's political and commercial action to conquer foreign markets and to favor and protect their investments abroad. In other words, in the face of big international financial capital, the big internal bourgeoisie, while interested in attracting foreign

investments to Brazil, also sought to preserve and expand the positions it held
in the national and international economy. To that end, it relied on the protective and active actions of the Brazilian state. It should be noted, in passing, that
contrary to the *manifest content* of the neoliberal ideology, the bourgeoisie did
not really aspire to a "minimum state" for the bourgeois class …

Let us indicate what the positions of these two big bourgeois fractions were
in the governments of the 1990s and 2000s. The two FHC governments were
not homogeneous, though they could be characterized as governments that
prioritized the interests of the big associated bourgeoisie and international
financial capital.

The first term was characterized by aggressive political action. FHC succeeded in imposing neoliberal reforms and proved to be successful where
Collor de Mello had failed. In his first mandate, FHC promoted a sharp reduction in customs tariffs, which, combined with the overvaluation of the exchange
rate introduced by the Plano Real, increased imports, including the import of
intermediate and final manufactured goods. In 1990, the average import tariff
rate was 40%, and the most frequent rate was 32.2%. In 1992, thanks to Collor
de Mello's measures, both fell to around 20%. Once in office, and still in 1995,
FHC imposed a new and drastic reduction in tariffs. The average rate dropped
to 12.6%, and the most frequent rate sank even further to the almost symbolic
value of 2% (Dieese, 1996). The result of such policy was that the Brazilian
trade balance started to show increasing deficits as of 1995, when it was 3.1
billion dollars; by 1997, it rose up to around 10 billion (see Charts 117–119 in
Dieese, 1996: 172–174). Still in his first term, FHC effectively pursued the privatization policy. After the steel, fertilizer, chemical, and other industries, the
time had come for the privatization of state banks, railroads, highways, electric
power distribution, telephony, sewage services, and other production and service industries.

The second term was marked by a defensive political action, in which the
government sought to circumvent the situation created by the 1999 currency
crisis and the increasing dissatisfaction in sectors of the popular movement
and the bourgeoisie itself. As neoliberal reforms were implemented, they
accumulated contradictions. Fiesp protested against the government's deindustrialization policy, and Força Sindical, the union force that had supported
neoliberal reforms and the FHC government, started to reassess its position.
This trade union central organized sit-down strikes at the workplace of its
main base, the metallurgical workers from São Paulo, to protest against trade
liberalization and the closing of companies. Fiesp, together with the National
Confederation of Industry (CNI), organized in May 1996 a national protest
in Brasília with industrialists from all over of the country. According to the

press at the time, most of the businesspersons who were in Brasília belonged to the sectors most affected by trade liberalization: capital goods, electronic components, textiles, shoes, and toys. The industrialists protested against the "dismantling of the industry" and the trade liberalization. They also demanded a devaluation of the exchange rate and reduced interest rates (Boito Jr., 2002a). This action enabled Fiesp to seek an approximation to the São Paulo workers' movement and to garner the support of the union centrals for the protest in Brasília. Fiesp's president took the initiative of visiting the president of CUT at its headquarters, posed for photos with Vicentinho and Luiz Antonio de Medeiros, from Força Sindical, and published an article in the mainstream press declaring that Fiesp would support the general strike that was being organized by the two union centrals. The general attitude of the industrialists was, at that moment, of radicalized opposition to trade liberalization and the interest policy.[4]

In the face of economic difficulties in the foreign sector – the exchange rate crisis – and internal political pressure, FHC fired Gustavo Franco from the presidency of the Central Bank and devalued the Brazilian real. This resulted in a moderation of the neoliberal opening, but did not lead to a break with the model. During FHC's two terms, the economic policy of trade opening – albeit mitigated by the devaluation of the Brazilian real in 1999 – together with privatization, financial deregulation, and the formation of the Free Trade Area of Americas (Alca, in Portuguese), was a manifestation of the hegemony of the big associated bourgeoisie and international financial capital within the bloc in power. This caused dissatisfaction and protests not only among members of the labor and popular movement, but also, and contrary to what most analysts suppose or claim, it caused dissatisfaction and protests in sectors of the Brazilian bourgeoisie, such as the big industrial bourgeoisie beset by the suspension of protectionism in the internal market.

Let us now examine the two Lula governments, which were not homogeneous either, but had an element of political continuity between them. As

---

4 At a meeting of the Fiesp board held in early May 1996, no less than 24 directors made a point of taking the floor to support, without restrictions, the protests organized by the entity's president against the trade liberalization policy. Some of them, such as Gerson Edson Toledo Piza, director of the São Paulo Center of Industries (Ciesp) in São Carlos, explained their stance on the proposal for a general strike: "You displayed a brave attitude, sir, in declaring that, if necessary, entrepreneurs and workers will come to a symbolic standstill"; Marcelo Kuañes, superintendent director of Kone Indústria de Máquinas, addressing Fiesp's president, stated: "I have in the past disagreed with your work philosophy, but today I have to congratulate you and join the general strike movement right away if it comes to happen." *Revista da Indústria*. São Paulo, May 6, 1996, *apud* Boito Jr., 2002a.

we have already indicated, the economic policy of the Lula era constituted a movement toward the big internal bourgeoisie to the detriment of the interests of the associated bourgeoisie and of international financial capital. While FHC's political tactic was to adopt an aggressive attitude in the first term to retreat to a defensive policy in the second term when difficulties arose, Lula did the opposite. He started out cautiously, with a first term marked by defensive tactics, whose main objective was not to clash with international financial capital. He changed as his second term began, adopting an intensive implementation of the neodevelopmentalist policy proposed by the big internal bourgeoisie. Ironically, it was the so-called *"Mensalão"* corruption crisis, considered by international financial capital and the associated bourgeoisie to be their opportunity to regain government power, which induced the Lula government to take aggressive action by enforcing the neodevelopmentalist policy. The deactivation of the FTAA (Alca), the diplomacy measures and foreign trade policy aimed at conquering new markets in the Southern Hemisphere, the strengthening of commercial relations with South American countries, the interruption of the privatization program, the boost offered to the remaining state-owned companies, and the new role of the BNDES in the formation of powerful Brazilian companies in many different segments of the economy – all these measures set up an economic policy that tended to prioritize the interests of the big internal bourgeoisie to the detriment of those of the big associated bourgeoisie and international financial capital.

In his second term, Lula invested heavily in the creation and consolidation of big national economic groups, with special credit and shareholding programs that also aimed at promoting investments by these groups abroad. Such policy led to a redefinition of the BNDES' role. From a bank that financed privatizations in the FHC governments, the BNDES was converted into a state bank for the promotion of predominantly national big capital.[5] In 2008, almost all the 20 largest Brazilian companies that operated abroad counted on BNDES as a shareholder, through BNDESPar, or through pension funds of state-owned companies, or even through a large contribution of interest-subsidized credit from the bank (see Table 2).

We must stress that the table does not show the data concerning the large loans, at favorable interest rates, granted by the BNDES to allow the formation and consolidation of these groups. From the data, first of all we gather the importance of companies and pension funds linked to the state for the big

---

5   For a comparison of BNDES's performance in the telecommunications sector in the FHC and
    Lula governments, see Cavalcante (2012).

TABLE 2   Investment of BNDES and public companies pension funds in the 20 largest
           Brazilian companies operating abroad in 2008 (net revenue)

1	Petrobras	Direct participation of BNDESPar in 7.62% of its capital
2	Petrobras distribuidora	Controlled by Petrobras
3	Companhia Vale	Direct participation of BNDESPar in 4.8% of its capital and of Previ, Petros, Funcesp, and Funcef pension funds in the controlling bloc
4	Ambev	
5	Companhia Brasileira de Petróleo Ypiranga	Sold to Petrobras, Braskem, and Grupo Ultra in 2007
6	Braskem S.A.	Direct participation of BNDESPar in 5.22% of its capital
7	Companhia Siderúrgica Nacional	Direct participation of BNDESPar in 3.64% of its capital
8	Gerdau Aços Longos S.A.	Direct participation of BNDESPar in 3.5% of its capital
9	Usiminas	Previ holds 10.4%; Grupo Votorantim, 13%, and Grupo Camargo Correa, 13% of its capital.
10	Sadia S.A.	Previ holds 7.3% of its capital, and BNDES participated in the merger with Perdigão in 2009.
11	Centrais Elétricas Brasileiras	Direct participation of BNDESPar in 11.81% and of the Brazilian Federal Government in 53.99% of its capital
12	TAM Linhas Aéreas S.A.	
13	Embraer	Direct participation of BNDESPar in 5.05%; of Previ in 14%, and of the Brazilian Federal Government in 0.3% of its capital
14	Cemig Distribuição S.A.	Participation of the state of Minas Gerais in 50.96% of its capital
15	Perdigão Agroindustrial S.A.	Previ holds 14.16% of its capital; Petros, 12.04%; Sistel, 3.98%; BNDESPar participated in the merger with Sadia in 2009
16	Gerdau Açominas S.A.	Indirect participation of BNDESPar through Gerdau Aços Longos

TABLE 2   Investment of BNDES and public companies pension funds (*cont.*)

17	Bertin S.A.	Direct participation of BNDESPar in 26.98% of its capital
18	Globo Comunicação e Participações S.A.	
19	J.B.S. S.A. (Friboi)	Direct participation of BNDESPar in 13% of its capital
20	Aracruz Celulosa S.A./ Votorantim Celulose e Papel S.A.	Direct participation of BNDESPar in 34.9% of the capital of the new company (Fíbria).

SOURCE: MANSUETO ALMEIDA. DESAFIOS DA REAL POLÍTICA INDUSTRIAL BRASILEIRA NO SÉCULO XXI. *APUD RETRATO DO BRASIL* 30, JAN. 2010, P. 11

Brazilian internal bourgeoisie. We can draw the following conjecture: an intensive privatization program would have left the big Brazilian private bourgeoisie vulnerable and defenseless in the face of big international financial capital. It was not the bourgeoisie as a whole that longed for indiscriminate privatization. We also observe that the big internal bourgeoisie basically comprised private capital, but also included state-owned companies and encompassed different sectors of the economy: mining, steel, agribusiness, processing industry, transportation companies, and others. The BNDES has been the state agent defending and strengthening these large groups. It is worth noting that the table does not include the banking sector. Incidentally, the PSDB leaders, headed by former president FHC and former governor José Serra, expressly argued against the new BNDES policy in the mainstream press. This policy would have increased the public debt, as the funds mobilized by BNDES were obtained through the issuance of government bonds. It would also have subsidized big companies, since the long-term interest rate that BNDES applied on loans to companies was lower than the basic interest rate, which is the rate paid by the government to raise the funds it allocates to this state bank. We would be facing a situation in which public money was offered to a handful of companies owned by friends of the government. However, the FHC government had done the same, only with a different objective: to privatize state-owned companies. In addition to the new role of the BNDES, the PSDB leadership symptomatically criticized other initiatives of the government's economic policy, such as large enterprises controlled by the state or by state-owned companies created or reactivated by the Lula government and that encompassed big companies that were predominantly Brazilian-based. Examples of that are the construction of the Belo Monte Plant, the project to build the high-speed railway between São Paulo and Rio de Janeiro, the nationalization and democratization of broadband internet, and others. After favoring national shipyards and the defense industry in state purchases, the Lula government issued in July 2010 the provisional measure regulating this priority.

The press reported the big international capital's dissatisfaction with these measures and the big international banks' longing for the return of the PSDB to the government command. In June 2010, at a conference in Vienna, the Institute of International Finance (IIF), a global association that gathers more than 500 large banks from the main capitalist economies, demonstrated its preference for José Serra's candidacy in the presidential election of that year and its distrust of then candidate Dilma Rousseff. Frederick Jaspersen, lecturer at the Vienna meeting, said to the hundreds of bankers in attendance that Dilma Rousseff as president would bring greater risk to the Brazilian economy than José Serra would. *Valor Econômico* newspaper obtained a copy of this lecture in which Jaspersen indicated the "central differences" between the two candidates. He associated Rousseff to increased public spending, relaxation of inflation control, and emphasized industrial policy, with state-owned companies playing a stronger role in the economy. He also highlighted Rousseff's lack of experience and asserted that with her in power there would be "a greater role of the state, a regulatory framework more influenced by political pressures, a greater risk of macroeconomic slippage, little progress in structural reforms, and limited increase of the potential growth of the economy."[6] The IIF economist presented Serra as the candidate who would respect and even tighten fiscal control, reduce interest rates, and devalue the Brazilian currency. His government would place less emphasis on state-owned companies, offer more support to the private sector, and employ tax policy to encourage private investment.

As we can see, the struggle within the large monopoly capital, which set the big associated bourgeoisie against the internal bourgeoisie, was reflected in the Brazilian party system. The majority wing of the PSDB, the electoral vanguard of neoliberalism in Brazil, had represented, despite the early stage of the party's history, big international financial capital and the interests of Brazilian entrepreneurs and bankers closely linked to that capital. The PT, born as a left-wing social-democratic party and linked to the union movement, had been

---

6   *Valor Econômico*, June 11 2010, article signed by journalist Assis Moreira, who covered the meeting of bankers in Vienna.

moving closer to the big internal bourgeoisie since the mid-1990s, when the so-called *Majority Sector* (Campo Majoritário) started the process of programmatic and organizational reformulation of the party. Underrepresented in the press and in the party system, this bourgeois fraction ended up being represented at the party level, and, due to particular circumstances, by a political party that was born out of the labor and popular movement.

2   The Political Relations of the Big Internal Bourgeoisie with the Lula Government

Addressing this subject in a systematic manner would require information and an analysis of the political action of the whole big internal bourgeoisie, of the institutions that represent the bourgeoisie, and of the decision-making process inside Lula's government. At present, we cannot fully develop this work. As an initial step, however, we will scrutinize the demands of São Paulo's big industrial bourgeoisie in face of some aspects of Lula's policy. Our intention is to indicate that the relationship established between the PT government and this bourgeois fraction is a relationship of political representation recognized by both. The year of 2004 was marked by the inauguration of Fiesp's new board of directors, chaired by Paulo Skaf. It is known that, as a candidate, Skaf had the support of the Presidency. One of the new board's first initiatives was to relaunch *Revista da Indústria*, a periodical that had not been published for six years, since the previous board had interrupted its circulation. Paulo Skaf turned the magazine's relaunch and his inauguration as Fiesp's president into a great political event, with the active participation of President Lula.

On the pages of the magazine, the new board proposed what they called a new and proactive attitude towards the Lula government; the magazine included articles signed by the association's president and the first and second vice-presidents, all of them criticizing monetarism, trade liberalization, high interest rates, and the tax burden that would be inherited from the 1990s. The function of *Revista da Indústria*, according to one of the articles, would be to collaborate in "Fiesp's new era" – a proactive era of joint action with government authorities so the decisions made would start to serve the interests of the industry. "Fiesp's new board aims to recover its prominence in major national decisions."[7]

---

7   See the reports and testimonies published in issue #101, November 2004, of *Revista da Indústria*, a monthly publication by Fiesp.

Besides the articles mentioned, there is in the same issue of the magazine an article signed by journalist Ricardo Viveiros commenting on the positions of the new board, presenting them as a real break with Fiesp's previous attitude.

Other articles criticize the predominance of "monetarism over the shop floor," "superlative profitability for the vicious financial cycle" (Skaf, 2004); the "current monetary terrorism that keeps interest rates at exorbitant levels and gives the financial sector unjustifiable preponderance over the productive;" "the costs of long-term financing" (Steinbruch, 2004); the excessive tax burden on the productive sector. They also present critical, albeit careful, considerations on the FTAA (Alca, in Portuguese) proposal, which might "suppress jobs in Brazil." The same articles propose that Fiesp and the industrial sectors should "raise again the flag of development and national production." In passing, and only subtly, they criticize the position of the entity's boards during the "FHC era." After praising the struggle of the industrial sector pioneers, Ricardo Viveiros states, "Gaps of omission do not do justice to the combative and active genesis of Fiesp and to the ability of many of its leaders to lead the São Paulo industrial sector to victory in the most diverse circumstances. It is this historic commitment to Brazil and its development that is being rescued by the entity's new management" (Viveiros, 2004).

Also in passing, Ricardo Viveiros's article mentions a possible alliance with workers and other segments of the productive sector: "In addition, it is necessary to reach a deeper understanding with workers' organizations and sectors such as agriculture, commerce, and services, thus articulating cohesive, viable actions and proposals to remove obstacles to production and the creation of jobs and income." (Viveiros, 2004). This alliance aimed at fighting monetarism. However, the author adds a caveat: "We are not opposing the financial area, which is already present in the public power; we just wish to see the business sector, represented by our entity, being active in the Legislative and Executive branches as well" (Viveiros, 2004). Fiesp's first vice-president advocated for a policy favoring the "indispensable formation of large internationalized national groups" (Steinbruch, 2004), which, as we have already seen, was promoted by the new role assigned to BNDES by the Lula government. There were also appeals for the valorization of the sugar and alcohol sector, which "was brought to a crisis in the 1990s," and "the advancement of reforms in areas such as social security, tributary, fiscal, political, labor, trade union and judicial" (Viveiros, 2004).

The following issue of *Revista da Indústria* covered the inauguration ceremony of the new board of directors.[8] The ceremony was a demonstration of Fiesp's strength and proximity to the federal government. The inauguration

---

8   *Revista da Indústria* #102, Dec 2004.

took place in the stately building of the Ipiranga Museum, in São Paulo, with the presence of four thousand guests, among whom were President Lula, Geraldo Alckmin, Marta Suplicy, governors of other states, and presidents of 18 federations of the industrial sector. The full-page picture shows Lula at the center. The tone of the text is proudly patriotic, ending in a grandiloquent and even ridiculous tone:

> On the stairs of the Museum, facing the famous Ipiranga [Brook], directors and counselors of the new Fiesp posed next to dozens of ambassadors, politicians, appellate judges, and secretaries for a picture that certainly will make history in São Paulo industry. In a fiery speech, the new president of Fiesp cried out in defense of the Industry as a legitimate productive authority. And the cry echoed![9]

After the celebrations, in the beginning of 2005, the new Fiesp board took the initiative to propose and draft the bill that authorized exporters to retain part of the values obtained and to open an account in foreign currency, as a compensation for the exchange rate appreciation. The Lula government embraced and approved the industrialists' proposal. Issue #103 of the magazine reported on this process, in which we can detect the proactive participation of the big internal bourgeoisie, as the Fiesp's board had promised.[10] Paulo Skaf's inauguration was an important indicator of the consolidation of the new arrangement within the bloc in power, in which the big internal industrial bourgeoisie established itself as the class base of the Lula government. In this hypothesis, the previous board was an "omission gap" in which Fiesp would have omitted or protested very timidly against the open and monetarist policies of FHC's governments.

Fiesp had participated in the *"Fora Collor"* campaign in 1992. However, in 2005, it did not abandon the Lula government during the *"Mensalão"* corruption crisis. *Revista da Indústria* remained silent for a long time regarding the corruption allegations. Of course, the silence was in itself favorable to the government. However, in the August 2005 issue, the industrialists' publication broke the silence to criticize the opposition, mentioning the political crisis, but without even mentioning the term *"Mensalão"* a single time. An interview with Paulo Skaf followed the same lines.

---

9   O Grito da Indústria. *Revista da Indústria,* # 102, Dec 2004.
10   *Revista da Indústria,* # 103, Jan 2005.

Both the article and the interview had the same central idea, which could be summarized this way: "Enough about the crisis, let's go back to work!"[11] Indeed, the PSDB's opposition was not well regarded by the industrialists.

In his interview, Paulo Skaf repeated verbatim the speech chosen by all the members of the government team, by the PT leaders, and by allied government parties: "let's go back to the positive agenda." Among other things, Skaf stated the following:

> It is not possible [...] There are projects that cannot be halted in Congress, in the Executive. Ergo, our effort has been to list the priority projects among the countless pending bills, and to make the country go forward in parallel with the Parliamentary Inquiry Committees (CPIs), which are important, but there are 150 million Brazilians who need and yearn for the advance of other issues.[12]

In the article "Nothing Holds Back Industry" by Jane Soares, we find the same catchphrase: "enough about the crisis, let's go back to work." The text also informs that a group of big businesspersons, all leaders of several business associations, formed a delegation and went to Brasília to express their veiled, but firm, support to President Lula. At the height of the *"Mensalão"* crisis, the newspapers exhibited a front-page photo of Lula accompanied by the cream of the big business community and several leaders of national business associations before the Presidential Palace.

But let us return to the August 2005 issue of *Revista da Indústria*:

> The business community wants the Executive and Legislative branches to leave the current immobility and adopt the necessary measures to stimulate production. [...] Currently, what concerns businesspersons is the unprecedented political crisis [...]. In this sensitive context, businesspersons once again become organized.[13]

> At the beginning of the month, in response to the request of the President of the Republic, [they] went to the Presidential Palace. The group of 24 businesspersons presented a list of modest claims [...]. What they want now is a minimum agenda to ensure governability. [...][14]

---

11   *Revista da Indústria*, # 110, Aug 2005. See the article "O tempo não espera," entrevista com Paulo Skaf, 17–19 and the article "Nada segura a indústria', 41–47.
12   *Revista da Indústria*, # 110, Aug 2005, 18.
13   *Revista da Indústria*, #110, Aug 2005, 43.
14   *Revista da Indústria*, # 110, Aug 2005, 42.

On the same day in Brasília, Fiesp's president and directors also met with Minister Dilma Rousseff to discuss projects that are waiting to be forwarded by Chief of staff to the National Congress. [...][15]

This is a time of awakening. Brazil cannot focus solely on investigating claims of deviations or privileges," reinforced Skaf.[16]

The next issue of *Revista da Indústria* (September 2005) addressed the political crisis again, but with a slightly different discourse. The emphasized message was: "Political reform is the way out of the crisis" (Junot, 2005.). In other words, the PSDB could not count on the support of the big Brazilian business community to promote an impeachment process against Lula. The problem would lie in the political system, not in this or that government. At no time the magazine expressed any animosity against the Lula government. On the contrary, while recognizing the legitimacy of the debate around corruption, the text returned, albeit with less emphasis, to "enough about the crisis, let's go back to work," an idea that disallowed and disqualified any criticism of corruption.

Parallel to [the political reform] debate which, together with the various Parliamentary Inquiries Committees (CPIs) in progress, seem to be draining all congressmen's and government's energy, society tries to maintain another debate, which before the crisis ranked higher on the list of priorities. This includes, for example, legal and foreign exchange reforms, and other measures to ensure the continuity of the economic expansion; in short, a minimum agenda as advocated by Fiesp and its president Paulo Skaf.

JUNOT, 2005, 48–49

Not only did the injunction "enough about the crisis, let's go back to work" returned, but also a warning was issued to the bourgeois parties that opposed the Lula government. After all, who was responsible for the fact that this "minor debate" was draining the energies of congressional representatives and the government?

Fiesp had strong reasons to support Lula, having established a smooth communication channel with the government. In the same September 2005 issue of *Revista da Indústria*, the article "Towards Modernity" by journalist Fernanda Cunha reveals how Fiesp took the initiative to draft the bill that gave exporters

---

15   *Revista da Indústria*, # 110, Aug 2005, 43.
16   *Revista da Indústria*, # 110, Aug 2005, 44.

the right to retain part of the foreign currency they obtained in their operations (Cunha, 2005, 38–39). Such measure was very important as it offset losses
in the export sector due to the exchange rate appreciation without the need
to interfere with the exchange policy, which was an important and sensitive
part of the whole development project. The bill was drafted by Fiesp and by
the Foreign Trade Studies Center Foundation (Funcex), and submitted for an
initial assessment to Antonio Palocci, Minister of Finance, and to Henrique
Meirelles, president of the Central Bank. The project was sent in September
to the National Congress, where it was approved and later sanctioned by
President Lula. The report in the Fiesp magazine describes the project in the
following terms:

> [...] the proposal endorses the floating exchange rate regime [...] and
> provides for the possibility of any Brazilian company registered in the
> Integrated Foreign Trade System (Siscomex) or in the Central Bank
> Information System (Sisbacen) to open a named account in foreign
> currency in the national financial system [...] Payments abroad for
> imports, freight, insurance, external financing, and royalties, for exam-
> ple, can be made directly from accounts in foreign currency that would
> eliminate spread expenses between the purchase and sale rate, the
> double incidence of provisional contribution on financial transactions
> (CPMF) on the entry and exit of foreign exchange, the double collec-
> tion of foreign exchange brokerage fees, and banking and bureaucratic
> costs.
>
> CUNHA, 2005, 38

> [...] it would also eliminate the mandatory conversion of export earn-
> ings into Brazilian reais within a maximum period of 210 days, allowing
> companies to exchange currency only according to the opportunity cost
> of investing financial assets and their need of cash flow. Thus, in the
> words of Roberto Giannetti da Fonseca, director of the Department of
> International Relations and Foreign Trade at Fiesp (Derex), companies
> would not be held hostage to the daily exchange quotation and would
> convert currency whenever the rate was more convenient.
>
> CUNHA, 2005, 39

Let us return to how Fiesp backed the Lula government during the crucial episode of the "*Mensalão*" corruption crisis. It should be noted that Fiesp's support
was key to the outcome of that crisis. Lula's relationship with organized workers

was strained. The political crisis was triggered by a vote-buying scheme involving parties and politicians who favored their own interests over the common good, and this scheme had been used to approve, among other government projects, the pension reform extinguishing civil servants' rights. The union movement and the Landless Workers' Movement (MST) were drawing away from the government. At the height of the crisis, a workers' demonstration in defense of the government, convened by the most representative leaderships in the union movement, gathered a paltry number of people, much fewer than those who had convened in another public act, also held in Brasília a few days earlier, to protest against the government and in support of subsequent investigations of corruption allegations. The latter act had been summoned by small left-wing organizations, such as the United Socialist Workers' Party (PSTU). When Lula realized that he had to "appeal to the masses," he did not resort to PT's traditional social base. He went to the Northeast region and held rallies among disorganized workers, whom Lulism had been approaching thanks to the "Family Grant" (*Bolsa Família*) program. In this scenario, the support of Fiesp – and, according to the press at the time, of the entire big internal bourgeoisie – was decisive for the government. The outcome of the crisis was the opposite of what the big associated bourgeoisie, the upper middle class, international financial capital, and the PSDB had expected: the *"Mensalão" crisis* strengthened the government's relationship with the big internal bourgeoisie. The replacement of Antonio Palocci with Guido Mantega at the Ministry of Finance proves our hypothesis.

The ministerial change took place in April 2006, less than a year after the crisis had begun. The April-May 2006 issue of *Revista da Indústria* featured the headline "A Developmentalist at the Ministry of Finance." The cover story title was "New Command, New Changes Possible" (Demarchi & Vieira, 2006). The text makes it very clear that Fiesp recognized two tendencies in the government. The first, defined as "monetarist," was represented by Palocci; the second, called "developmentalist" and backed by Fiesp, was represented by Guido Mantega. This detail matters: it means that the internal bourgeoisie identified politically with Lula's neodevelopmentalism. Some points of the article deserve mention.

The text indicates that the São Paulo business community welcomed the change of ministers and applauded Mantega's developmentalism. It featured testimonies from more than ten leaders of various industry sectors as well as some of Fiesp's directors, and they all harped on the same string: Mantega valued development and would probably reduce the interest rate. The ideas they associated with Mantega were: developmentalist, interest rate reduction, man of production, deserves support, deserves trust, open to dialogue. In addition, the report approved the fact that Mantega, upon taking office, declared that he would not undertake another round of import tariff reductions. This proposal, described as "insane" by Fiesp's director Paulo Francini, had been planned by Palocci and Planning Minister Paulo Bernardes.

The report pictured Palocci pejoratively as orthodox and monetarist. It acknowledged that he freed Brazil from an inflation rate of 12.5% per year, increased foreign exchange reserves from 16 to 59 billion dollars, and the trade balance from 13.3 to 44.8 billion dollars. However, it emphasized that he sacrificed development, presenting the following data: 0.5% of GDP growth in 2003, 4.3% in 2004, and 2.3% in 2005. The report reserved some irony for Palocci: the "ex-Trotskyist" who "became a monetarist." His ideas "did not coincide with those of the productive sector," in the words of Paulo Francini.

The industrialists were divided between two groups: the optimistic and the pessimistic. The former bet that Mantega would bring a real "path reversal," an optimistic expression employed by Boris Tabacof, president of the Deliberative Council of the Brazilian Pulp and Paper Association (Bracelpa). The pessimistic group, comprising the majority, thought that it would not be possible to change much, especially because Lula had only eight months left as president. Entrepreneur Mário Cesar Martins de Camargo, president of the Brazilian Association of Graphic Industries (Abigraf), was skeptical. He stated, "Anyone who is appointed Finance Minister will suffer from Pedro Malan's syndrome." In other words, s/he "will try to contain the inflation through interest" (Demarchi & Vieira, 2006, 22). The references to government authorities and former authorities make it clear about whom the industrialists had a positive or negative opinion.

Although this research among industrialists has not been exhaustive, it is worth mentioning that there was an ostensible demonstration of preference for the Lula government and of veiled hostility towards the PSDB from a historical representative of the sugar and alcohol sector in the state of São Paulo, Luiz Guilherme Zancaner, owner of the Unialco group – comprised of three alcohol and sugar mills – and also director of the Bioenergy Producers Group (Udop), an entity of mill owners located in the Western region of the state of São Paulo. In an interview with *Valor Econômico* newspaper, Zancaner declared his support for the Lula government, his recognition that the government's policy favored his economic sector more than the previous administrations had, and also presented a negative assessment of José Serra, then governor of the state of São Paulo (Grabois, 2010). One aspect of Zancaner's interview is especially interesting for our analysis: he emphasized the demand for the participation of Petrobras in Brazilian ethanol production mills, lest they be swallowed up by the growth of foreign capital. Similar to other industry sectors, sugarcane mills wanted protection from the state – in this case, from a powerful state company – against foreign competitors. Below are two excerpts from the interview.

1. Support for the Lula government and criticism of candidate Serra

VALOR: How do you assess Lula's attitude toward your industry?

ZANCANER: During the crisis, the government played its part and offered credit, even though there was a lot of bureaucracy involved. The Lula government has been outstanding for our business, and I am moved by that. The industry has done a lot for Brazil, but the government is doing a lot for the sector, too. Never before has there been such a good policy for us. President Lula misses no opportunity to be kind. Other people miss no opportunity to be unpleasant, arrogant.

VALOR: Are you talking about the pre-candidate for the Presidency José Serra? Has he been against sugar-cane plantations?

ZANCANER: I can only say that Serra is an excellent administrator, but I believe he does not see our industry as Lula does. [...] In my opinion, Lula led a better government. FHC laid the groundwork, but Lula and Dilma have established the channels with us.

VALOR: And do you think Dilma will carry this policy further?

ZANCANER: Dilma was very clear when she was here, in Araçatuba. She intends to give continuity to Lula's policy.

VALOR: Have you met her?

ZANCANER: Yes, I have talked to her. I feel that the majority of the industry, even taking into account the problems with the MST, has an affinity and a very good dialogue with her. Governor Serra is more reserved; we have no dialogue with him. [...]

..
.

2. Claim for restrictions on foreign capital

ZANCANER: The government, for example, is concerned about the denationalization of the industry, which is important for us. But balance is also important; foreign capital is welcome, because it improves the price of our assets. And we need that capital. But balance is necessary. Their capital cost is much lower because of the interest they find abroad.

VALOR: Minister Dilma defends the strengthening of national groups in the ethanol sector. Is there a way to do this except by increasing funding?

ZANCANER: Why can't Petrobras take part in national groups? The government should strengthen and support national groups to balance national capital. Currently, foreign capital produces 25% of all sugarcane in Brazil.

VALOR: How would the participation of Petrobras work?

ZANCANER: Petrobras has a better chance of entering ethanol production at the plant. The company has already had export contracts with Japan, and a distribution structure.

This interview is relevant because it shows clearly that this part of the big internal bourgeoisie had a positive image of the Lula government, and also explains why this fraction of the big internal bourgeoisie kept distance from the PSDB. However, this is not an exceptional statement. The sugar and alcohol mills in the countryside of São Paulo state – responsible for most of the country's production – and the Lula government were lavish in their demonstrations of reciprocal political recognition, appearing together numerous times in the daily press.

There was mutual political recognition as well as efficient communication channels between the big internal bourgeoisie and the Lula government. The government served important interests of the large industry, agribusiness, and the entire internal bourgeoisie. Precisely for this reason, Lula was able to count on them when he faced difficulties.

3   Contradictions within the Internal Bourgeoisie and the Neodevelopmentalist Front

The idea that agribusiness has supported the Lula government may not have convinced the reader. Landowners feared the action of landless groups (MST) and understood that the Lula government was complacent with this social movement. Big landowners wanted to have the Forest Code revised in order to increase the country's agricultural area, and they considered that the Lula government created difficulties in this area. Big landowners also criticized the Lula government for its policy of granting land to indigenous peoples and the remaining *quilombo* populations;[17] senator Kátia Abreu of the Democrats party (DEM), also president of the National Confederation of Agriculture and

---

17   *Quilombo* populations are the descendants of Afro-Brazilian slaves who escaped from slave plantations that existed in Brazil until slavery was abolished in 1888.

Livestock of Brazil (CNA), displayed a strong opposition to the government in the National Congress. It is true that the Lula government did not have the support of the entire agribusiness sector. We state that it did so in general terms because its top, most powerful segment had its interests covered by the government policy.

Agribusiness is a broad and heterogeneous industry, composed of segments with very unequal economic power and profitability. The active functions in agribusiness are land ownership, agricultural or livestock production, product commercialization, financial intermediation, and the processing industry itself. One of Fiesp's important departments deals with agribusiness. The representatives of the countless associations linked to the different segments and cultures of this sector usually say that agribusiness is segmented upstream and downstream of the farm: it is located "before the gate," "inside the gate" and "after the gate" (Bruno, 2009). In this chain, land ownership, which has so much weight in the Brazilian socioeconomic structure, is the weakest link in political terms. There are large multifunctional economic groups that invest in all stages of this capital appreciation cycle, as well as companies or family groups that specialize in one of these functions. The vast majority of landowners is made up of suppliers of sugarcane, orange, soybeans, beef, fish, coffee, or cotton to the agro-industry and to slaughterhouses, both of which have power to impose prices and demands about financing and planting. The economic support supplied by the Lula government to the Brazilian Friboi, which became in just a few years the largest meat processing company in the world, was not very beneficial for cattle breeders in Brazil's Midwest region. The mainstream press published reports in which breeders associations lamented the monopsony exerted by Friboi in the region. Periodically, landowners mobilized to roll over the debts they had with the banking system. The few and large slaughterhouses, juice processors, mills, and banks were in the hands of groups that wielded much more economic power than landowners, and the interests of the two parts did not exactly coincide.[18] As these powerful groups of the agribusiness segments supported the government, we have included them in the big internal bourgeoisie.

The big internal bourgeoisie and, even more so, its neodevelopmentalist front, had innumerable contradictions. They comprised forces and segments that had been united, but not merged. The difficulty here is to distinguish the

---

18 See Denise Elias's work on agribusiness in the Ribeirão Preto region (Elias, 2003). This separation of land, industrial, commercial, and banking capital in agricultural production is not new in Brazil. It is present throughout the history of the Republic. See in this regard the work of Sérgio Silva on the coffee economy (S. Silva, 1981).

conflicts and criticisms that never went beyond the front's boundaries from the conflicts and criticisms that did extrapolate these boundaries and that may lead to a change in the positioning of some segment or force in the national political process. The elements below will help us reflect on this situation.

Let us start with the contradictions within the big internal bourgeoisie itself. The first and most evident is the opposition between the big Brazilian industry and the Brazilian banking system. These two sectors required state protection against foreign capital: the banks demanded governmental control over the entry of foreign capital into the sector. And the big industry wanted protection for their products in the domestic market, prioritization of national companies in public purchases, low-cost BNDES credit, and foreign policy in the service of their exports. These two sectors were united around preserving the participation of Brazilian groups in the country's economy. However, *Revista da Indústria* frequently criticized the Lula government because of the Central Bank's interest policy. High basic interest rates increased public spending, hampering the expansion and improvement of infrastructure services. The banks' freedom to fix spread, which increased the borrower's costs, were also criticized.[19] The solution found by the Lula government was the expansion of the BNDES budget, which was almost quadrupled during Lula's mandates, and the multiplication of subsidized credit programs for the big industry and agribusiness.

Another contradiction placed big industry and agribusiness in opposite sides. It came up during the so-called Doha Round when agribusiness was favored in its main objective: easier access to the American and European markets. To this end, and contrary to what the big industry intended, the Brazilian government started a new round of trade liberalization to foreign manufacturers.

Finally, we have the contradiction between state and private capital, which does not exclude a simultaneous relationship of unity. Big national private companies have state-owned companies as their partners, buyers, suppliers, and financiers. However, the delimitation of which part of production and the market belongs to each segment is a cause for dispute within the internal bourgeoisie. Reflecting this contradiction, there were two wings within the

---

19   One of the many reports in the *Revista da Indústria*, especially dedicated to this subject, notes that governmental expenditure on payment of interest on public debt in 2006 reached 160 billion reais, i.e., 7.6% of that year's GDP, while investment spending reached only 0.6% of GDP. Many scholars note that the large industry also invests in government bonds. However, by consulting the financial statements that banks publish in the mainstream press, they, and not the industrialists, are the main holders of these bonds.

Lula government: the statist wing disputed political space with the privatizing wing. Carlos Lessa's dismissal from the presidency of the BNDES in Lula's first term was a victory of the privatizing over the statist wing. Later on, the privatizing wing formulated the policy of creation and consolidation of big Brazilian private companies – the "national champions" – in different segments of the economy to compete for a position in the world market. A good example was the formulation of the broadband universalization policy: in this case, the result has been a compromise in the form of a division of work between Eletrobras, which was being recovered and reactivated by the government, and the private company Oi.

Contradictions also placed the big internal bourgeoisie as a whole and the labor and popular movement in opposite sides. Two important elements here were public spending on the working population and the agrarian issue.

The edition of *Revista da Indústria* that celebrated the replacement of Antonio Palocci with Guido Mantega at the Ministry of Finance had some criticism for the new minister. The magazine referred to a certain malaise that Mantega had caused "[...] on March 29, the day of his inauguration, when he discarded the adoption of a long-term fiscal plan, as advocated by Palocci and Paulo Bernardes, Minister of Planning." (Demarchi & Vieira, 2006, 23). Fiesp's president Paulo Skaf stated that Mantega "would not relax fiscal policy irresponsibly," (Demarchi & Vieira, 2006, 24) which was a way to both supporting the minister and putting pressure on him at the same time. We transcribe the last excerpt of the report.

> Businesspersons and economists fear the deterioration of public accounts, since the surplus has already fallen from 5.15% in October 2005 to 4.38% in February [2006]. And measures such as the 1.5% real increase for pensioners starting in April helped reinforce the perception that public spending might be getting out of hand.
>
> DEMARCHI & VIEIRA, 2006, 25

In analyzing the neodevelopmentalist front, we find a complex problem regarding public spending. The big internal bourgeoisie was reluctant to make the small concessions required by the Lula government in order to maintain the front itself. Big businesspersons wanted: lower interest rates, state investment in infrastructure, customs protection, the BNDES at their service, business diplomacy and other benefits, but they rejected the hiring of new employees, salary increases for the workforce, minimum wage readjustment, social security spending, and so on. It was a well-known situation: they wanted a lean state for workers and a generous one for businesspersons. The Lula government sought to maintain some marginal gains for workers, but it was not easy to find the balance that would avoid defections on the political front it represents.

Instructive in this regard was the article "The Government in the Opposite Direction," signed by journalist Lúcia Kassai (Kassai, 2007), which is the cover story of the magazine. It is accompanied by an illustration that speaks for itself. The photo shows four stacks of bills of 100 reais, side by side. Three of the stacks are tall and have inscriptions associated with them: the first stack corresponds to "civil servants," the second, to "social security," and the third, to "interest." The fourth stack is short and withered and corresponds to "investment." In other words, the Lula government was spending a lot on employees' salaries, social security, and interest payments, and very little on investment, which would be of interest to industry and production. According to the report, in 2006, the federal civil service payroll would have corresponded to 16.3 billion reais. On average, a public sector worker receives a salary four times as high as that of the worker who performs an equivalent function in the private sector. The report also criticizes retirement plans for the rural population and elderly people in need, both established by the 1988 Constitution. It also denounces the expansion of trust positions without public exams, the salary amounts paid to congressional representatives, and the creation of new municipalities with the aim of providing public positions for local political leaders. However, the emphasis is placed on civil servants. For Fiesp, even the problem of high interest rates would be solved if only government public spending (aimed at the working class) were reduced. The reasoning is simple.

> If the government cut expenses and reduced the tax burden, interest rates would naturally fall, and the dollar would appreciate. In China, the tax burden is much less than in Brazil, and state investments are higher. [Newton de Mello, president of the Brazilian Machinery Builders' Association (Abimaq)].
>
> KASSAI, 2007

In short, Fiesp strongly insisted on the need to implement a reduction in civil servant's wages and to carry out a new and more radical pension reform.

Another source of instability on the neodevelopmentalist front was the opposition between the big bourgeoisie, particularly agribusiness, and the peasant movement. In the aforementioned interview with mill owner Luiz Guilherme Zancaner, this conflict becomes clear:

> VALOR: Do you have ideological differences with the federal government and with Minister Dilma?

ZANCANER: I was the founder of the Rural Democratic Union (UDR) in the city of Araçatuba, in 1988. I am very close to Ronaldo Caiado. I have ideological disagreements with both Lula and Minister Dilma. We disagree on the Landless Workers' Movement (MST) and also on the issue of human rights; I am very critical of Minister Vannuchi (Minister of Human Rights). Concerning the amnesty issue, we should let bygones be bygones. But if you want to re-examine the amnesty issue: those who have kidnapped, robbed banks, or killed, all of them should be brought to justice. There must be equality.

VALOR: Do you mean that this support for the Lula government and Dilma is a matter of pragmatism?

ZANCANER: It is a matter of pragmatism, of our business.

GRABOIS, 2010

It was impossible for the Lula government to preserve its political proximity with agribusiness and, at the same time, implement a land reform. Therefore, the government devised a strategy to circumvent this contradiction. Credit for family farming was greatly increased, taking into account the interests of landed peasants and, therefore, favoring one of the social bases of the MST and other peasant movements. However, the poor and landless farmhands, who constituted the other social base of the peasant movements, were abandoned by the Lula government. If we take into account the social class Lula's government represented, that was all it could have done. The question that arose at that point was: how long would the poor peasantry remain on the neodevelopmentalist front?

The big internal bourgeoisie did want state intervention in the economy. It wanted the state to intervene both as an investor and as a facilitator of private investments (improving infrastructure, science and technology, subsidized credit, etc.). However, the bourgeois class had a hard time accepting the concessions necessary to maintain the common front with the wage earners and the peasantry, without which the state could not overcome or circumvent the political resistance that challenged neodevelopmentalism.

An analysis of the situation suggests that there was a real possibility of one of these fractions abandoning the neodevelopmentalist front. The PSDB sought to attract the big internal bourgeoisie by suggesting – though not openly – that it would drastically reduce the state's social spending and clip the wings of the peasant movement in Brazil. The far-left organizations sought to get the unions and the peasantry to withdraw their support for the Lula government. Up to when this chapter was written, the front unity had prevailed. However, those who wish to undermine it do not suffer from the lack of motives or argumentations.

CHAPTER 3

The Political Bases of Neodevelopmentalism

In Brazilian sociology and political science, the relations between political process and capitalist development are a classic subject. Our study revisits that subject in order to examine it in new historical conditions: the two first decades of the twenty-first century.[1]

Our study is informed by the idea that capitalism in Brazil, in order to develop, has depended greatly on some kind of political participation by the popular classes. This dynamics stems from structural characteristics of Brazilian economy, society and state that became a part of global capitalism at a later stage as a dependent player. Running the risk of being too generic, we wish to point out that this phenomenon was noticed in the most significant moments of the process of Brazil's capitalist modernization, such as in 1888–1889, and in 1930.

To avoid lingering too long on this matter, let us consider the case of the political break of 1930. During the so-called Oligarchic Republic, particularly after Prudente de Moraes's inauguration in 1894, the state's social and economic policy favored coffee-based capital's interests (Perissinoto, 1994). While it is true that coffee had created the minimal conditions for industrial growth, it is also correct that it hindered an economic policy that would have advanced the industrialization process (Silva, S., 1981). The annihilation of the coffee bourgeoisie's hegemony within the bloc in power allowed the unification of the national market and the removal of political obstacles to the implantation of an industrializing economic policy; but this annihilation only became possible thanks to the Tenentista movement,[2] which channeled popular dissatisfaction regarding the Oligarchic Republic in a politically efficient manner (Santa Rosa, 1976). Historic research has shown that São Paulo's industrial bourgeoisie – hypothetically the fraction of the ruling class that held the most interest in industrialist politics – chose to support in the election of March 1930 the incumbent from the Paulista Republican Party instead of the dissident candidate Getúlio Vargas (Fausto, 1970).

---

1 This chapter was written in 2012, during Dilma Rousseff's first term.
2 Tenentismo was the political-military movement of various rebellions by young officers (mostly lieutenants) of the Brazilian army that occurred during the 1920s. The tenentes (lieutenants) called for reforms in the power structure.

In addition, during the entire populist period, in face of the industrial bourgeoisie's commitments and hesitation, it was the urban workers who became the key political resource to overcome or bypass the persistent – and neglected by most of the historiography – resistance of the old coffee bourgeoisie and the U.S. capital to the capitalist industrialization policy (Boito Jr., 1982). The various political crises between 1930 and 1964 show the intersection of two contradictions: successive attempts to restore the coffee bourgeoisie – in 1932, in 1945, and in 1954 – combined, differently in each occasion, with the pressure of the demands from the labor and popular movement. The populist governments defended themselves from the coffee bourgeoisie's political action for restoration by relying on the labor and popular movement (Saes, 1979). During the 1954 crisis, for example, the industrial bourgeoisie ended up joining the coup conspiracy, as it was concerned with the increasing demands from urban workers and, more specifically, with the Vargas government's attitude – thought to be too condescending – towards these demands. The result was a retrocession enforced by Café Filho to the industrialization program (Boito Jr., 1982). Although the popular classes were excluded from the political system by the 1964 coup d'état, there was for certain, after a period of crisis and stagnation, a five-year period of strong capitalist development between 1968 and 1973. Nevertheless, by the end of the 1970s, when the core countries started pressuring for trade liberalization in the periphery, the big Brazilian bourgeoisie, isolated both socially and politically, could not resist for long. The result was alternating periods of stagnation and weak economic growth in the 1980s and 1990s, as well as a loss of status for the Brazilian bourgeoisie in the national economy (Diniz & Boschi, 2004; Bielschowsky & Stumpo, 1995; Boito Jr., 2002a).

It was in the 2000s, when candidates from the Workers' Party (PT) rose to the country's presidency, that Brazilian capitalism went back to displaying somewhat higher rates of economic growth. We understand that this was a new episode in which the workers' political intervention gave a new boom to capitalism in Brazil. We were not witnessing anything as remarkable as the end of big coffee capital's long hegemony. Nonetheless, the popular element proved to be an important factor in the Brazilian political history, making it possible for the Lula da Silva and Dilma Rousseff governments to overcome, however cautiously and indirectly, the stagnation that predominated in the 1990s. It was the PT – a party created by the labor and popular movement – that returned to the proposal of the state intervention aiming at developing Brazilian capitalism.

1   The Neodevelopmentalist Political Front

In this chapter, we wish to elaborate on the idea that in the twenty-first century a political front was formed in Brazil, which we call neodevelopmentalist: the broad, heterogeneous base supporting the policies of economic growth and cash transfer initiated by the Lula da Silva and Dilma Rousseff governments. In those years, we lived in a political situation that showed similarities, in its more general aspects, to the situation of the populist developmentalist period mentioned above.

Brazilian capitalism had changed, and class structure had been transformed considerably. Now, in the private sector, urban wage earners were a group with a long experience with the union struggle; in the public sector, most of them were permanent employees with, consequently, more leverage. Since the military dictatorship crisis, over 30 years before, civil servants have been learning to practice unionism. Wage earners also counted on the Unified Workers' Central (CUT), the longest living union central in Brazil's history. This situation differed considerably from that of the workers right after the 1930s: having just migrated from the countryside, without experience in organizing or struggling for demands, they were very susceptible to the populist appeal. Brazilian companies, in turn, were more integrated to international capitalism than the industrial and service companies during Vargas's presidency had been. Now, the nationalist appeal no longer found among the ruling class the same engrossed audience it had had in the past. At this point, however, just as during the populist and developmentalist period, we discern the existence of a broad, cross-class, somewhat unstable political front that formed the support base of the development policy. And although populism and nationalism now lacked the relevance they had in the Vargas period, they were also present in this twenty-first-century political front.

Right from the start, we highlight those that seemed to be some key characteristics of this political front: a) it was steered by the big Brazilian internal bourgeoisie (see Chapter 2 above); b) it included working classes that found themselves excluded from the bloc in power – the lower middle class, blue-collar workers, peasants, and the marginal mass of workers (Kowarick, 1975; Nun, 1978); c) it maintained a populist relationship with the marginal workers; d) it became the main political resource on which the big internal bourgeoisie relied in order to rise politically within the bloc in power; and e) it faced, in the national political process, what we might call the orthodox neoliberal camp. In our work, we hypothesize that this camp encompassed big international financial capital, the Brazilian bourgeois fraction perfectly integrated and subordinated to that capital, sectors of big landowners, and the upper middle class allocated both in the public and private sector, but particularly in the latter. We are discussing here, therefore, the relations between fractions of the ruling class, present in the bloc in power, and the working classes, situated outside that bloc; and, in particular, we are discussing the political advantages that the big Brazilian internal bourgeoisie had acquired as it managed to establish, through the actions taken during the Lula da Silva and Dilma Rousseff governments, an alignment with broad popular sectors.

The neodevelopmentalist political front started to form in the 1990s. In the previous decade, certain aspects of political and economic order caused key instruments of the sociopolitical struggle – PT, CUT, and the Landless Workers' Movement (MST), all of them recently created by the working class – to become averse to any political approximation with big business. These movements had great strength, and the inflation aggravated wages disputes (Almeida, 1996). However, in the beginning of the 1990s, the situation changed. The most significant part of the bourgeoisie unified around the neoliberal program, unemployment rose severely, and the labor and popular movement, with the exception of MST (Coletti, 2002), entered an ebbing period (Boito Jr., 2002a). In the second half of the 1990s, signs of change began to appear. A sector of the big internal bourgeoisie, which had also supported – although selectively – the neoliberal program, went on to accumulate contradictions regarding this same program (Boito Jr., 2002a; Bianchi, 2004). It was this picture – marked, on the one hand, by growing difficulties for the labor and popular movement, and, on the other, by the fact that a sector of the bourgeoisie was starting to reconsider its position regarding some of the so-called market-oriented reforms – that facilitated the conditions for the construction of a political front that would encompass sectors of both the ruling and ruled classes.

This front, organized mainly by the PT, rose to governmental power in 2003 with the inauguration of the first Lula da Silva government (Boito Jr., 2002b). At this point, it was not a front that could call itself populist, nor could its program be identified as that of the old developmentalism. Let us thus present, synthetically and introductorily, this front's program and characters.

2   The Neodevelopmentalist Program

Why should we resort to the term "developmentalism"? Tentatively and introductorily, we would say that it is because this is a socioeconomic policy program that seeks economic growth for Brazilian capitalism via cash transfer in a way that does not cross the boundaries established by the neoliberal economic model still prevailing in the country. To achieve economic growth, the Lula da Silva and Dilma Rousseff governments employed some key socio-economic policy elements that had been absent during Fernando Henrique Cardoso's presidency. We shall number here a list – by no means exhaustive – of some of the elements that have been highlighted by part of the bibliography: a) policies to recover the minimum wage and promote cash transfer, both of which increased purchasing power for the lower classes, i. e., those that display a stronger propensity to consumption and, therefore, have a greater impact on demand growth; b) steep rise in budget allocation by Brazilian Development Bank (BNDES) to finance big national companies at favored or subsided interest rates; c) foreign policy of supporting big Brazilian companies or companies situated in Brazil for export of goods and capitals (Dalla Costa, 2012); d) anti-cyclical economic policy – measures to keep aggregate demand in moments of economic crisis; and e) more state investment in infrastructure. Later, the Rousseff government initiated changes in interest and exchange policies, reducing basic interest rates and the bank spread, and meddling in the exchange market to depreciate the Brazilian currency, aiming at lowering the cost of productive investment and offering protection – albeit hesitant – to the internal market. Because of these elements, and in spite of the fact that they did not break with the neoliberal economic model inherited from the 1990s, we have decided to employ the term "developmentalist" to address this program.

And why the prefix "neo"? Because the differences between this and the old developmentalist program of the 1930–1980 period are significant. *Neodevelopmentalism is the developmentalism of the neoliberal capitalism period.* The problem is complex, and this is a subject about which we do not wish to be exhaustive. For now, we highlight six differences. Neodevelopmentalism: a) promotes a much more modest economic growth than the one propitiated by the old developmentalism, although it is considerably greater than that observed in the 1990s; b) attaches less importance to the internal market, while maintaining the trade liberalization inherited from Collor and FHC; c) assigns less importance to the development of the local industrial park (Bresser-Pereira, 2012); d) accepts the restraints of the international division of labor, promoting in a new historic situation a reactivation of Brazilian capitalism's primary-export function; e) has a lower cash distribution capacity; and f) is driven by a bourgeois fraction that lost all velleity to act as a nationalist anti-imperialist social force. All these six characteristics, which are narrowly linked to one another, make neodevelopmentalism much less ambitious than its predecessor, and such characteristics stem from the fact that neodevelopmentalism is the developmentalist policy that is possible within the boundaries dictated by the neoliberal capitalist model.[3]

In fact, this latter model may be succinctly defined as the result of a double pressure: from imperialist states over the dependent economies, and from the capitalist class over the workers (Boito Jr., 2002a; Duménil & Lévy, 2006; Harvey, 2005). In the historic conditions prevalent in the three last decades of the twentieth century, this double pressure was successful and led to the so-called "market-oriented reforms": trade liberalization for goods, services, and financial markets in the periphery; prominence of the financial accumulation circuits; privatization of public companies and services; suppression of social and labor rights. As we pay attention to each one of those pillars of the neoliberal capitalist model, we will have no trouble seeing that the neodevelopmentalist policy cannot significantly raise public investment, prioritize the internal market, or start a vigorous cash distribution policy – not without breaking with such pillars. After this initial characterization of the neodevelopmentalist program, we shall introduce, also briefly, the characters of this story.

3   The Classes and Class Fractions Integrating the Neodevelopmentalist Front

Let us number the classes and class fractions that, performing as active social forces, were responsible for crystallizing and implementing this developmentalist policy. The big internal bourgeoisie, driving force of the neodevelopmentalist front, was distributed over several economic sectors – mining, heavy construction, the apex of agribusiness, the processing industry, and, to some extent, big private and state banks of predominantly national capital. These big companies were unified in their demand for the state's favor and protection

---

3   This denomination leads to controversy. Several economists have emphasized the process of deindustrialization in Brazil during the period studied here. We maintain, at least for now, this denomination because: a) both the Lula and, most specially, the Rousseff governments tried to counteract, without breaking with the neoliberal model, the deindustrializing effects of such model. During 2011 and 2012, Rousseff adopted a number of measures – concerning exchange, interest, taxes, and state purchases – that followed in that direction; b) it seems to us that it is possible to discuss neodevelopmentalism even though the processing industry no longer had the role it used to have in the days of the old developmentalism (Bresser-Pereira, 2012); and c) neodevelopmentalism also involves a social policy of cash transfer and distribution – real raise of the minimum wage and compensatory policies. For an approach that may put in question the "neodevelopmentalist" denomination, see texts by Wilson Cano (2012) and Reinaldo Gonçalves (2012).

when competing with foreign capital. Some authors have actually claimed that the so-called globalization was producing a global homogeneous bourgeoisie (Miglioli, 1998). That was not the case in Brazil (Martuscelli, 2010). At any rate, the way the Lula da Silva and Dilma Rousseff governments prioritized the interests of this fraction of big internal capital was evident in countless aspects of the economic policy. One of its key elements was the effort to maintain a surplus in the trade balance, which immensely favored agribusiness, mining, and other sectors linked to exports of products from agribusiness and natural resources. The financing policy offered by the Brazilian Development Bank (BNDES), the powerful state financial institution that made it unscathed through the wave of privatizations of the 1990s, was given a budget several times larger than that of the 1990s, and started prioritizing a small number of predominantly national companies as receivers of loan programs at favored or subsided interest rates (Bugiato, 2012). The purchase policy of the Brazilian state and the big state companies also changed under the neodevelopmentalist governments, and started prioritizing big companies that were predominantly national or implanted in Brazil. Ultimately, the Brazilian foreign policy concatenated with this new economic policy, so as to offer priority to the big internal bourgeoisie's interests. A crucial fact regarding this aspect was the closure of the negotiations about Alca, as well as Mercosur's growing strength. Actually, in this important foreign policy episode, big businesspersons and the labor and popular movement ended up converging to the same position (this is developed in greater detail in Chapter 5 below). The big internal bourgeoisie is the most favored force in the neodevelopmentalist policy.

As for the ruled classes, the urban workers and the lower middle class had an organized participation in the neodevelopmentalist front, by virtue of unionism and the Workers' Party. Indeed, these were the forces that created the party that would become the instrument of that front – the PT. Since then, this party, which in the 1990s fought for the enforcement of a social welfare state in Brazil and for the strengthening of state capitalism, grew closer to the big internal bourgeoisie, which had been offering lukewarm criticism to neodevelopmentalism. In the turn from the 1990s to the 2000s, combining its original tradition with the bourgeois dissatisfaction, the PT became empirically the creator and party tool of neodevelopmentalism in response to the circumstances. The working class and the lower middle class remained present in the PT, but, although they occupied a position of social base, now they were no longer the party's driving force. Wage earners had something to gain from neodevelopmentalism. The economic growth allowed a significant employment recovery, and the minimum wage readjustment policy increased the purchasing power of the base of the wage pyramid. The new economic and political conditions favored considerably the union organization and struggle, leading to a great increase in the number of strikes and allowing the workers to obtain new wage gains, in sharp contrast with what had happened with unionism in the 1990s (Boito Jr. & Marcelino, 2010).

The wages dispute, an economic conflict between employers and employees, should not overshadow the political unity of both parts around common political goals. The workers' unions had their representatives, standing beside big business's representatives, in many consulting organisms of the government. There were also frequent joint campaigns organized by big industry businesspeople associations and the union centrals in order to pressure the government into offering the local industry customs protection and lowering the economy's basic interest rate. Later, as a result of that joint pressure, the Rousseff government started changing its interest and exchange policies.

The peasants were also present in the neodevelopmentalist front, also in an organized way. The second term of FHC's presidency had persecuted and criminalized the peasant movements; with the rise of Lula da Silva to power, these movements had their demanding rights recognized by the government. Organizations of struggle for land – the most important of which is the Landless Workers' Movement (MST) – and organizations based on peasants and wage-earning rural workers – such as the National Confederation of Agricultural Workers (Contag) – represented the diversity of the rural workers' situation. We can distinguish, besides the class difference between wage-earners and peasants, different segments within the peasantry. The peasants whose finances were modest but enough to meet their needs, present mostly at Contag and at the sector of settled peasants inside MST, demanded technical assistance, financing for production, market and price for their products. The neodevelopmentalist governments partially met these demands by financing family agriculture, which grew considerably in comparison with its progress during FHC's presidency, and by starting programs of governmental purchase of peasant production – for example, in the supply of products for school meals (MST, 2009). The poor peasants, those with little or no land, demanded the expropriation of idle lands and an aggressive policy to liberate new settlements. This peasant segment was the most marginalized by the neodevelopmentalist front. The Lula and Rousseff governments reduced considerably the land expropriations. Agribusiness was an important factor in neodevelopmentalist policy, a fact that hindered the expropriation policy (Scarso, 2012).

The unemployed, the under-employed, and those living on odd jobs or "living on their own" represented the outermost point of the neodevelopmentalist front, maintaining with it a very particular relationship. These "marginal workers" inhabited mostly the outskirts of the country's big urban centers and the

Northeast countryside. We must distinguish two sectors in the marginal mass. One part was organized in popular demanding movements, known as "urgency movements," such as the movement seeking habitation and the unemployed workers' movement. The latter was weak in Brazil when compared to similar movements in countries like Argentina and France (Amorim, 2012; Figueiredo Filho & Souza, 2012). The former was more important due to its sociopolitical status. It encompassed many varied organizations acting in large and medium Brazilian cities; these organizations mobilized dozens of thousands of families and had several political orientations. There was a variety of movements, from those that demanded only home ownership for its members to those that pressured for a change in the government's housing policy, or that even promoted the need to struggle for a change in the prevalent economic model as a whole. These movements' victories were evidenced, at the local level, by the acquisition of real estate and urban land through direct action, and, at the national level, by government measures addressing housing policies. The most important effect of the movements for housing was the alteration of the Brazilian state housing policy. In the 1990s, the country had abandoned the policy of building popular houses. During Lula's second term, a broad housing program called "My House, My Life" was created, breaking with the country's omission in that area. This program was extended during Rousseff's presidency (N. C. Oliveira, 2010) and propitiated a convergence of interests between the landless and a whole branch of civil construction – a convergence of interests that did not exclude the struggle around house models, financing forms, and other points of the program (Hirata & Oliveira, 2012).

The other part of the "marginal mass of workers" was disorganized both socially and politically. It was included in the neodevelopmentalist front thanks to the cash transfer policies of the Lula da Silva e Dilma Rousseff governments. The "Family Grant" program, offered to families below the poverty line, and the "Continuous Benefit Program," offered to senior citizens and persons with disabilities, were the main tools of this policy. This impoverished mass did not take part in the neodevelopmentalist front's policy in an organized manner. The Lula and Rousseff governments chose to hand them out cash without bothering – neither these governments, nor their party, the PT – to organize them. They formed a passive, disorganized electoral base that was invited to participate in the political process only through voting for candidates from the neodevelopmentalist front. The relationship between the front's governments and their electoral base allowed the populist tradition of Brazilian politics to continue. In the populist political relationship, workers achieve real gains – contrary to what liberal observers, for whom populism is mere "demagogy," have claimed. However, these gains are very limited, precisely because their

beneficiaries remain politically and ideologically dependent on the government's initiatives.

Albeit broad and contradictory in its class composition, the neodevelopmentalist political front existed and acted as such. The forces that integrated
it – even though they might clash (often fiercely) about economic issues like
wages, social and labor rights, land expropriation, and others – have acted
jointly at crucial moments of the national political process. That was the case
in 2002, when Lula da Silva was elected president; in 2005, during the political
corruption crisis known as the *"Mensalão,"* which threatened the continuity
of the Lula government; in 2006, when Lula da Silva was reelected to the presidency; and again in 2010, during Dilma Rousseff's victorious electoral campaign. In all these crucial situations, the survival of the neodevelopmentalist
governments had been at risk, and, in all of them, important employers' associations, union centrals, peasant movements, popular movements for housing,
as well as the poor, disorganized voters supported the Lula da Silva and Dilma
Rousseff governments and candidacies with manifestations of all kinds or simply with their vote. In acting like that, these social forces, even though moved
by different interests, showed that they were part of the same political camp.[4]

4   The Contradictions in the Core of the Front

A study of the contradictions inside the neodevelopmentalist front would
require its own separate chapter. Such contradictions encouraged centrifugal
movements and, on the left as well as on the right, the forces interested in
breaking down the front exploited them to achieve this goal. A reflection upon
this subject might allow us to conjecture on this political front's solidity and
likely duration. Given our space limitations, we shall make only a few considerations on the issue.

---

4 We are basically considering the class struggles because they were prevalent in Brazilian society. However, there were conflicts that crossed and transcended the class struggle in varied,
   complex ways: the women's, the black, the homosexuals', and the indigenous' movements.
   In these cases, the political boundaries of the class struggle can be tenuous, particularly in
   Brazil's situation, which is not a revolutionary situation. Regarding such conflicts, the governments of the neodevelopmentalist front have usually presented a more progressive position
   than that of the PSDB governments; that also ensured stronger popular support to the front.
   In the case of racial quotas for public universities, for example, meritocratic bias displayed by
   the upper middle class, which is PSDB's active social base, limits the reforming action of this
   party's legislators and governments in this area.

There were contradictions in the core of the big internal bourgeoisie: between the banking capital and the productive capital concerning interest policy and the refinancing of the public debt (Dias, 2012; Minella, 1994), between the processing industry and agribusiness concerning international agreements (see Chapter 5 below), and among regional sections of this bourgeois fraction (Farias, 2009).

There were also contradictions among the working classes and the different bourgeois fractions: between the different groups of peasants and agribusiness, between the wage earners in the private sector and the bourgeoisie, and between the wage earners in the public sector and the bourgeoisie that aimed at reducing state spending on staff.

This picture becomes even more complex when we consider that international relations influenced internal politics. Venezuela's entry into Mercosur divided opinions in the core of the developmentalist front. Part of the big internal bourgeoisie – such as the big construction companies – saw in it new prospects for investment, while another part displayed concern regarding the likely impacts of that decision in the relations with the United States and the European Union.

In the labor and popular movement, these contradictions were translated into the creation of new organizations and into inner struggle and dissidence in already existing organizations. Two union centers were created to oppose the Dilma Rousseff government – Conlutas and Intersindical (Galvão, 2012). These union centrals basically gathered workers from the public sector (Galvão, Marcelino & Trópia, 2011, 2012), and, although they were minor centrals, the unions affiliated to them played a major role in a series of civil service strikes during Rousseff's presidency. Inside the MST, a struggle between two groups erupted – the broad majority group, which defended that the movement should remain offering critical support to Rousseff's presidency, and the minority group, which intended to break with the government (L. H. Silva, 2012).

Such contradictions and dissidences, however, did not compromise the overall unity of the neodevelopmentalist front. The contradiction that remained polarizing national politics placed the neodevelopmentalist camp and the orthodox neoliberal camp in opposite sides.

CHAPTER 4

Lulism, Populism, and Bonapartism

Lulism is one of the most important political phenomena of 21st-century Brazil.[1] Some have compared it to Varguism, which dominated Brazilian politics between 1930 and 1964. There are indeed similarities. Both phenomena present a broad popular base that is, however, devoid of organization; both implemented a state intervention policy in the economy to stimulate economic growth, give the federal government greater room for maneuver vis-à-vis the imperialist countries, and promote a moderate income distribution. Some analysts and observers of Brazilian politics have characterized Lulism as a new variant of Brazilian populism.[2] Some years later, André Singer and other authors introduced a new element into the debate by characterizing Lulism as a variation of Bonapartism (Singer, 2012).

In this chapter, we want to indicate, firstly, why it is correct to characterize Lulism as populism and, more precisely, as a neopopulism. A warning is in order here: Lulism is not restricted to Lula's political leadership. Only in appearance does populism depend exclusively on the personal figure the leader. Although a part of reality, this appearance is deceptive. In its deepest determinations, populism transcends the leader figure. Unaware of this fact, many have been surprised by the election and re-election of Dilma Rousseff, since they had attributed Lula's leadership abilities to his "charisma," which they had erroneously assumed to be a personal, non-transferable trait of his. Secondly, we intend to point out the misconceptions of those authors who characterize Lulism as a kind of Bonapartism. Finally, and throughout the text, we shall stress the importance of the political and theoretical issues involved in this discussion, which might seem, at first glance, merely a taxonomic discussion.

1   The Concepts

Much of contemporary Brazilian historiography has abandoned the concept of populism. Among those who have done so are historians who are critical

---

1   This chapter was written in September 2017.
2   I myself have published a text in which I characterize Lulism as a kind of neopopulism. See Boito Jr., 2003. The reemergence of populism in Brazil and Latin America was already analyzed in the 1990s by several political scientists. See Saes, 1994.

of Getúlio Vargas's legacy as well as some of those who defend it. We think, however, that this concept has resisted criticism and remains valid. More than that, the concept of populism is essential for the understanding of the current political situation in Brazil and Latin America. Scenes from the 2017 "Lula's Caravan for Brazil," – showing the former president, though persecuted and defamed by the Judiciary and the media, being enthusiastically welcomed by the impoverished and politically disorganized mass in the Northeastern *sertão* [backlands] – should serve as a warning to authors who have tried to ban the concept of populism from the historiography of republican Brazil. Throughout this chapter, and in order to inform the reader and clarify our concept of populism, we will make critical references to this historiography.

Both concepts, populism and Bonapartism, are the subject of extensive discussion in the social sciences; but what many do not realize is that both terms serve to designate more than one concept. "Populism" and "Bonapartism" are polysemous words. Now, in order to avoid delving into exclusively terminological discussions, which may erroneously be perceived as conceptual discussions, it is important not to confuse, as linguists would say, the signifier with the signified. The signifier "bat" can signify both an implement used to hit a ball and a nocturnal flying animal; the signifier "ball" can signify either a spherical object or a formal gathering for social dancing. The signifiers "populism" and "Bonapartism" can mean several different things, too. When we read "populism" or "Bonapartism," it is necessary to ask about the concrete meaning that such words assume in the text. In a conceptual discussion, although the word is not totally indifferent, what really matters is the sense in which it is used, that is, the idea it represents, i.e. the concept that the word assumes in that context.[3]

In the discourse of liberal observers and analysts, the word populism merely means demagogy, an unscrupulous leadership that deceives the uninformed masses; among the Weberians, it refers to a charismatic leadership that stems from the leader's personal and non-transferable attributes; finally, in Marxist texts, the word populism points to a leadership supported by a popular base that aspires to income distribution and remains politically disorganized, since it harbors illusions about the state's function. Only in this last case it is proper to speak of a populist ideology. Authors who employ the concepts of demagogic and charismatic leaders (characterizations that, by the way, may merge) understand that populism would be, by its very nature, a politics devoid of any

---

3   For the definition of the concept of populism, I will refer back to some of my earlier works in which I discussed it. The debate on Lulism requires revisiting the concept of Varguism and other discussions (Boito Jr., 1982 and 2005a).

ideology. In Brazilian intellectual life, this type of analysis was carried out by the so-called Itatiaia Group, formed by intellectuals of the 1950s from which emerged the former Superior Institute of Brazilian Studies (Iseb) in Rio de Janeiro. The group's magazine, *Cadernos do Nosso Tempo*, published in 1954 a pioneering article that became very influential in the analysis of Brazilian populism, titled "What is Adhemarism?" The answer to the title question was that, unlike bourgeois liberalism and workers' socialism born in Europe, Adhemarism would be not a class politics, but a mass politics, devoid of ideology and under the tutelage of a charismatic leader.[4] Therefore, in spite of the vocabulary coincidence in their use of the word populism, analysts differ significantly in terms of the concept: some are talking about demagogy, others about charisma, and still others about ideology.

There are also important differences in the realm of political action that, though differing from theoretical analysis, is not disconnected from it. The liberal notion of populism characterizes a political phenomenon and, in one and the same act, denounces and combats it from an elitist and anti-popular point of view. The Marxist conception of populism, while having both a progressive aspect (income distribution) and a conservative facet (keeping the masses in a state of political disorganization), may, either provide critical support to the populist leadership or combat its action, depending on the situation. And when combating it, it will do so by aiming at the political organization of the masses, not the elimination of their political participation, which is the liberals' goal. These theoretical and political differences between diverse concepts of populism often go unnoticed, not only because the word employed by different authors is the same, but also because the historical phenomena to which these authors refer are, broadly speaking, also the same: the political leaderships of Getúlio Vargas, Leonel Brizola, Jânio Quadros, and others.

---

4   "O que é Adhemarismo?, *Cadernos do Nosso Tempo* 2, 1954. The article is apocryphal, but is currently attributed to Hélio Jaguaribe. Marxist authors have criticized the formalism and misconceptions of this definition (See Saes, 1994). An alternative analysis is presented by Francisco Weffort (Weffort, 1978). Unfortunately, to this day, many historians who criticize the concept of populism act as if the aforementioned formalist definition were the only existing one. In so doing, they promote their own rejection of the concept of populism, but do not contribute to an understanding of the phenomenon. Jorge Ferreira (2001), for example, criticized and rejected the concept of populism, attempting to rescue the Vargas heritage in a positive light. His objective was to bring the Brazilian labor movement close to the old European social democracy. In our opinion, his historical analysis is unsuitable. Mass working-class parties such as the European communist and socialist labor parties succeeded in establishing a welfare state in Europe, while the Brazilian Labor Party (PTB), being a cadre party dependent on the union structure, could only achieve a limited, unequal social citizenship.

Let us move one step forward. We define populism, in a synthetic manner, as the fetish of the protective state. The individualization or personalization of politics is as much remarkable in populism as in Bonapartism and actually transcends both, since it is present, to a greater or lesser degree, in all bourgeois and petty-bourgeois political orientation of capitalist societies. This personalization of politics is, in this case, a manifestation of a statist ideology. The cult of the leader figure indicates the cult of the state as an institution.

We can develop the idea of a fetish of the state by drawing on Marx's well-known analysis of the relationship between the peasantry and Louis Bonaparte, as well as between the peasantry and the Second French Empire, and also on Lenin's texts on the peasantry's relationship with the state. Both works present, at least in practical terms, the idea of the fetish of the state (Lenin, 1975). And it is worth observing that the fetish of the state is common to populism and Bonapartism; there is a formal similarity between the two phenomena. The peasantry, disunited by the individualism of the small landowner, finds it difficult to organize as a group, hence tending to assign to the capitalist state, formally a universalist institution, open to everyone's interests, the task of acting on its behalf and in its place. The peasants, awaiting the action of the state, remain politically unorganized. The notion of fetish is used because the peasants are unaware of the fact that state action depends, first and foremost, on the political correlation of forces. On the contrary, they imagine that the state is a free and sovereign entity, which allows peasants to attribute to the state a strength and a capacity for action that, in many cases, actually come from the political action of the peasantry itself. The main source of Louis Bonaparte's power was the electoral support of the peasantry, the majority class of the French population, in his election as a congressional representative, as president of the Republic, and also in the successive plebiscites of the Second Empire. The phenomenon is the same as that of commodity fetishism. Just as the producer attributes to the commodity qualities that result from his/her own labor activity, the peasantry attributes to the state the strength that actually comes from the political participation of the peasants themselves.[5]

However, we have said that populism is the fetish of a particular kind of state, the state conceived as a protective force. It is the adjective "protective," describing the content of state policy, that differentiates populism from

---

5   To avoid conceptual confusion, it must be made clear that fetishism is not alienation. The similarity between the former concept, present in *The Capital,* and the latter, present only in drafts and short texts by young Marx, is merely formal. These are distinct concepts related to distinct theoretical issues: fetishism is a concept belonging to historical materialism; alienation is related to theoretical humanism issues (See Boito Jr., 2013a).

Bonapartism. The latter is the fetish of the state based on order. Formally similar, populism and Bonapartism differ in content. Workers who serve as a social base for a populist relationship expect the state – a supposedly free, sovereign, universalist entity – to take the initiative to protect them economically and socially; by contrast, workers, whether peasants or not, who are at the base of a Bonapartist relationship expect that the state – which they also consider to be free, sovereign, and universalist – will take the initiative to impose social order, which is threatened by disruptive and subversive forces.[6] The first supposition was nurtured by workers who formed the social base of Varguism, and also by the workers who were the social base of Lulism; the second supposition was nurtured by the French peasantry that expected Bonaparte to eliminate the growing labor movement in Paris, which they perceived as a threat to social order and private property.

2   Varguism and Lulism

It is evident that Brazil from the 1930s to the 1950s was very different from Brazil in the 2000s and 2010s. The objectives, the social bases, and the political methods of Varguism and Lulism are different, but they have common general features. We will indicate why these are two variants of populism, what they have in common, and what differentiates them. In the next section, we will offer a critique of the analyses that characterize Lulism as a type of Bonapartism.

The goal of Varguism was the capitalist industrialization of the country by integrating in the political game, although still in a subordinate and controlled position, the young working class newly arrived from the rural hinterlands. This young working class was sufficiently strong to compel national politics to take it into account, but, at the same time, it lacked organization, making it possible for Varguism to integrate it in a controlled manner. The opponents of Varguism were the bourgeois fraction that had been hegemonic between 1894 and 1930, namely the big associated bourgeoisie linked to exports and imports (See Perissinotto, 1994); US imperialism, which, more than European imperialism, was reluctant to accept Vargas's industrialist policy; and, finally, the upper middle class. The associated bourgeoisie and imperialism were the leading forces of the former National Democratic Union (UDN), while the upper middle class was its social base. Vargas, to defeat or circumvent the interests

---

6 The personalistic, authoritarian, xenophobic political leaderships that proliferate nowadays in Europe and in the United States cannot, from this perspective, be described as populist.

of UDN, counted on the support and control of the young post-1930 working class, whose political and socioeconomic profile was distinct from that of the Old Republic workers. Support was obtained through the expansion and consolidation of labor law. Vargas clashed against the old Communist Party (PCB) over control of this working class and obtained it mainly through the implementation of the corporative union structure of the state.

Coming from the countryside with no experience in organization or class struggle, these workers were attracted by the appeal of the head of the federal state addressed to them. The workers became organized and fought at the level of trade unions, but in part they did so within the state union and, above all, were unable to organize in a mass labor party with its own political agenda (Boito Jr., 1991). And this was due not to these workers having a traditional "cultural background" that would have induced them to personalize social and political relationships – which would indeed be contrary to the assumptions of the modernization theory. The willingness to respond to the political call of a modern and bureaucratic capitalist state actually represents an overcoming, not the continuity, of the ideology of subordination to the landowner.

But Varguism, in addition to being a type of populism, served as a foundation for the organization of populist governments – unlike what happened, as we will see, with Lulism. Populism is politics, ideology, and, contingently, government. These different dimensions are present or absent in different periods and are articulated in a particular way. On the one hand, there may be a populist disposition in the popular classes, without a leadership or movement to catalyze it. In periods like this, this disposition remains latent, being potentially glimpsed in sporadic and politically impotent manifestations, such as riots expressing popular dissatisfaction, or through broad, in-depth opinion polls. On the other hand, there may be a populist political movement without there being a popular government. An evident example of this situation was "Lula's Caravan for Brazil," a tour that former president Lula da Silva undertook through the Northeast region. The government at that time, headed by Michel Temer, was thoroughly antipopular, while a populist government is necessarily characterized by minimally meeting popular demands.

What is more interesting is the fact having a populist leadership at the head of the government is not in itself a reason to characterize this government as being necessarily populist. The characterization of a government depends, fundamentally, on the composition of the bloc in power, and not on its social support base, which, as such, is excluded from state power.[7] It is the bloc in

---

7 Here I refer to Nicos Poulantzas's concept of support-class (1968), which is characterized by a social class that is devoid of political organization and serves as a diffuse and inorganic

power during Getúlio Vargas's governments that allows us to characterize that government as populist. In this bloc in power, the state bureaucracy acted as an autonomous social force implementing a political program of development of Brazilian capitalism that was not supported, in its fundamental features, by any of the bourgeois fractions that comprised it. Such policy was actively and persistently opposed by the old associated bourgeoisie, which was bumped from its hegemonic position in 1930. And if the internal bourgeoisie, whose most important and most benefited segment was the industrial sector, accepted this policy, it was only with many reservations, restrictions, and conflicts (Farias, 2017). What happened in this period was, in fact, a prolonged crisis of hegemony in the bloc in power. It was this crisis and the fact that the president had popular support (though diffuse and inorganic, as it is typical of populism) that granted the state bureaucracy great room for maneuver when dealing with different bourgeois fractions. In other words, although the Vargas governments acted to develop Brazilian capitalism and privileged the interests of the bourgeoisie, especially its industrial segment, they were not bourgeois governments in the strict sense of the term (Boito Jr., 1982).

In the case of Lulism, although its social bases, objectives, and enemies were similar to those of Varguism, the two movements differ in several respects. The common feature is that the social bases of both aspired to state protection and did so for popular and progressive reasons: economic growth, income distribution, and, to a greater or lesser extent, a willingness to support a strong position of the Brazilian state before the imperialist powers. Part of the Brazilian left-wing today may not realize this, but Varguism had more ambition than Lulism. Varguism struggled to reshape the former international division of labor and to industrialize the country. To this purpose, it had to break with the legality of the First Republic, resort to armed action to liquidate the hegemony of the old associated bourgeoisie in 1930, win a civil war in 1932, and change the entire political system of the country. Once in power, Varguism was supported by a working class committed to unionism, with a significant part linked to a communist party and potentially threatening to the bourgeois order. The populist crises of 1954 and 1964 were caused by the rise of the labor movement (and, in 1964 in particular, also of the peasant movement); this rise went far beyond the limits of populist politics. The support from this social base cost populism the implementation of social and labor rights that still plague the Brazilian bourgeoisie. The eradication of Varguism from Brazilian politics

---

support for a government or a political regime. This class does not integrate the bloc in power and may, in an extreme situation, offer its support due to ideological motivations, even if its minimum interests are not fulfilled by government policy.

required a coup d'état and the implementation of a military dictatorship that lasted two decades. Lulism, in turn, arose in a different historical situation, when the labor movement grew stronger both domestically and internationally. Moreover, Lulism had more modest ambitions.

Lulism's main – albeit not only – social base was the marginal mass of workers (Boito Jr., 2003). This base did not have as much potential as the base of Varguism to pressure and destabilize the political process. By "marginal mass of workers," we refer to the segment of workers that – as is typical of dependent capitalist countries – fails to be integrated, in a relatively stable and lasting way, into the strictly capitalist production, that is, the production of goods based on wage labor (Kowarick, 1975; Nun, 2001; Pereira, 1971). This segment was as large as it was heterogeneous: part-time informal wage earners, impoverished segments of the peasant economy, self-employed urban workers, street vendors, male and female workers in the informal labor market of personal and domestic service, the underemployed, the chronically unemployed, and others. The complexity of the political game is highlighted by the fact that the social base backing Getúlio Vargas, a professional politician and big landowner, was the working class; the social base backing Lula da Silva, a professional politician and a metalworker, was the marginal mass of workers, not the working class. While Vargas addressed his speeches at the São Januário Stadium to the working class, Lula organized his "Caravan for Brazil" in the Northeast region and spoke mainly to the impoverished and disorganized workers, not to the metalworkers of São Paulo ABC region, where he emerged as a national labor leadership.

Just like the young post-1930 working class, albeit for different reasons, the marginal mass of workers also found it difficult to organize itself into an autonomous social force, that is, into a party with its own political program. The heterogeneity and fragmentation of their working conditions, as well as their low capacity to put pressure on capitalists or governments, made these workers prone to populism. In the Brazil of Lulism, while the industrial working class lost relevance in terms of the economy and trade unions, the segment of marginal workers grew considerably due to the establishment of the neoliberal capitalist model. The political trajectory of Lula and of the Workers' Party (PT) itself describes a gradual shift from its original social base – grounded in the new unionism that was emerging in the metallurgical industry of São Paulo's ABC region in the late 1970s – to the marginal mass of workers who today form the majority of the Brazilian population. The social policy of the PT governments was focused not on labor law and social rights, but rather on policies of cash transfer favoring the marginal mass. The establishment of labor rights would not even reach the members of this population – with the exception of domestic workers, for whom Dilma Rousseff's government rightly guaranteed access to labor rights enshrined in the Consolidation of Labor Laws (CLT).

Being a variation of populism, Lulism did not organize its social base, which remained politically dispersed and was kept as a "deposit of votes" for the presidential candidates of the PT. Let us return for a moment to the analysis of Varguism.

Vargas had created state unionism and the Brazilian Labor Party (PTB). Neither of these institutions meant overcoming populist statism. The state union worked – and still works today – as a union apparatus attached to the state that gives it legitimacy through the provision of the union charter, a monopolistic representation based on the legal guarantee of union unity; and the financial resources necessary for the operation of unions, originated in mandatory union fees also guaranteed by the state. This is the type of unionism in which the state poses, and is seen by workers, as the neutral, sovereign entity that organizes unionism for them. The Brazilian Labor Party (PTB) was a kind of extension, at the parliamentary level, of state unionism. It was never a mass labor party like the European communist and socialist parties. Its *gaucho* core, better organized and programmatically better defined, was an outlier in the history of that party. As for the Brazilian Communist Party (PCB), it undoubtedly took the first steps to become a mass workers' party in 1945–1947. If the party had succeeded, populism might have been aborted. However, what was aborted was the PCB, when the Dutra government declared it illegal and banned it from the union movement.[8]

Lulism, on the other hand, resulted from a revitalization of the union movement that reformed the unionism of the state, and, in the critical

---

8   Historians influenced by Thompson's work have rejected the concept of populism because they think it conceals the fact that in Brazil, between 1930 and 1964, workers struggled hard for social and labor rights. An example of this line of research is the book *Na Luta por Direitos. Estudos Recentes em História Social do Trabalho,* by Fortes et al. (1999). The concern of these authors is fair, but I feel the solution they found is faulty. The concept of populism does not assume that the masses do not fight for their interests. In fact, under the hegemony of populist ideology, it is possible that workers organize, and they in fact do so, but in order to struggle for what they want. What the populist ideology precludes is the organization of workers specifically in terms of political parties (See Saes, 1979). For this reason, the positive work of these historians retracing the union and strike movement of the Brazilian proletariat cannot be accepted as an argument for rejecting the concept of populism. To do so, it would be necessary to demonstrate that the old Brazilian Communist Party (PCB) had succeeded in constituting in Brazil a mass labor political party, similar to the European communist and socialist parties, or that the old Brazilian Labor Party (PTB) had assumed the profile of a party based on an organized mass, with a continuing political action (not restricted only to election periods) and an active internal life revolving around debates over policy issues.

scenario of the military dictatorship, it came close to breaking with that institution. It had a unionist dimension, a typical labor economism focused on economic demands, but based on the self-organization of the workers, and not on a state-based unionism. However, since its birth, it did not fail to exhibit traces of the Brazilian populist tradition – plebiscitary assemblies at the Vila Euclides Stadium that did not contemplate any possibility of discussing the conduction of strikes, an exacerbated personalization of Lula's leadership during strikes, and a difficulty to get rid of the alleged benefits of official unionism. Later on, as we have already indicated, Lula's political activity based itself primarily on the marginal mass of workers and its populist component became dominant.

During Lula's first term in office, a discussion arose within the government team about the need for the government and/or the PT to organize the marginalized workers that were benefiting from the programs of cash transfer and offers of goods and services, but the proposal was rejected. At the time, the program in question was the "Family Grant" (*Bolsa Família*), which provided monthly cash allowances to the poor. The proposal to organize the base was defeated. Then came the programs "Light for All," "Cisterns," "My House, My Life," and others. The policy of keeping beneficiaries disorganized was not altered. What the government got from the workers/beneficiaries was, to borrow an expression from journalist Breno Altman, their gratitude, but not their conscious identification with a reform program. It is true that, unlike what happened during Varguism, there is not a systematic field research on the ideological disposition of the marginal mass of workers who supported Lula, particularly about their perception of the state, of politics, and of the former President of the Republic. Here we have to fill the gaps through inference from the sorts of political practice of the agents involved in this relationship – the practice implies a discourse – and also by referring back to the scarce material available.

Lula's discourse as a union leader in the 1970s was that of a reformist and combative workers' union leadership. As the newspapers of the time show, though, in speeches addressed to popular audiences, particularly during his first presidential term, he started to explicitly convey the image of a father figure who would protect the citizens/children. Linguists who have analyzed his speeches called attention to this component, and there is also at least one field research that, although without statistical representativeness, points in the same direction. And maybe the most important: the aforementioned "Lula's Caravan for Brazil" provided new and very significant empirical material on this point. Suffice it to read the title of the report published on the PT website about the experience of the caravan: "For many Northeasterners, Lula is known as a father!"[9] In short, these workers were not politically educated to rely on their own strengths. What was encouraged with this policy was the fetish of the protective state, that is, the spontaneous populism of the marginal mass.

Lulist neopopulism is the key to understanding the weak popular resistance to the parliamentary coup that was perpetrated in Brazil in 2016. In the fight against Dilma Rousseff's impeachment, the leaders and activists of the popular movements that organize workers of the marginal mass – such as the Landless Workers' Movement (MST), the Homeless Workers' Movement (MTST), the Movement of People Affected by Dams (MAB), and others – were a constant and prominent presence in street demonstrations. These movements, however, organize but a very small portion of the workers of the marginal mass, though they strive to educate these masses politically by helping them to overcome populist illusions. But this huge number of workers of the marginal mass was completely absent from the protests against the parliamentary coup. The masses, deluded by the fetish of the state, failed to organize or defend their leaders; as a matter of fact, they imagined that these leaders were powerful enough to overcome difficulties by themselves, and expected to be protected by them. Moreover, had the PT or the Rousseff government decided – at the last minute, as they saw the growth of the enemy's strength – to appeal to these masses, they would have found it hard to make up for the time lost as they left these groups dispersed and politically passive. The marginal mass only reappeared in national politics in August 2017, a year after the parliamentary coup, during "Lula's Caravan for Brazil," and it reappeared as a mass at Lula's rallies and marches, welcoming him enthusiastically, but showing no political organization. Lula visited the nine states of the Northeast region and dozens of cities. He revitalized Lulism, achieving great popular enthusiasm and zero organizational balance. Lulism again asserted itself as neopopulism.

---

9   <http://www.pt.org.br/para muitos-nordestinos-lula-e-conhecido-como-pai>; checked on December 30, 2020. See also the report of the Brazilian edition of *El País* titled: "If Today I Have a Car, a House, and Can Dress Like This, It's Because of Lula," containing the following statement: "During Northeast tour, the PT politician was called 'father' by his voters and told them not to be discouraged by politics." Available at: <https://brasil.elpais.com/brasil/2017/09/03/politica/1504475928_990903.html>; checked on December 30, 2020. Walquiria Leão Rego and Alessandro Pinzani, after interviewing 150 women beneficiaries of the Family Grant program in the Northeastern backlands, reported the following results: "A relevant majority of the interviewees (75%) stated that the Family Grant program is an indulgence from the government, or an act arising from the fact that Lula was poor ... Only a few said that the government has the duty to help the poor, and only five of them used the word "right." (Leão Rego & Pinzani, 2013). For the purposes of our discussion, "indulgence" and "the government has the duty to help the poor" may be the same thing. On the presence of the father figure in Lula's discourse, See Tomaz & Gouvêa, 2017.

Also, because Lulist populism was based on the workers of the marginal mass, unionism had but a very weak participation in the fight against President Dilma Rousseff's impeachment, due to two factors: the peripheral position of the union movement in the PT governments' social policy, and the existence of a large group of conservative union leaders who were shaped by the very structure of state unionism.

Lula and Rousseff were presented with historical claims of unionism at crucial moments of great symbolism, but these were ignored by the PT governments. Among them were the reduction of the workweek, the approval of International Labor Organization Conventions 151 and 158 (which prevent terminations without cause and grant collective bargaining rights to public sector workers), the end of the welfare factor, restriction of outsourcing regulations, revision of the income tax table, and others (Marcelino, 2017). The union struggle gained more space as the policy of economic stimulus reduced unemployment from 13.5% in 2003 to 4.6% in 2014. This increased the workers' willingness to fight, multiplied the number of strikes, and greatly improved the collective agreements and conventions (Boito, Galvão & Marcelino, 2015). However, the only important economic or social measure that targeted exclusively the union movement and met its demands was the policy of minimum wage appreciation.

There were 12 union centrals in Brazil at that time, and when the crisis erupted, threatening the Dilma Rousseff government, only three of them backed the demonstrations in defense of the president's mandate – the Unified Workers' Central (CUT), the Men and Women Workers' Central of Brazil (CTB), and the Intersindical.[10] However, this political position only resulted in material and logistical support for the protests. In Brazil, union centrals do not have the power to direct the action of their member unions, and the large unions in these centrals abstained from participating in the movement against the parliamentary coup. Some of them were absent for fear of not being able to mobilize their bases for the demonstrations. In state unionism, the relationship between leader and social base is, by definition, distant, and the right-wing uproar over corruption scandals during the PT governments neutralized sectors of wage earners. Other unions, mainly conservative ones, did nothing

---

10   We say defense of the president's mandate because her economic and social policy was indefensible and perceived as such by the labor movements. After promising economic growth and cash distribution during her campaign, in which at the same time she accused the opposing candidate of planning to implement a policy of expenditure cuts and fiscal adjustment, Dilma Rousseff, once in office, betrayed her promises and put in place a strongly recessive economic policy.

simply because they supported the right-wing parliamentary coup against the PT center-left government. An interesting topic for research would be a comparison between the union mobilization in defense of Getúlio Vargas in 1945, in the so-called "Movimento Queremista," and the very weak union mobilization in defense of Dilma Rousseff in 2015 and 2016.

We should add that the analysis of the weak union and popular mobilization in defense of Dilma Rousseff's mandate should also take into account that the government did not seek to mobilize the masses in its defense. The president confined her resistance actions to the institutions of the capitalist state. She and her Justice Minister, José Eduardo Cardozo, consciously and systematically adopted the strategy of restricting themselves to the legal dispute, trying to prove, based on arguments – which were technically correct, but politically irrelevant – the legality and insignificance of the administrative acts that were presented as grounds for Dilma Rousseff's impeachment.

Lula's and Rousseff's governments, despite having established a neopopulist type of relationship with the marginal mass of workers, were not, unlike the Vargas governments, what we could characterize as populist. They were in fact governments of the Brazilian big internal bourgeoisie, the hegemonic fraction in the bloc in power. Populist politics was an important, but subordinate dimension of the PT governments. Two rival bourgeois fractions were competing for hegemony in the Brazilian state bloc in power in the period of the neoliberal capitalist model: the big internal bourgeoisie, which aggregated segments of agribusiness, industry, and banking, and the associated bourgeoisie, represented by companies linked, in several different ways, to foreign investments in Brazilian capitalism. Fernando Henrique Cardoso (FHC)'s government represented the hegemony of the associated bourgeoisie and international capital; Lula's and Rousseff's governments, in turn, represented the hegemony of the big internal bourgeoisie. We have no space here to develop these theses, but we understand that the social, foreign, and economic policies of these governments justify such claims (see also Chapters 2 and 8 in this volume). The implementation of the hegemony of the big internal bourgeoisie, which was expressed in the neodevelopmentalist economic policy, was made possible because the PT governments built a broad, unstable, heterogeneous political front that supported the rise of this bourgeois group to the condition of hegemonic fraction in the bloc in power. The marginal mass of workers joined this front, which I call here the neodevelopmentalist front, by means of populist politics. Nevertheless, this fact alone does not justify the characterization of the PT governments as populist. They were bourgeois governments – specifically, governments of the big internal bourgeoisie.

3   Bonapartism and Lulism

André Singer, inspired by Karl Marx's classic text *The Eighteenth Brumaire of Louis Bonaparte*, maintains that Lulism is a type of Bonapartism. In our view, this characterization is inaccurate (See Boito Jr., 2013b).

We have already characterized the political relationship between the Bonapartist leadership and its base as the fetish of the state based on order. Firstly, here the individualization or personalization of politics, just as in populism, is a manifestation of the statist ideology, an ideology that maintains the Bonapartist base politically disorganized, since it would be up to the state, not the workers, to act, particularly in the political sphere (Bluche, 1981). Secondly, as we have already indicated, the longing for order, which nourishes the fetish of the Bonapartist state, is the conservative and antipopular trait that distinguishes Bonapartism from populism. We should also point out that Bonapartism is a notion that, as it is well known, refers to a specific type of bloc in power.

Several Marxist scholars agree that the Bonapartist bloc in power is characterized by the constitution of a government: a) that is endowed with ample room for maneuver regarding social classes; and b) whose policy zigzags among conflicting interests. Due to their own characteristics, governments of this type arise at moments of important political crises. The room for maneuver and the strength of the government stem from two factors that act in conjunction: a) the "balance of forces in weakness" both among the fundamental classes and the fractions of the dominant class; and b) the fact that the government has a popular base. This is the understanding that appears in *The Eighteenth Brumaire of Louis Bonaparte* (Marx, 1963), where Marx wrote phrases like: "the bourgeoisie could no longer rule, while the proletariat was still unable to do so;" "the conflict between large landed property and capital split the ruling classes between different dynastic houses;" "Louis Napoleon seems to be hovering above classes, but he represents the most numerous class in French society: the peasantry." The idea that the Bonaparte government served sometimes one and sometimes the other without successfully implementing a coherent policy is an aspect that must be examined carefully. Marx wrote this book in the heat of the moment, when Louis Napoleon's government was beginning to organize itself and the political crisis had not yet been overcome. The government did take measures that were sometimes incongruous, as it had not yet managed to stabilize. The subsequent story of the Bonapartist regime does not fit well into this analysis.

Louis Bonaparte remained in power for two decades and implemented a policy of capitalist modernization in France (Plessis, 1973). Engels himself went on to make a somewhat different analysis of Bonapartism. He continued to see it, as in Marx's *Eighteenth Brumaire*, as characterized by governments with ample room for maneuver in their relationship with the ruling classes due to the balance of forces but indicated that such governments could use this greater autonomy to promote a capitalist modernization in their countries, that is, to implement a coherent economic policy. Engels mentions Bismarck's as an example of Bonapartist government, since it pursued a capitalist industrialization of Germany. Since then, this concept has been widely used within the Marxist tradition. The Japanese State of the Meiji era is considered to be Bonapartist, and even in Brazil there is a long tradition of considering the Vargas state as a Bonapartist state (See Demier, 2013). In all these cases, this characterization is due not to the fact that such states zigzagged among social classes, but because they used their greater autonomy to promote a capitalist modernization.

Let us examine André Singer's analysis. He considers the electoral realignment that took place in the 2006 presidential election as the initial milestone of the phenomenon of Lulism. During that election, as Singer rightly shows, a double movement took place: while part of the middle class electorate moved away from Lula, broad low-income segments approached the PT candidate. Lula's leadership has since then become the political representation of this group, which André Singer calls, following economist Paul Singer, the "subproletariat." Most of this subproletariat integrates the class that we have been calling in this chapter "the marginal mass of workers." The subproletarians would be those workers who "[...] offer their workforce in the market without finding anyone who is willing to buy it for a price that ensures its reproduction in normal conditions."[11] This subproletariat, whose income the author indicates to be in the range of up to two minimum wages, represents 47% of the entire Brazilian electorate, which makes it by far the most numerous (fraction of) class in the country and capable of deciding a presidential election. This group integrates domestic servants, employees of small businesses, and workers deprived of organizational capacity and incapable of exerting pressure, all of which makes them unable, in Singer's opinion, to participate in the class struggle. The relationship that the PT governments started to establish with this politically disorganized social base is classified by Singer as a Bonapartist relationship.

The dynamics of the power game in Brazil would be, according to Singer, as follows: the PT governments, supported by a politically amorphous but

---

11   The definition is by Paul Singer. André Singer rescued it in his own work (2012).

electorally powerful base, would practice arbitration between the fundamental classes to keep any of them from becoming prevalent, and promote, in this
game of equilibrium, the interests of the subproletariat, which was the fraction of the working class represented by Lula's and Rousseff's governments
(See Singer, 2012, 159, 165, 196, 200 and 219). The idea of representation here
is different from the one found in Marx's *Eighteenth Brumaire*. When Marx
claims that Louis Bonaparte represents the peasantry, he is indicating that
there is an ideological relationship in which the peasantry imagines that
Louis Bonaparte's government will promote the peasants' interests. This illu-
sory or ideological representation is implied in the general thesis of Marx's
book, according to which the Bonapartist regime replaced the political power
exercised directly by the bourgeoisie to guarantee this class's economic domination; Marx develops this topic more explicitly in Chapter VI of that book,
where he analyzes the peasantry's relationship with Louis Napoleon. The
illusion of representation was highlighted by Nicos Poulantzas's commentary
on Marx's work, and was, moreover, what allowed Poulantzas to develop the
aforementioned concept of support-class: a dominated class, *excluded from
the bloc in power*, that nevertheless deludes itself into offering a given government or regime a support base.

In André Singer's analysis, by contrast, Lulism removed the subproletariat from the influence of the bourgeoisie (Singer 2012, 44), elevated it to
the condition of the main force in government power, and accomplished
the political program of that specific fraction of the working class – neither the political program of the bourgeoisie, nor the political program of
the proletariat. According to Singer, the bourgeoisie's program is neoliberalism; the proletariat's is a break with neoliberalism; and the weak reformism
without breaking with the established order, which was the policy of the PT
governments, is the "complete implementation of the program of the subproletariat" (Singer 2012, 44, 76, 219). Even the fact that Lula's and Rousseff's
governments did not completely break with the neoliberal model reflected
their subproletarian social base's interests and values (Singer 2012, 74,196).
In Singer's analysis, the PT governments' state policy prioritized the interests
of the subproletariat, not those of the bourgeoisie or of any other fraction of
that social class.

> The democratic wave of the 1980s – a time when strong reformism was
> constituted in the country as a perspective of the organized working class
> – came up against the obstacle on which this book has been commenting
> since its beginning: the vast subproletarian fraction, the poorer half of
> the Brazilian population, who wanted (and wants to) integrate with the

capitalist order and thrive in it, not to transform it from the bottom up, particularly since this is not within their reach.

SINGER 2012, 196

• •
•

Against the backdrop of economic orthodoxy, Lula's stroke of genius was to build a substantial policy to promote an internal market focused on the least favored group – a policy that, together with the maintenance of stability, corresponds to nothing less than the accomplishment of a complete program favoring a class (or a fraction of a class, to be precise). Not the organized working class, [...] but the group that Paul Singer called the subproletariat.

SINGER 2012, 76

• •
•

In my opinion, the "continuity between Lula's and Fernando Henrique Cardoso's governments" regarding macroeconomic policy [...] [was] the means to ensure a vital element in winning the support from the poorest: the maintenance of order.

SINGER, 2012, 74–75

• •
•

Lula's and Rousseff's governments, supported by the subproletariat, seek to balance the fundamental classes – the proletariat and the capitalists – because their success depends on neither of them having the strength to impose their own designs: strong reformism, which aims to rapidly increase equality [...], or neoliberalism, which tends to increase inequality by imposing loss on workers.

SINGER, 2012, 200

• •
•

What is the [government's] objective in maintaining the balance between capital and labor? It is not only about preserving order and avoiding political radicalization, but also about guaranteeing the subproletariat two fundamental conditions: low inflation and increased buying power

SINGER 2012, 159–160

> In short, that is the subproletariat platform, which Lula's and Rousseff's
> governments have been supporting
>> SINGER 2012, 229

We will present some critical observations about this characterization. The first is very brief and merely illustrative. When Lula was elected president in 2002, there was not in Brazil any major political crisis, which historically tends to be a factor in the formation of Bonapartist and populist governments. It is widely recognized that Lula became president at a moment when the labor and popular movements had for some years been living through a regressive and defensive phase. As for Singer's other observations, two of them refer specifically to the relationship the popular classes maintained with the capitalist state and with the PT governments, and the other concerns specifically the relationship that the state and those governments maintained with the ruling classes.

Let us first note that André Singer overestimates the political power of the "subproletariat." To assert that the capitalist state prioritizes the interests of a *dominated* class would require, at the very least, more development and explanation. Furthermore, if the heterogeneous popular sectors that he groups together under the notion of subproletariat are characterized, according to the author himself, for not being able to participate in the class struggle, how can they be said to have a "program"? When we say that a sector or a social class is disorganized, this means that this sector or class does not have its own political program to intervene in the situation. There is no doubt that the impoverished and disorganized mass that votes for the PT candidates does so to pursue certain aspirations, but these are diffuse aspirations, not articulated in a clear and conscious way as they would be in a program. Moreover, the PT governments were the ones that organized these diffuse aspirations with the creation of the "Family Grant" program. We should add that this program, though it offered cash transfers to workers from the marginal mass and actually improved their living conditions, was not the priority of state policy. If we add, for example, the budget of the Brazilian Development Bank (BNDES) for subsidized loans to large national companies, to the costs of rolling over the public debt – in both cases, amounts aimed at a small number of Brazilian businesspersons and big bankers – we will reach a sum that is a hundred times greater than the total amount of resources of this main cash transfer program that was destined to millions of workers. It is necessary to distinguish, on the one hand, the bourgeois fractions that integrate the bloc in power and, on the other, a popular class or tier that serves as a mere support-class for a particular government.

Secondly, it is difficult to maintain that the subproletariat that sided with Lulism was conservative, in the sense that it defended the maintenance of neoliberalism. In Marx's analysis, the identification of the peasantry with Louis Napoleon was conservative: the peasants wanted him to restore social order because they were frightened by news of workers' and popular uprisings in 1848 and 1849 in Paris and other French cities. Now, in the Brazil of Lulism, the "subproletariat" aspired to income redistribution and this aspiration was progressive and popular. Singer recognizes this aspiration, but asserts that it conformed to a conservative attitude that did not admit of a break with the neoliberal order. He is so emphatic in his assertion that he attributes the fact that Lula and Rousseff did not definitively break with neoliberalism not to the interests of the big bourgeoisie in the bloc in power, but to an alleged conservatism of the subproletariat.

It is true that there is popular conservatism, but in the Brazil of Lulism, this conservatism favored candidates who opposed the PT governments and did not vote for the PT candidates. After all, it was not the whole "subproletariat" that had sided with Lulism. As of 2006, Lula had a large majority in this social tier, but a significant fraction of it continued to vote for right-wing candidates (a fraction that unfortunately is disregarded in Singer's analysis). Now, if we characterize the "Lulist subproletarians" as conservative, how should we characterize the portion of the subproletariat that, yesterday and today, voted or declared intention to vote for right-wing or extreme right-wing politicians, such as João Dória, of the Social Democratic Party (PSDB) in São Paulo, and Jair Bolsonaro, of the Social Christian Party (PSC) in Rio de Janeiro?

Singer offers the reader few arguments to support his thesis of the subproletariat's widespread conservatism or to present that conservatism as the reason why the PT governments maintained neoliberalism. He cites surveys that indicate the rejection of strikes by low-income groups, but we should add that these same surveys demonstrate tolerance of strikes by high-income groups. One would then have to explain these *two* results, and legitimately ask whether they are not the outcome of the same and only cause. In Brazil in the 2000s and 2010s, most strikes were led by public service workers, and most were corporate strikes of specific segments fighting for specific interests. Strikes in the public sector generate problems mainly for the low-income population, not for the high- or very-high-income population. Could this not be the explanation? Could such rejection of strikes by the poor population be characterized as conservative? The fact is that this rejection is no more corporatist than the Brazilian strikes of the period meant to be taken as standard of a progressive position. Moreover, why would rejection of strikes mean a specific attitude of adherence to neoliberalism? There is a missing link in this causal chain. Rejection of strikes, even when motivated by conservatism, could mean different kinds of interests or aspirations. Again: the arguments that support this thesis are scarce. What the political and economic literature indicates as certain is that the maintenance of the neoliberal model, merely reformed by neodevelopmentalist policy, serves the interests of big companies, and it is possible to demonstrate that a great part of the bourgeoisie fought and still fights for the pillars of this model to be maintained. It is not appropriate to attribute to those below a political responsibility that belongs to those above.

Our last observation concerns the relations the ruling class maintains with the Brazilian state and the PT governments. There is in Singer's hypothesis an abuse of the concept of Bonapartism. Characterizing Lula's and Rousseff's governments as Bonapartists simply because they have made, at one time or another, concessions to conflicting demands from existing social forces would be tantamount to assuming that the capitalist state is a mere passive instrument in the hands of the ruling class or its hegemonic fraction. In fact, the capitalist state has an active role that puts itself above the immediate interests of this or that class or fraction, and that enables it to seek *an unstable balance of compromise among the existing forces.* It is true that the capitalist state is the arena of a *distributive* conflict among the fractions of the bloc in power, and even among the fundamental classes, but it is at the same time an active actor in these conflicts. What characterizes Bonapartism is something more than an active state in search of an *unstable balance of compromise,* which is a stabilizing element of class domination. Bonapartism is a situation in which the socioeconomic policy of the state, *considered in its fundamental aspects,* fails to express both the objective interests and the explicit demands of different fractions of the bourgeoisie. It turns out that, in their fundamental aspects, the economic policy of Lula's and Rousseff's governments addressed primarily the interests of the big internal bourgeoisie. And it is possible to demonstrate that this fraction of the bourgeoisie was contemplated, at least until Rousseff's second term, in the economic policy of the PT governments. Not only were its objective interests prioritized by state policy, but it also identified politically with the PT governments which, in stark contrast to what happened in the Fernando Henrique Cardoso era, created several forums for the big internal bourgeoisie to express its interests.[12] In the

---

12   The participation of big Brazilian businesses in advisory bodies for the determination
       of economic policy during Lula's governments is analyzed in two works by Eli Diniz and
       Renato Boschi (2004; 2007). Tatiana Berringer (2015) analyzes the participation of the
       business community in determining the foreign policy of Lula's governments.

2005 corruption scandal known as the *"Mensalão"* crisis, the Federation of Industries of the State of São Paulo (Fiesp), already under the presidency of Paulo Skaf, and the most important national associations of the big bourgeoisie mobilized in defense of Lula's government, dismantling the first attempt at a parliamentary coup, which was outlined at the time by the Brazilian Social Democracy Party (PSDB).[13]

In the period that encompasses Lula's both terms and Rousseff's first term, it is possible to detect a growing affirmation of the program of socioeconomic policy that we can call neodevelopmentalist.[14] It was not a path that zigzagged at the mercy of the molecular alterations in the correlation of forces. Lula's first government was marked by important concessions to the international financial capital, concessions that ended up neutralizing and dividing the conservative opposition forces. However, already in that first term, there were changes to its foreign policy and the role of the Brazilian Development Bank (BNDES) in order to serve the interests of the big internal bourgeoisie (Berringer, 2015; Bugiato, 2016). In his second term, the neodevelopmentalist profile of the government's socioeconomic policy became evident with the launch of the "Growth Acceleration Program" (PAC), the anti-cyclical economic policy measures in the context of the international economic crisis, and the creation of the housing program "My House, My Life." Rousseff moved even further in the same direction: she depreciated the exchange rate, reduced the basic interest rate, pressed for a reduction in banking spreads, reduced the primary surplus through various means, established a new regulation for public purchases that favored local production, and implemented protectionist measures, among others. This rise of neodevelopmentalism shows that state policy under the PT governments followed a clear path and aimed at capitalist development without, however, breaking with some of the pillars of the neoliberal model – we can mention the rollover of the public debt, which inhibited the investment capacity of the state, and the trade liberalization, which undermined domestic industry. But the reduced scope of this neodevelopmentalist economic policy, limited by the impositions of the persisting neoliberal capitalist model,

---

13   On the support of the big bourgeoisie to Lula's government during the "Mensalão crisis," see Martuscelli (2015). In Rousseff's second term, a crisis of political representation occurred between the government and the big internal bourgeoisie. Important segments of the processing industry and agribusiness that were members of this bourgeois group either abandoned the government or turned against it (See Boito, Jr., 2017).

14   Which can be defined as the merge of an economic policy aimed at stimulating growth by means of the state intervention with the maintenance of the pillars of the neoliberal capitalist model (See Saad-Filho & Morais, 2011).

is explained not because it would have addressed interests of the "subprole-tariat," but because it addressed the interests of segments of the Brazilian big bourgeoisie and of the international capital that may have lost some of their prominence during the PT governments, but were never removed from the bloc in power.

CHAPTER 5

Neodevelopmentalism, Social Classes, and Foreign Policy in the PT Governments

In this chapter, we analyze Brazilian politics with the help of a conceptual framework that is not dominant in Brazilian political science.[1] For different reasons, the prevalent approaches are currently institutionalism and neo-elitism, which separate politics from society, while our perspective unites these two fields through the concepts of class and class conflict. Therefore, we resume the process of linking politics to the interests of classes and class fractions, and thus to society and economy.

We should also clarify that our focus on class conflict is unlike what seems to be the most usual, which consists of considering the "bourgeoisie" and the "working class" as two homogeneous blocs, without internal divisions, in a constant and often fierce opposition to each other. In contrast, our approach takes into consideration the fractions that subdivide these two social classes, as well as the existence of intermediate classes – such as the middle class and the peasantry. It also provides for the possibility of the formation of fronts and alliances that may moderate, in certain circumstances, the conflict among the fundamental classes of a capitalist society like Brazil. As a result, this complex treatment of social classes identifies numerous groups intervening in the political process to form a multipolar scenario, establish complex relations of unity and struggle, and provide varied viewpoints on the political game according to context and to what is at stake.

To analyze the bourgeoisie, we have used the concept of bloc in power, which has some characteristics that are worth highlighting. In the first place, it contemplates the asymmetry in the relations among social classes: the bloc in power is composed only of the ruling classes and their fractions. Thus, the concept distinguishes the position occupied in the political process by the ruling classes – whose historical interests are organized by the state – from the position attributed to the working classes. Secondly, the concept of bloc in power enables us to consider the relations of unity and struggle that bring the interests of fractions of the ruling class closer or put them in opposition, proving to be a fundamental instrument to explain most political conflicts that

---

1   This chapter was written in coauthorship with Tatiana Berringer in September 2013.

do not necessarily pit the bourgeoisie against the working class. Thirdly, this concept offers a criterion to analyze the existing power hierarchy among the bourgeoisie's various fractions. It includes the notion of hegemonic fraction, whose interests are *prioritized* by the state's economic policy even when this prioritization harms the interests of the other fractions of the bloc in power. And fourthly, regarding the analysis of foreign policy, the concept of bloc in power allows us to overcome the most evident flaws of political realism (a dominant theoretical framework in international relations studies) by making it possible to understand a given state's foreign policy as an extension of the internal arrangement of power – especially the interests of the hegemonic fraction – in the international scenario. Therefore, the concept of bloc in power makes it possible to distinguish the close links between national and international politics, as well as to detect the real (class) content of what realists call "national interest," which the ideological discourse claims to be the interest of all the people.

Finally, there is room yet for two clarifications: one on the division into fractions that we believe to exist in the Brazilian bourgeoisie; and the other on the concept of internal bourgeoisie, which plays a central role in our analysis. We believe that the bourgeois fraction we call big internal bourgeoisie disputes with the big bourgeoisie associated with international capital the primacy in the orientation of the state's economic policy. Nicos Poulantzas (1974; 1975) analyzed both this division into fractions and the concept of internal bourgeoisie in a pioneering way with the aim of identifying three positions that may appear within contemporary bourgeoisies. The internal bourgeoisie is the fraction that occupies an intermediate position between two extremes in the bourgeoisie: on the one hand, the national bourgeoisie, which could assume an anti-imperialist position in dependent and colonial countries; on the other hand, the so-called "comprador" bourgeoisie, which is a mere extension, in the dependent social formation, of the core countries' capital. However, we prefer to replace the expression "comprador bourgeoisie," which refers to earlier stages of the economic relations between imperialist and dependent countries, with the expression "associated bourgeoisie." But still in regard to the concept of internal bourgeoisie: it allows us to avoid two symmetrical and opposite errors. One is imagining that there truly exists a national bourgeoisie in contemporary Brazil; and the other, much more common, is imagining that the new wave of internationalization of the capitalist economy might extinguish all differences and conflicts of interests between Brazilian companies and international capitalism.

1   The Bloc in Power and the Neodevelopmentalist Political Front[2]

Lula da Silva's victory in the 2002 presidential election was evidence of important changes in Brazilian politics that were consolidated during his two terms (2003–2010) and the subsequent Rousseff government. In the first place, there was a change within the bloc in power. Brazil's big internal bourgeoisie, a fraction of the capitalist class that maintained its own capital accumulation base and disputed positions with international financial capital, rose politically to the detriment of the interests of the big bourgeoisie associated with international capital. Thus, big international capital and its internal allies, whose interests had guided the Brazilian state's actions in the Collor de Mello (1990–1992), Itamar Franco (1993–1994), and Fernando Henrique Cardoso (FHC) [1995–2002] administrations, lost the hegemony that they had undisputedly enjoyed in the 1990s and found themselves in a subordinate position and opposing the Workers' Party (PT) governments. Secondly, this change was linked to a broader change in national politics that transcended the limits of the bloc in power. The political rise of the big internal bourgeoisie was only possible thanks to the formation of a political front that brought together this bourgeois fraction and the main sectors of the popular classes.

This political front, which we call neodevelopmentalist, was broad, heterogeneous, and full of contradictions. At the party level, it was represented mainly by the PT. This front brought together Brazil's big internal bourgeoisie – which was its leading force –, the lower middle class, the urban workers, and the peasantry. The front also incorporated the broad, heterogeneous social sector that includes the unemployed, the underemployed and self-employed, impoverished peasants, and other sectors that comprise what the 20th-century Latin American critical sociology called "marginal mass of workers" (Nun, 2001; Kowarick, 1975).

The neodevelopmentalist front distinguished itself from the conservative political field that, with its orthodox neoliberal orientation, was represented at the party level mainly by the Brazilian Social Democracy Party (PSDB). Despite its name, this party had no resemblance to European social democracies. Roughly speaking, the orthodox neoliberal field brought together big international financial capital and the fraction of the Brazilian bourgeoisie fully associated with it, part of the big landowners, and the public and private sectors of the upper middle class.

---

2 This is covered in greater detail in Chapter 3 above, which already analyzed the neodevelopmentalist political front.

Let us take a closer look at this front's characters and how the neodevelopmentalist program addressed – most unequally, it is important to stress – the forces that supported it. Why resort to the term developmentalist? Because this program was oriented to the economic growth of Brazilian capitalism. However, it did so without breaking with the neoliberal economic model still in force in the country. To pursue economic growth, the Lula and Rousseff governments employed a few important elements of socioeconomic policy that had been absent from FHC's mandates: a) policies to restore minimum wage and promote cash transfer, both of which increased purchasing power for the lower classes, namely those that display a stronger propensity to consumption; b) higher budget allocation by the Brazilian Development Bank (BNDES) to finance big national companies at subsided interest rates; c) foreign policy supporting big Brazilian companies or companies situated in Brazil for export of goods and capitals; d) anti-cyclical economic policy – measures to keep aggregate demand in moments of economic crisis. Later, the Rousseff government started to implement changes in interest and exchange policies, reducing basic interest rates and the bank spread, and meddling in the exchange market to depreciate the Brazilian currency, aiming at lowering the cost of productive investment and increasing that of imported products. These elements, even though they did not lead to a break with the neoliberal economic model inherited from the 1990s, are the reason why we have decided to employ the term "developmentalist" to address this program.

And why the prefix "neo"? Because the differences between this and the old developmentalist program of the 1930–1980 period are significant. *Neodevelopmentalism is the developmentalism of the neoliberal capitalism period.* There are six differences worth highlighting. Neodevelopmentalism: a) promotes a much more modest economic growth than the one promoted by the old developmentalism, although it is still considerably greater growth than the one observed in the 1990s; b) attaches less importance to the internal market; c) assigns less importance to the development of the local industrial park; d) accepts the restraints of the international division of labor, promoting in a new historic situation a reactivation of Brazilian capitalism's primary-export function; e) has a lower cash distribution capacity; and f) is driven by a bourgeois fraction that has lost all velleity to act as a nationalist anti-imperialist social force. All these six characteristics, which are narrowly linked to one another, make neodevelopmentalism much less ambitious than its predecessor. They stem from the fact that neodevelopmentalism is the developmentalist policy that is possible within the boundaries dictated by the neoliberal capitalist model. The lowest rates of GDP growth were what was possible for a state that compromised about 40% of its budget for the payment of interest and public debt repayments, undermining its own investment capacity; the lesser role attributed to the internal market was due to the commitment to maintain trade liberalization. The reactivation of the primary export function was the possible growth option for an economic policy that did not intend to revoke the offensive that imperialism had carried out against the Brazilian industrial park. All these characteristics prevented or discouraged a stronger cash distribution policy.

Let us now examine the classes and class fractions that, as active social forces, were the characters responsible for establishing and implementing such development policy. The big internal bourgeoisie, the driving force of the neodevelopmentalist front, was distributed over several economic sectors: the processing industry, shipbuilding, civil construction, mining, and the apex of agribusiness, represented by companies that processed and/or exported agricultural products, such as meat, sugar cane, soy, citrus, and others. What unified such diverse companies was their demand for the state's favor and protection when competing with foreign capital. Thus, contrary to what some authors have argued, the so-called globalization has not produced a homogeneous global bourgeoisie (Martuscelli, 2010). At any rate, the way the Lula da Silva and Dilma Rousseff governments prioritized the interests of this fraction of the big internal capital became evident in countless aspects of the economic policy. One of its key elements was the effort to maintain a surplus in the trade balance, which immensely favored agribusiness, mining, and other sectors linked to exports of products from agribusiness and natural resources. The financing policy offered by the Brazilian Development Bank (BNDES), the powerful state financial institution that made it unscathed through the wave of privatizations of the 1990s, was given a budget several times larger than that of the 1990s and started prioritizing a small number of predominantly national companies as receivers of loan programs at favored or subsided interest rates (Bugiato, 2012). The purchase policy of the Brazilian state and the big state companies also changed under the neodevelopmentalist governments and started prioritizing big companies that were predominantly national or implanted in Brazil. Ultimately, the Brazilian foreign policy concatenated with this new economic policy, so as to offer priority to the big internal bourgeoisie's interests. The big internal bourgeoisie is the most favored force in the neodevelopmentalist policy.

As for the ruled classes, the urban workers and the lower middle class have an organized participation in the neodevelopmentalist front, by virtue of unionism and the Workers' Party. Indeed, these were the forces that created the party that would become the instrument of that front – the PT. Since then, this party, which in the 1990s fought for the enforcement of a social welfare state in Brazil and for the strengthening of state capitalism, grew closer to the big internal bourgeoisie, which had been offering lukewarm criticism to neoliberalism. In the turn from the 1990s to the 2000s, combining its original tradition with the bourgeois dissatisfaction, the PT became empirically the creator and party tool of neodevelopmentalism in response to the circumstances. The working class and the lower middle class remained present in the PT, but, although they formed the party's social base, now they were no longer its driving force.

These wage earners had something to gain from neodevelopmentalism. The economic growth allowed a significant employment recovery, and the minimum wage readjustment policy (see Table 3 below) increased the purchasing power of the base of the wage pyramid. Data from the Brazilian Institute of Geography and Statistics (IBGE) show that between 2002, which was the last year of the FHC government, and 2010, the last year of the Lula government, the unemployment rate fell from 12.6% to 6.7%. During the Rousseff government, the downward trend continued and, in 2012, the unemployment rate was only 5.5%, i.e., less than half of the unemployment rate that had been inherited from the FHC era. Moreover, the minimum wage increased by 53.67% during Lula's two terms.

TABLE 3   Evolution of the minimum wage in constant R$, January 2010

Period	Value (R$)	Real increase (%)
April/2002	331.88	--
April/2003	335.96	1.23
May/2004	339.96	1.19
May/2005	367.93	8.23
April/2006	415.91	13.04
April/2007	437.12	5.10
March/2008	454.74	4.03
February/2009	481.05	5.79
January/2010	510.00	6.02
Total*	-	53.67

* Real increase from April/2002 to January/2010

SOURCE: INTER-UNION DEPARTMENT OF STATISTICS AND SOCIO-ECONOMIC STUDIES (DIEESE 2010)

The new economic and political conditions favored considerably the union organization and struggle, leading to a great increase in the number of strikes and allowing the workers to obtain new wage gains, in sharp contrast with what had happened with unionism in the 1990s. According to Boito and Marcelino (2011), from 2003 to 2012, the number of strikes saw an almost constant growth, which even the 2008 economic crisis could not deter. In 2004, there were 302 strikes. The number grew steadily until it reached 411 in 2008, the year of the economic crisis. Four years later, in 2012, the union movement carried out 873 strikes.

Although the annual average of strikes in the 2000s and 2010s remained below the annual average of the 1990s, research by the Inter-Union Department of Statistics and Socio-Economic Studies (Dieese) indicated that the former were mostly offensive strikes, that is, in the 2000s and 2010s, workers fought for real wage adjustments, improvements in working conditions and new rights, while in the 1990s the prevalence was of defensive strikes – i.e. movements against the dismissal of workers and the disregard of clauses of the wage agreement, and for the payment of back wages (Dieese, 2013b).

During the PT governments, there was an exponential growth in the number of collective agreements and conventions with wage adjustments above the inflation rate, confirming the recovery of Brazilian unionism in the 2000s and 2010s. In 2003, only 18.8% of collective agreements and conventions had obtained salary increases above inflation. In 2008, this percentage jumped to 76.1% (Boito Jr. & Marcelino, 2011); and in 2012, no less than 95% of the 704 trading units analyzed by Dieese achieved real wage increases. In around 4% of them, wage adjustments were equal to inflation; and in 1%, they were lower. However, the real average increase obtained by workers was not very high, remaining in the range of 1.96% above the National Consumer Price Index (INPC) (Dieese, 2013a).

The workers' unions had their own representatives, who stood beside big business representatives in many consulting organisms of the government. There were also frequent joint campaigns organized by associations of big industry businesspeople and the union centrals to pressure the government into offering the local industry customs protection and lowering the economy's basic interest rate. Later, as a result of such combined pressure, the Rousseff government started reducing the interest rate and taking measures to stimulate the exchange rate depreciation to favor exports, protect the domestic market, and make investments cheaper.

The peasants were also present in the neodevelopmentalist front, also in an organized way. The second term of FHC's presidency had persecuted and criminalized the peasant movements; with the rise of Lula da Silva to power, these movements had their demanding rights recognized by the government. The world of rural labor was very diverse, and workers were represented by different associations. Peasants were represented by the Landless Workers Movement (MST), the Movement of People Affected by Dams (MAB), the National Confederation of Agricultural Workers (Contag), and others. The wage-earning peasants were represented by the network of official unions and by Contag, the Brazilian association that congregated them. Considering the different layers of the peasantry, we can say that the average peasant was present mainly in Contag and secondarily in MST's group of settled peasants. This group demanded technical assistance, financing for production, as well as market and price for their products. The neodevelopmentalist governments partially met these demands by financing family agriculture, which grew considerably in comparison with its progress during FHC's presidency, and by starting programs of governmental purchase of peasant production (MST, 2009). The poor peasants, those with little or no land, demanded the expropriation of idle lands and an aggressive policy to liberate new settlements. This peasant segment, also organized by the MST, was the most marginalized by the neodevelopmentalist front. The Lula and Rousseff governments reduced land expropriations considerably. Agribusiness was an important factor in neodevelopmentalist policy, a fact that hindered the expropriation policy (Scarso, 2012).

The unemployed, the under-employed, and those living on odd jobs or "living on their own" represented the outermost point of the neodevelopmentalist front, maintaining with it a very particular relationship. These "marginal workers" inhabited mostly the outskirts of the country's big urban centers and the Northeast countryside. We must distinguish two sectors in the marginal mass.

One part was organized in popular demanding movements, known as "urgency movements," such as those fighting for land, housing, and employment. We have already discussed the movements fighting for land. As for the other two, the housing movement was more important due to its sociopolitical status. It encompassed many and varied organizations acting in big and medium Brazilian cities; these organizations mobilized dozens of thousands of families and had several political orientations (N. C. Oliveira, 2010). There was a variety of movements, from those that demanded only homeownership for its members to those that exerted pressure for a change in the government's housing policy, or that even alerted to the need to struggle for a change in the prevalent economic model as a whole. These movements' victories were evidenced, at the local level, by the acquisition of real estate and urban land through direct action, and, at the national level, by government measures addressing housing policies. The most important effect of housing movements was the alteration of the Brazilian state housing policy. In the 1990s, the country had abandoned the policy of building popular houses. During Lula's second term, a broad housing program called "My House, My Life" was created, breaking with the country's omission in that area. The Rousseff government continued implementing this housing program (N. C. Oliveira, 2010) and, in three years, financed the construction of two million dwellings, spending more than 50 billion Brazilian reais (Agência Brasil, 2012).

The other part of the "marginal mass of workers" was disorganized both socially and politically. It was included in the neodevelopmentalist front thanks to the cash transfer policies of the Lula and Rousseff governments. The "Family Grant" program, offered to families below the poverty line, and the "Continuous Benefit Program," offered to senior citizens and persons with disabilities, were the main tools of that policy. The "Family Grant" program covered more than 13 million families with a budget of around 15 billion Brazilian reais (MDS, 2013). This impoverished mass did not take part in the neodevelopmentalist political front in an organized manner. The Lula and Rousseff governments chose to hand them out cash without bothering – neither these governments nor their party, the PT – to organize them. They formed a passive, disorganized electoral base that was invited to participate in the political process only through voting for candidates from the neodevelopmentalist front. The relationship between the front's governments and their electoral base allowed the populist tradition of Brazilian politics to continue. In the populist political relationship, workers achieve real gains – contrary to what liberal observers, for whom populism is mere "demagogy," have claimed. However, these gains are very limited precisely because their beneficiaries remain politically and ideologically dependent on the government's initiatives.

Albeit broad and contradictory in its class composition, the neodevelopmentalist political front existed and acted as such. The forces that integrated it – even though they might clash (often fiercely) about economic issues like wages, social and labor rights, land expropriation, and others – have acted jointly at crucial moments of the national political process. That was the case in 2002 when Lula da Silva was elected president; in 2005, in the political crisis that came to threaten the continuity of the Lula government, known as "Mensalão"; in 2006, when Lula was re-elected, and again in 2010, during Dilma Rousseff's victorious electoral campaign. The fact is that, in all these crucial situations, the survival of neodevelopmentalist governments had been at risk, and, in all of them, important employers' associations, union centrals, peasant movements for agrarian reform, popular movements for housing, as well as the poor, disorganized voters supported the Lula and Rousseff governments with manifestations of all kinds or simply with their vote. In doing so, these social forces, even though moved by different interests and objectives, proved to be part of the same political field.

2   Foreign Policy and the Neodevelopmentalist Front

The foreign policy of the Brazilian state during the Lula and Rousseff governments must be considered in the context of the political changes of their time. First and foremost, we should picture them as part of the change that took place within the bloc in power in Brazil. It is our understanding that a state's foreign policy stems from the characteristics of the bloc in power that controls that state. Secondly, it results, for different reasons and to a lesser extent, from the new political presence of the popular classes in national politics. In other words, differently from the self-appointed realist and neorealist trends, we refuse to consider the state as a homogeneous institution, endowed with its own interest and power, with foreign policy detached from domestic politics. It is the changes that occurred in Brazilian domestic politics – which emerged in association with the changes in the international scenario – that explain the new foreign policy of the Lula and Rousseff governments.

The foreign policy of the Lula governments was an important tool for strengthening the big internal bourgeoisie. During this period, there was a change in the international performance of the Brazilian state that was determined by the interests of this class fraction. At the international level, the Brazilian internal bourgeoisie united around common interests, which were fundamentally the following: state support in the conquest of new markets for its export products and direct investments abroad; priority for its products and services in purchases by the state and state-owned companies; and greater state protection in the internal market. In our view, this is why the main targets of the Brazilian state's international actions were: the emphasis on South-South relations; the priority given to South America; the creation of the G-20 to act in the Doha Round of the World Trade Organization (WTO); the creation of the Ibas Forum (India, Brazil, and South Africa); the negotiations and filing of the Free Trade Area of the Americas (Alca, in Portuguese) proposal; the postponement of the Mercosur-European Union negotiations; and later, Brazil's performance in the BRICS (Brazil, Russia, India, China, and South Africa) forums.

It is worth remembering that the FHC governments' foreign policy was focused on the monetary stabilization plan, thus aiming at attracting investments and loans from the IMF and the World Bank. To achieve all that, Brazil had to assume a submissive attitude towards the centers of world power.

The strategy employed was the approximation with the imperialist states – the United States and Europe – and the ratification of international regimes, among them the Treaty on the Non-Proliferation of Nuclear Weapons (NPT), which was signed in 1997, 29 years after the Brazilian state refused to adhere to this discriminatory agreement. Also, it is worth recalling the signing of Protocol 505, of April 18, 2000; the agreement, on the one hand, provided for the transfer of defense equipment at low cost and, on the other hand, completely yielded control of the Alcântara Base, Maranhão, to the United States. The Brazilian state was prevented from using the base and from supervising the import of equipment (spaceships, vehicles, etc.) that the United States brought to stock or launch. This agreement was rejected by the Senate after Lula took over the presidency in 2003.

The proposal to create the Free Trade Area of the Americas (FTAA, Alca in Portuguese) was one of the elements that led the big Brazilian internal bourgeoisie to become organized during the FHC governments. It brought the interests of that fraction closer to the interests of the popular and labor movements that had been campaigning against the FTAA proposal. Let us look at this in detail.

Although there were contradictions within the big internal bourgeoisie regarding the FTAA proposal, they declined in importance as the process progressed. The internal bourgeoisie, especially the industries focused on the Brazilian and Latin American production of manufactured goods (paper and cellulose, electronics, chemicals, food, and capital goods), had expressed its opposition to the FTAA proposal as soon as the negotiations began. In turn, industries whose production was oriented to the foreign market (agribusiness, steel, footwear, and textiles) welcomed the project, given that they were the least negatively affected by the commercial liberalization of the 1990s.

To defend its interests and determine its demands regarding foreign policy, the big internal bourgeoisie created the Brazilian Business Coalition (CEB) in 1996. CEB's goal was to organize the demands of the business community to pressure the government in the planning and execution of hemispheric negotiations. For the first time in the history of Brazilian foreign policy, the ruling classes came together around a common agenda with national, multi-industrial scope. CEB was created after the participation of some Brazilian businesspersons in the II Business Forum of the Americas, which took place in Cartagena in 1996 (a meeting of Latin American bourgeoisies to negotiate the FTAA proposal). At that event, which was part of the FTAA negotiation meetings, the Brazilian bourgeoisie was surprised by the competence and readiness of the USA businesspersons and felt threatened by their technical knowledge and capacity to influence their state. Coincidentally or not, they agreed that the next Forum would be in the Brazilian city of Belo Horizonte. That led the National Confederation of Industry (CNI) to realize the need to expand its influence and volunteer to organize the next forum (Oliveira & Pfeifer, 2006).

In organizing the Forum, the CNI managed to bring together broad sectors of the Brazilian bourgeoisie to participate in the formulation, discussion, and elaboration of decisions during international negotiations. The most intense activism at CEB came from protectionist sectors, notably large and medium-sized companies of the South and Southeast of Brazil. Agribusiness displayed a relatively independent performance from CEB (Oliveira & Pfeifer, 2006). In fact, this sector aimed at accessing the U.S. market, and could only achieve that if the United States agreed to reduce its protective policies regarding their agriculture (A. J. Oliveira, 2003). Since American governments refused to do so, Brazilian agribusiness had no reason to pressure the Brazilian state to sign the free trade agreement and ended up joining the group of industries that opposed the FTAA.

CEB became a benchmark for the other international economic negotiations then underway, especially the Doha Round of the World Trade Organization (WTO) and the negotiations on the Mercosur-European Union agreement. In order to institutionalize channels for dialogue and consultation with the bourgeoisie, the Ministry of Foreign Affairs (Itamaraty) created special sections for debate on international economic negotiations (Senalca and Seneuropa) and a Permanent Business Committee.

The labor and popular movements, in turn, were organized around the National Campaign Against the FTAA (CNA), which brought together 55 organizations, with emphasis on the Unified Workers' Central (CUT), the MST, the pastoral sections of the Episcopal Conference of Brazil (CNBB), the Popular Consultation, the World March of Women, the Unified Socialist Workers' Party (PSTU), and some sectors of the PT. Most of these organizations arose in the outcome of the fights for the country's re-democratization and against neoliberalism, and they also held a plebiscite on the foreign debt in 2000. The movement against the FTAA started in 1997, but the campaign did not become organized before 2001. Its goal was to raise awareness and mobilize the population to dissuade governments from signing the treaty (Silva, 2008). The idea of the campaign against the FTAA was born at the World Social Forum (WSF) in the Brazilian city of Porto Alegre in 2001. It was a continental campaign that helped to strengthen a progressive camp that succeeded in electing several e presidents between 1998 and 2011, among which were: Hugo Chávez in Venezuela, the Kirchner couple in Argentina, Michele Bachelet in Chile, Fernando Lugo in Paraguay, Tabaré Vasquez in Uruguay, Evo Morales in Bolivia, etc. The good relationship between Lula and these presidents was fundamental for continental geopolitics and contributed to overthrow the proposal of the FTAA creation, as well as to strengthen regional integration.

In Brazil, the campaign held a popular referendum in 2002, in preparation for which massive training courses were conducted on the political and economic impact of the FTAA approval. Various teaching materials were produced and distributed to the people, such as booklets, videos, and leaflets. The campaign organized state and local committees that spread across the Brazilian territory and carried out discussions in schools, neighborhoods, universities, churches, local radio, and TV stations, to mobilize the population and collect subscriptions. The plebiscite collected more than ten million votes, of which 95% were against Brazil's participation in the FTAA. This articulation, in addition to bringing together a large section of the Brazilian left-wing, strongly influenced the decision of the Labors' Party, whose base had participated intensely in this mobilization. The fight against the FTAA joined wide popular sectors in resisting the deepening of neoliberalism in the region (S. A. Silva, 2008). We could say that the fight against the FTAA contributed to consolidate a neodevelopmentalist platform with particular – and even contradictory – objectives and definitions, a platform claimed both by the organizations of the working classes and by the representatives of the big Brazilian internal bourgeoisie.

The FTAA was one of the main subjects that marked the opposition between the PSDB and the PT in the 2002 electoral campaign. For it was precisely from 2001 on, a year before the election, that the FHC government began to take a stand in favor of the agreement, while the PT's aversion to it grew stronger. According to Lula's statements, due to hemispheric asymmetries, the FTAA would have worked less as an integrative project than as a plan to annex Latin American economies to the United States (A. J. Oliveira, 2003).

The PT's position became even more explicit at the beginning of the Lula government when ambassador Samuel Pinheiro Guimarães was appointed secretary-general of the Ministry of Foreign Affairs. Guimarães had been discharged from the presidency of the Institute of Research on International Affairs (IPRI) in 2001 after declaring his opposition to the FTAA during a meeting of the Brazilian Machinery Builders' Association (Abimaq) (Bandeira, 2004).

However, the Lula government did not abandon the FTAA negotiations in the first years of mandate and started defending a "light FTAA," by which countries would enter into different levels of commitment with the FTAA, conducting bilateral or plurilateral negotiations. This attitude caused great discomfort to the organized sectors of the National Campaign against the FTAA and ended up dividing this big left-wing articulation into opponents to the government (PSTU), its support base (PT and CUT), and critics that advocated structural reforms and changes in Brazilian society (MST and Popular Consultation).

It is important to stress that the Brazilian state used the WTO negotiations and the perspective of a Mercosur-European Union agreement as a counterweight to the FTAA negotiations. According to Thorstensen (2001), these three negotiations were intertwined and allowed the Brazilian state to play strategically in the international scene. From the Brazilian point of view, these negotiations meant: asymmetric relations between imperialist and dependent states, a threat to Brazilian industry, and the prospect of a reduction in agricultural protectionism To stall for time and gain leverage in the FTAA negotiations, the Brazilian state sought to show a positive attitude in negotiating with the European Union and, at the same time, served at the WTO Dispute Settlement Body on the cotton and sugar panels, demonstrating its capacity to act contrary to the United States and the European Union in multilateral spheres (Vigevani & Mariano 2005). On the other hand, the United States sought to diminish Brazil's influence in Latin America and pushed for the signing of the FTAA by negotiating bilateral agreements with Andean countries (Chile, Colombia, and Peru), Caribbean countries, and with other members of Mercosur, particularly Uruguay and Paraguay.

That is why the Lula government, right from the start, sought to strengthen Mercosur and other integration initiatives in South America – such as the approximation between Mercosur and the Andean Community of Nations as well as the South American Infrastructure Integration Initiative (Iirsa) – as a way to counterbalance its relations with imperialist states (in particular, the United States and Europe) and introduce new aspects in the regional integration policy in areas such as energy, transport, and communications.

It is worth mentioning that the Brazilian state respected the Bolivian state's decisions on the nationalization of gas and oil that interfered with Petrobras' operations; it also renegotiated the Itaipu hydroelectric plant treaty with Paraguay at the latter's request and participated in a series of economic cooperation initiatives, such as contributing voluntarily with resources to Paraguay for the construction of a 500kw line between the Itaipu hydroelectric plant and Paraguay's capital, Asunción. An important milestone of the Lula governments' foreign policy was the creation of the Union of South American Nations (Unasur) in 2008, which, in addition to incorporating Iirsa, created the South American Defense Council (CDS) to oppose the OAS' Inter-American Reciprocal Assistance Treaty (Tiar). In 2008, the Brazilian state also played an important role in containing the attempted coup d'état in Bolivia and Ecuador, as well as arbitrating the conflict between Colombia and Ecuador.

Some of the actions of the Brazilian state displayed its opposition – albeit occasional – to the United States' positions in the international political arena: condemning the 2003 invasion of Iraq; sheltering Honduran President

Manuel Zelaya in the Brazilian embassy; taking a dissenting position regarding the production of enriched uranium in Iran and the installation of US military bases in Colombia.

In addition, the foreign policy endeavored to expand and deepen South-South relations, created coalitions such as the G-20 at the WTO, participated in the IBSA Dialogue Forum (involving India, Brazil, and South Africa), took part in the UN peacekeeping mission in Haiti (Minustah), and approached states in Africa and the Middle East, as well as China, Russia, and South Africa, through BRICS. These relations brought great benefits to the Brazilian internal bourgeoisie by increasing access to new markets for the export of commodities and manufactured products, as well as securing the installation of Brazilian companies in these territories. Between 2003 and 2010, in addition to a reversal in the balance of trade situation from a deficit to a large surplus, there was a clear change in the destination of Brazilian exports. The increase in exports to Latin America and other regions contributed, along with other elements, to decrease unemployment in the country.

Brazilian companies not only grew but also became internationalized. There were almost a thousand Brazilian companies with a relevant presence abroad at the time – with more than 10% of the branches' capital and direct investment superior to US$ 10 million. The most internationalized Brazilian companies were: JBS, Gerdau, Stefanini IT Solutions, Metalfrio, Marfrig, Ibope, Odebrecht, Sabó, Magnesita, Suzano Papel e Celulose, Vale, Weg, Brasil Foods, CI&T, Artecola, Embraer, Camargo Correa, Marcopolo, Petrobras, among others. Brazilian transnational companies invested mainly in agriculture, livestock, and natural resources; consumer goods such as food, beverages, and textiles; intermediate goods in the area of chemicals, equipment, and construction; and commerce and transportation, with emphasis on profitable activities in natural resources, civil construction, and food (Fundação Dom Cabral, 2012).

After the FTAA failed in 2005, the Brazilian Business Coalition (CEB) had its role reduced and transferred to foreign trade departments of the National Confederation of Industry (CNI), the Federation of Industries of the State of São Paulo (Fiesp), and major economic groups. In 2004, the Brazil-China Business Council was formed; it was led by Vale do Rio Doce Company and consisted of national corporations dedicated to mining, energy, paper, pulp, food, and construction. These corporations were interested in exporting to China or accessing its huge market.

After the 2008 crisis, there was an increase both in imports of Chinese products and in foreign direct investment in Brazil. To contain the negative impacts of this situation, the Brazilian state encouraged the devaluation of its currency, created new protectionist tariffs, reduced the Tax on Industrialized

Products (IPI), and required that a portion of government purchases be made from Brazilian companies. At the same time, state representatives began to condemn the "currency war" and the fiscal austerity policies advocated by the European Union and the United States. Together with the other BRICS's members, Brazil criticized the policies adopted by international financial organizations and started to fight for a new international structure (a new development bank).

In short, we can say that the filing of the FTAA proposal, the postponement of Mercosur negotiations with the European Union and the Doha Round, the strengthening of Latin American integration and the deepening of relations with dependent states, and the changes in tariff policy, exchange rate policy, interest rates, and BNDES investments were all part of the Lula and Rousseff governments' policy to guarantee state protection to the big internal bourgeoisie, both nationally and internationally.

3   Conclusion

During the PT administrations, the political debate in Brazil about the government, an electorally viable opposition, the media, and major political parties was dominated by economic issues. Among them, prevailed the issue of economic growth and, secondarily, the distribution of income, and the reduction of economic and social inequalities. Two lines of economic thought clashed against each other in this debate: the monetarist and the neodevelopmentalist. According to our analysis, this debate must be associated with the conflict between the bourgeois fractions that composed the bloc in power.

Still, the big internal bourgeoisie and the big bourgeoisie associated with international capital were not as separate as oil from water. These two fractions were part of a bigger group called big capital, with common interests in many sectors and circumstances. On the one hand, many national companies sought out foreign partners to increase their economic power and to incorporate technology; on the other hand, foreign companies searched for national partners, intending to insert themselves more easily into the Brazilian economy and politics. In the processing industry, which aspired to the protection of the domestic market, there were a large number of foreign companies. And the big banks, which, coupled with international financial capital, held the bulk of government bonds and were interested in expanding financial gains, were mostly national companies. The two fractions considered in our analysis had, in addition to a well-defined central core, a periphery comprised of companies that oscillated between two poles due to the multiple aspects that conditioned them: national or foreign capital, financial or productive sector, production for export or for the domestic market, agriculture or industry, region of the country where their plants were located, etc. However, none of this denied the fact that the two different conceptions and strategies of economic policy – the monetarist and the neodevelopmentalist – polarized different sectors of the big bourgeoisie.

A group of big companies with exclusively or predominantly Brazilian capital maintained a mighty presence in the areas of heavy construction, mining, processing of some agricultural products, processing industry, shipyards, defense industry, and others. These companies pressured the state for a neodevelopmentalist policy that would increase investments and public spending on infrastructure, reduce the interest rate, depreciate the Brazilian currency to increase the income of exporters, and protect the internal market. In turn, big international capital and the Brazilian bourgeois fraction associated with it pushed for a monetarist policy that would reduce state investments, maintain primary surplus and interest rates at high levels, keep the Brazilian real appreciated, and increase trade liberalization. Their goal was to ensure that the state would remunerate public debt securities. They aspired to the maintenance of financial gains. They longed to purchase the dollars they sent abroad at low prices and claimed free access to the Brazilian domestic market. Despite the points in common between the two bourgeois fractions, the conflict was established.

This was the main conflict in Brazilian politics during the PT governments, affecting the conditions of life and struggle of the working classes, not to mention the Brazilian state's performance in the international arena.

The instance of greatest international prominence of the Brazilian state stemmed mainly from the strengthening of the big internal bourgeoisie; it was when Brazil questioned the organizations' rules and the international order itself – starting with the trading system, when the Brazilian government, via the G-20, sought to question the unilateral opening of dependent economies in contrast to the maintenance of agricultural protectionism by the imperialist states. Next, the Brazilian position on the Iran-Turkey agreement on uranium enrichment revived the criticism of the strategy of using access to technology to maintain the gap between imperialist and dependent states. Finally, criticizing the international financial system – with the support of the BRICS countries –, Brazil consolidated a position that challenges the order that Europe and the United States have imposed since the end of World War II. These initiatives had modest concrete results, but the comparative difference between this foreign policy and that of the FHC governments was remarkable.

The national and popular elements, after being relegated to the museum of political antiquities in the 1990s, bounced back – although timidly – into Brazilian politics in the 21st century.

Neodevelopmentalism and the Recovery of the Brazilian Union Movement

This chapter discusses Brazilian unionist activities at the time the Workers' Party (PT) held the country's presidency, a period that began with Lula da Silva's inauguration in January 2003.[1] It is an important period, since for the first time in Brazil's political history a party born mainly from the union movement took over the federal government. Unions and social movements held high expectations for the PT governments, faced some positive results, and met with a number of frustrations. The support from the union and social movements played a decisive role in Lula da Silva's reelection in 2006 and in Dilma Rousseff's election in 2010.

The period in question is also relevant from the perspective of the economy. On the one hand, the international economic situation – marked mostly by the growth of the Chinese economy and a sharp increase in the demand for commodities – and the PT governments' policies led Brazil's economy to grow faster than it had during both terms of Fernando Henrique Cardoso.[2] Big Brazilian companies from agribusiness, mineral production, heavy construction, shipbuilding, processing industry, and other sectors were greatly benefited by this policy. On the other hand, the PT governments' social policy fostered an improvement of the working population's life conditions. The reduction in unemployment, the governmental policy to restore the minimum wage, and the policies regarding cash transfer and construction of popular houses favored workers employed by the formal market as well as informal workers, the unemployed, and the marginalized populations – those living in *favelas* (slums), workers from the shrinking peasant economy, and others. These socioeconomic policies allowed the PT governments to gather diverse sectors and social classes to build a large, contradictory political front, which we shall call the neodevelopmentalist front. This political front was the social

---

1 This chapter was written in coauthorship with Andréia Galvão and Paula Marcelino in 2014.

2 The annual average of the GDP expansion in the eight years under Cardoso (1995–2002) was 2.3%, against 4% during the eight years under Lula (2003–2010). It continued to grow even after the international crisis that was unleashed in 2008, but the average of the Rousseff government diminished considerably, dropping to 1.8%.

base of these governments, ensuring their political and electoral success (see Chapter 3 above).

Almost the entire union movement was integrated to the neodevelopmentalist front. The Unified Workers' Central (CUT), linked to PT; the Union Force (FS), PT's traditional adversary, which became part of the governmental support base during Lula's second term; the General Workers' Central of Brazil (CGTB); the Workers' Central of Brazil (CTB); the New Workers' Union Central (NCST), created in 2006; the Workers' General Union (UGT), created in 2007; and finally, the Brazilian Union Central, formed by dissidents from CGTB that became organized in 2012. However, the downgrade of PT and CUT's political program spawned tensions and conflict in the unions and left-wing organizations (Galvão, 2006; Galvão; Tropia & Marcelino, 2013). CUT's support to the Lula government caused a rift inside that central, leading some of its minority groups within it to create two new organizations seeking to achieve a national scope: Conlutas (National Struggle Coordination) in 2004, and Intersindical in 2006. These organizations, in spite of their minority status, formed a pocket of resistance pole to the hegemonic unionism and contributed to invigorate the union landscape by challenging the hegemonic unionism for the ability to represent the workers. These organizations' actions may have also influenced the orientation of the unions that supported the government, leading them, in some cases, to be more critical of the neodevelopmentalist policy.

This chapter is divided into three sections: the first addresses the union movement's participation in the neodevelopmentalist political front; the second analyzes the actions of the union centrals that took part in the neodevelopmentalist front; and, finally, the third studies the strike struggle during Rousseff's government, its characteristics and results.

1   Neodevelopmentalism and the Union Movement

In the 1990s, the decade of the neoliberal reforms and economic stagnation, two factors marked the Brazilian union movement (Boito Jr., 1997). Firstly, regarding the political process, the largest, most active wing of the union movement, organized by the Unified Workers' Central (CUT), opposed the Collor(1990–1992), Itamar (1992–1994), and Cardoso (1995–2002) governments. The programs for trade liberalization, privatization, social security reform, and deregulation of the labor market set the neoliberal governments against CUT's demands and historical platform. Secondly, at the base of the union movement, the number of strikes dropped to less than half the number recorded in the previous decade – see Chart 1 – and the strikers' demands became mostly defensive – to have their

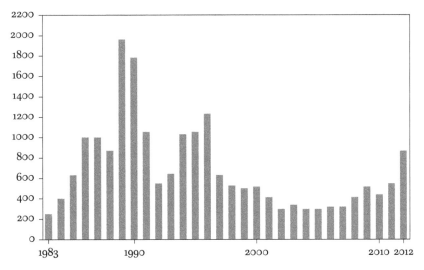

CHART 1   Number of strikes in Brazil recorded in each year

jobs maintained, to have late wages paid, to have their rights respected, to ensure the compliance with contractual clauses that had been agreed upon, etc. These two factors, namely the poorly efficient resistance to the neoliberal reforms and the reduction in the number of strikes, led most scholars and observers to suggest that the Brazilian unionism was facing a profound crisis.

In the 2000s and also in the 2010s, the situation of Brazilian unionism changed considerably. The new political and economic scenario – which we will discuss ahead – had a strong impact on the union movement. The great majority of the union movement, represented by the seven largest union centrals, became a support base, in spite of the criticism it offered, to the PT governments; the strikes became more numerous and frequent – see Chart 1 – and the workers were successful as their demands started seeking actual wage increases. The number of strikes, which had been falling since 1997, began to grow in 2003, the first year of Lula's government. At a first stage, between 2003 and 2007, the number reached a plateau around a little over 300 strikes per year, while at a second stage, from 2008 to 2012, the number rose even more.[3]

---

3   The number of strikes remained, however, distant from that of the 1980s, an exceptional period in the history of Brazilian unionism, as it combined "explosive factors" of politics and economy: the military dictatorship crisis, and annual inflation rates between three and four figures. In 1989, when there was a record number of two thousand strikes, there was also a record inflation rate: 1,764%.

Later, some analysts of the union movement came to consider that Brazilian unionism was going through a phase of recovery (Boito Jr. & Marcelino, 2010).

The changes that occurred in Brazil were part of a larger picture of changes in Latin America. The neoliberal model experienced a crisis in the continent; the neoliberal ideology and governments, after a brief period of political and ideological success, started being contested in most countries in that region. Three groups of countries represented three very different situations (Boito Jr. *et al.*, 2007)). In a first group, we had countries with conservative governments where neoliberalism not only survived, but also barely saw any meaningful process of reforms. That was the case of Mexico, Colombia, and Peru. At the other end, we had a group of countries whose governments attempted, with varying degrees of success, to break with the neoliberal capitalist model. These were the countries that relied on an economy based on minerals and oil, had low industrial diversification, and were ruled by left-wing governments with a strong popular base: Venezuela, Bolivia, and Ecuador. A third group, in an intermediary position of the political spectrum, was formed by countries – such as Brazil and Argentina – that had a more developed capitalist economy, a diversified industrial park, and, in the 2000s and 2010s, governments composed by parties supported by the working class and the waged lower middle class – the Peronist Justicialist Party in Argentina, and PT in Brazil. In the third group, the governments established a political front uniting, at one end, the big internal bourgeoisie, whose interests conflicted more and more with the neoliberal model in its most orthodox form, and, at the other end, the working class and the lower middle class. While in Venezuela, Bolivia, and Ecuador the popular base of the post-neoliberal governments was composed mainly by peasants, indigenous people, and a very diversified range of urban popular classes, in Brazil and Argentina the movement driven by the unions and the lower middle class was the social force that stood out as the support base of the governments that were reforming the neoliberal capitalist model. It was this political front that served as foundation to neodevelopmentalism in Brazil and Argentina, and that fostered the recovery of Brazilian unionism.

How was this political front formed? What was its program? What sort of recovery did it foster in regard to Brazilian unionism? In the 1990s, both the union movement and the businessperson's associations went through a process to redefine their political positions. CUT, after defending in the 1980s the implantation of a welfare state in Brazil and being cornered by the neoliberal reforms, abandoned that program and showed a willingness to make concessions, moving closer to a political platform that we may call neodevelopmentalist. On the other side of the barricade, businesspersons from the industrial sector felt their interests were conflicting more and more with those of

Cardoso's neoliberal program, which they had supported at first. The industrial businesspersons criticized mainly the trade liberalization, the high interest rates, and the economic stagnation (Boito Jr., 2002a). In June 1996, CUT, FS, and the General Confederation of Workers – a minor, conservative union central – called for a general strike against recession and unemployment. The strike occurred on June 21 of that year, and around 12 million workers stopped working in the whole country. What was new – and even surprising – about that strike was the official, active support from the powerful Federation of Industries of the State of São Paulo (Fiesp). This convergence between the union movement and the businesspersons was not an isolated fact, but it can be considered, due to its importance and unusualness in the history of Brazilian strikes, the initial landmark of the political front that would be formed to support the PT governments. In fact, in the 2002 presidential election, won by Lula da Silva, the businesspersons' position was very different from the one they had taken in the 1989 election. At the time, the president of Fiesp had stated that, if Lula won, not only capital, but the businesspersons themselves would leave the country. However, right from the beginning of his government in 2003, Lula da Silva chose to keep close, institutionalized political relations with both Fiesp, his old political nemesis, and the union movement, from which he had come, and which had cast him into the national political scene.

The neodevelopmentalist socioeconomic policy did not reach as far as the classical developmentalist policy that had predominated between the 1930s and the 1980s, but it was also distinct from the orthodox neoliberalism of the Cardoso governments.[4] It was neodevelopmentalist because it emphasized economic growth and because it perceived the state as a fosterer of growth, goals that had been absent from or very secondary during Cardoso's presidency. Its most characteristic tools were: direct investments from the state; public banks financing private investors at subsidized interest rates; the creation of new protectionist measures that prioritized local companies in purchases by the state and by state companies; and the implementation of a foreign policy that favored commercial/diplomatic relations with the south and aimed at facilitating the international expansion of big Brazilian companies. Such policy did not reach as far as the old developmentalism because it did not break with some basic factors of the neoliberal capitalist model that limited the economic growth policy itself: refinancing of the public debt, which devoured great part

---

4   This sort of classification – orthodox, heterodox – always depends on the comparative term. If we change the term of reference, the classification may change. Compared to the neoliberalism of the Menem government in Argentina, the Cardoso government's neoliberalism was moderate.

of the state budget and hindered its investment capacity; maintenance of a high interest rate that discouraged private investment; and maintenance of trade liberalization, which threatened local industrial companies.

Even though it did not break with some basic factors of the neoliberal model, the neodevelopmentalist policy attempted to relax them, moderate them, with the goal of stimulating economic growth and seeking space for a social policy to reduce poverty. Regarding the economic policy, the PT governments raised immensely the budget allocation for the Brazilian Development Bank (BNDES) and put it in service of Brazilian companies; reduced, on the long term, the basic interest rate – although it remained at a high level – and the primary surplus; and suspended the program to sell public companies. Regarding social policy, they implemented a mechanism to recover the minimum wage, created or stimulated cash transfer programs ("Family Grant" and "Continuous Benefit Program"), developed a program for building popular housing ("My House, My Life"), and established a policy to support small agriculture.

The neodevelopmentalist economic program halved unemployment and created much better conditions for the unions' organization and struggle. Between April 2003 and January 2013 – in other words, in ten years of PT government – the minimum wage went from R$ 240 to R$ 678 in nominal values. Accounting for that period's inflation, this increase represented an actual gain of 70.49% (Dieese, 2013c). It is a known fact that unemployment reduction (see Chart 2) improves not only the workers' life conditions, but also the circumstances of the union struggle.

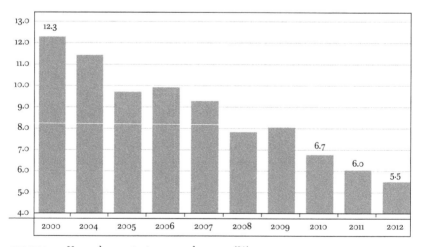

CHART 2   Unemployment rate – annual average (%)

It is important to emphasize that the recovery of Brazilian unionism, given the factors that facilitated it, had some unique characteristics. We believe it is fundamental to underline that the recovery of the struggle for demands – the object of our analysis in the third part of this chapter – was combined with a downgrade of the union movement's political platform, as we will see ahead.

2   The Union Movement's Political Moderation

The PT governments encouraged two apparently contradictory union prac-tices: i) they fostered political moderation on the part of the movement's leadership, by expanding for the unions the institutional mechanisms in their relationship with the state, and by promoting an alliance between the union movement and part of the employers; ii) they stimulated the struggle for demands and the procuring of improvements in collective agreements and conventions, by reducing unemployment and enabling a recovery of the eco-nomic growth. We will elaborate on these considerations in a moment.

However, we must first explain our understanding of political modera-tion. In the 1990s, as we have indicated above, CUT abandoned the struggle to implement a social welfare state. In fact, its focus changed. The proposals for nationalizing banks and health, education, and transportation services started losing ground, and the documents and practice of the unions affiliated to this union central started focusing on defending the resumption of the economic growth (Giannotti & Lopez Neto, 1992; Galvão, 2002). However, even though Brazilian unionism's political moderation was an identifiable trait since the 1990s, the union movement's interlocutors in this period were a government considered adversarial, and employers who had unleashed an offensive against the workers, either through the threat to workers' rights, or through the compa-nies' productive and managerial restructuration. As the PT governments took over, the interlocutors became an allied party, and a group of employers that partly integrated the political front sustaining these governments. Therefore, if the favorable economic situation during these governments offered union-ism more opportunities to succeed, this political arrangement commended caution, lest the achievements credited to the governments were threatened. Thus, political moderation was not the fruit of the unionists' mere taking part in the governmental institutions and holding positions in the government, but the result of a broader process that was not restricted to the union leaderships.

Having clarified that, we shall resume our analysis of union practices during the PT governments. The Lula government, during his first term, expanded the unions' participation in governmental agencies – a possibility opened by the 1988 Constitution and put in practice in the 1990s, with the Deliberative Council of the Worker Support Fund (CODEFAT) and the Trustee Board of the Guarantee Fund for Time of Service – through the creation of two tripartite organizations, the National Labor Forum (FNT) and the Socioeconomic Development Council (CDES), to discuss the reforms that the administration intended to implement. Furthermore, the Lula government promoted a series of conferences to discuss public policies in various areas, ensuring new spaces for workers' intervention through their union organizations and social movements. At the end of his presidency, Lula approved a law that established that workers from public companies with more than 200 employees would have representatives taking part in the management boards.

The intensification of the unions' participation in administrative agencies allows us to speak of an increase in the unions' influence in politics, but that does not mean that unionism drove governmental politics. Therefore, the ability to form unions was at odds with the unions' limited intervention in the decision-making process, since, as we will see, only a small part of the unions' propositions was effectively discussed in the institutional spaces ensured by the government, and an even smaller part was put in practice. However, the expansion of the participation channels in the government's consulting agencies, as well as the closeness between the government and a significant portion of the union movement, affected the unions' conceptions and strategies, strengthening the perspective of joint actions being performed by the unions, the PT administrations, and the Brazilian bourgeoisie.

The union centrals prioritized institutional action and showed willingness toward political alliance, but that did not translate into an absence of conflict. The third section of this chapter will address precisely the growing strike struggle during the PT governments. Priority was also offered to the defense of corporative economic interests of workers from different segments – as it was observed in strikes by specific categories seeking actual wage increase – but that did not mean an absence of more general political demands. The union centrals introduced a long list of demands, particularly the appreciation of minimum wage, the reduction of the workweek from 44 to 40 hours, the end of dismissal without cause, the signing of ILO Convention 151 to make collective negotiations mandatory in the public sector, the end of the social security factor,[5] the end of outsourcing, the increase in resources for education, and the boost in public investment.

---

5   A reducing factor instituted by the welfare reform implemented by the Fernando Henrique Cardoso government in order to encourage workers to stay active for longer.

CUT was the big force behind the "Development Project from the Standpoint of the Working Class" (2005), which culminated in the "Working Class's Agenda for Development with Sovereignty, Democracy, and Work Appreciation," a list of demands composed during the 2010 presidential campaign. That agenda, also supported by the other union centrals that formed the government's support base, proposed to review, and not revoke, some measures – instituted by the Cardoso administration – that reduced the state's investment capacity, such as the goals of primary surplus, the law regarding Public-Private Partnerships, and the Fiscal Responsibility Law. At the same time, CUT supported measures that interested the big internal bourgeoisie and promoted initiatives in partnership with the bourgeois fraction, as in the case of the "Brazilian Seminar on Dialogue, Production, ad Employment," organized by Fiesp, CUT, and FS in May 2011.

This seminar proposed a pact in defense of the industry, demanding a reduction on taxes and employers' contributions, in order to, in the words of the seminar's organizers "prioritize productive investments and the national industry, to the detriment of financial speculation and the import of goods" (Fiesp, CUT & Força Sindical, 2011). This episode of workers and industrial employers acting against deindustrialization was not an isolated case. Throughout 2011, union centrals and industrial federations organized joint manifestations in several state capitals against high interest rates, which inhibited investments; against the valued exchange, which facilitated the import of manufactured goods; and against the tax burden, which reduced Brazilian industry's competitiveness. Such episodes attested to unionism's participations in the neodevelopmentalist front. This participation hindered, however, the efficient, consequential advancement of the struggle for proposals that met stronger resistance from the employers. That is the case of the already mentioned proposals to decrease the workweek to 40 hours without wage reduction, to set a stern regulation to outsourcing, and to extinguish the social security factor. Among all the demands presented by the unions, the only one effectively met was the policy of minimum wage appreciation – the outcome of a 2007 agreement between the union centrals and the government that established the minimum wage's annual readjustment according to the inflation rate plus the variation of the previous year's GDP. The ratification of the ILO Convention 151 was passed into law by presidential decree in 2013, but it was not regulated.

As it was previously mentioned, prioritizing institutional participation in the agencies created by the PT administrations did not mean the absence of mobilization or conflict. Between 2003 and 2009, all union centrals, along with other social movements, promoted six national marches of "the working class" for the restoration of the minimum wage, for employment, and for social rights; in 2009, they organized two unified acts against the effects of the economic crisis; in 2013, they promoted the seventh march of the working class and two national days of struggle were summoned after the "June demonstrations," with the stated goal of "advancing the workers' agenda into Congress."

During this entire period, the union centrals maintained a busy calendar with mobilization days against layoffs and for job stability, strikes against precarious working conditions in the private sector, and against the noncompliance with agreements negotiated with the government in the public sector.[6] In 2011 and 2012, there were important strikes by education, mail, private and public banking, oil, and civil construction workers.[7] An important part of these manifestations was caused by the PT governments' contradictions, as they not only failed to advance the list of claims presented by the union centrals, but also contradicted some of their bases' interests, like in the matter of privatization. Although Dilma Rousseff, as a presidential candidate, had maintained a discourse criticizing the privatization process, once in power she promoted the resumption of the process of auctioning oil wells and the privatization of airports, inciting criticism and protests, even from the centrals that had backed her.

The unity of action did not quash, as we have stated, the differences between hegemonic unionism and the minority pole represented by Conlutas and Intersindical. Those differences were observable in the negotiation of items that apparently constituted unanimity among the union centrals. Three examples may indicate some of those divergences. Although all union centrals demanded the end of the social security factor, the centrals linked to the neodevelopmentalist front (except for CTB) negotiated with the government a formula that eliminated this reducing factor only for some workers, failing to defend it as a valid measure for all workers without exception. Likewise, while Conlutas and Intersindical defended the end of outsourcing of any kind, the remaining centrals, even as they held up the banner of getting rid of outsourcing, understood that it would be wiser to regulate it instead of prohibiting it peremptorily. Finally, the divergences among the union centrals reached also some measures that represented the risk of flexing labor relations. One of CUT's most important unions, the ABC Region Metalworkers Union, introduced to

---

6   Since 2003, the federal government had been negotiating with workers through a National Table of Permanent Negotiation, but negotiations were established and interrupted at the whim of circumstances, and the agreements were not respected by the government.

7   In Brazil, strikes are summoned by grassroots unions, which are not necessarily linked to union centrals, though most of them are: 75% of the 10,274 unions registered with the Ministry of Labor and Employment are affiliated to the centrals.

the government in 2011 the Collective Bargaining Agreement with Specific Purpose proposal, which authorized the unions to negotiate with the company's collective agreements whose clauses derogated norms from the Brazilian labor code – the Consolidation of Labor Laws (CLT).

These examples make it possible to illustrate the political moderation that characterized the unionist leadership. At the base of the movement, though, we notice that the strikes followed a clear upward line, and that the great majority of the agreements signed led to actual wage gains.

3   The Growth of the Strike Struggle

The neodevelopmentalist period in Brazil, under the PT administration, was marked by a resumption of the workers' strike struggle. In 2004, two years into Lula da Silva's first term, a new cycle of strikes began, amid a climate of recuperation of unionist activity in terms of its historical pattern of operation: meaningful, organized strikes almost exclusively during the period of wage readjustment,[8] demands that were very restricted to wage issues, and workers lacking an organic participation in union life.[9] At the base, strike activity remained at a reasonably high level, and the large majority of the strikes led to actual wage gains; at the movement's leadership, as we have previously established, the political dispute escalated as new union centrals appeared.

Let us consider some indicators referring to the strikes between 2004 and 2012.[10] We shall offer special emphasis to three aspects: strike activity level, types of demands, and the results that workers obtained from the strike struggle in relation to wages. Most of the strikes that we will analyze were organized by unions of professional categories – few strikes were summoned by union centrals.

In the second half of the 1980s, a period when Brazilian unionism was exceptionally active, there was an average of 2,200 strikes per year. In that decade,

---

8   In Brazil, per legal determination, each professional category has a specific month of the year devoted to wage negotiation.

9   The reasons for this form of operation were directly related to the structure of Brazilian unionism. For about 80 years, this structure had remained the same in its fundamental aspects. Its main consequence was to keep the unions dependent on the state's custody for virtually everything, beginning with the acknowledgment of which union is representative of a given category, as well as its financial support and the regulation of all sorts of conflicts (Boito Jr., 1991).

10   Data sourced from the Inter-Union Department of Statistics and Socioeconomic Studies (Dieese), maintained by Brazilian unionism as a whole.

Brazil's social, political, and economic circumstances were favorable to strike activity. Firstly, the country was leaving behind, partly thanks to pressure by the union movement, a military dictatorship that had lasted over twenty years; this transition opened to the movement a channel to set in motion demands that had been repressed by the military governments, such as political participation, and compensation for the workers' successive losses in purchasing power during the dictatorial period. Secondly, the quantitatively remarkable strike activity of the 1980s was caused by hyperinflation;[11] the strikes aimed, in the first place, at wage restoration.[12] In the 1990s, a period of implementation of neoliberal policies in Brazil, the annual average of strikes dropped to around 930. In the 2000s, particularly after 2004, although the strikes diminished in absolute numbers (between 2004 and 2012, the average numbers were 450 strikes and 1.7 million strikers per year[13]), they gained strength in terms of demands and accomplishments, and later advanced quantitatively.

It is possible to observe that the public sector – workers in public service and state companies – made most of the participants in that period. This is a historical pattern in Brazilian unionism. Be that as it may, in four of the nine years analyzed, between 2008 and 2012, the number of strikes was higher in the private sphere than in the public sphere. The participation of the private sector workers, even before 2008, was high and mounting during the 2004–2008 quinquennium, no matter whether we consider the number of strikes or the number of strikers. The balance between the number of strikes in the public and private sectors does not reflect directly the number of strikers distributed in the two sectors. Out of the studied period, only in 2009 and 2012 was the number of private sector strikers higher than that of the public sector.

The near equilibrium between the number of strikes triggered in the public and private sectors shows that other factors beyond stability, which is typical of public servers, had motivated the strikes, and the main one was the evaluation that, in an environment with better overall work conditions, the union movement could be more aggressive in its demands.

Most of the strikes had been offensive, or, in other words, had sought new achievements. They were strikes that increased the amount destined to work remuneration, advancing over the companies' revenue or the state's resources,

---

11   In the course of the 1980s, according to the official Brazilian index, the annual inflation was never below 57%, and reached the impressive mark of 1,764% in 1989.

12   A similar situation could be observed in Spain, a country where the number of strikes in the 1980s was also exceptionally high for its historical standards.

13   The Economically Active Population (PEA) in Brazil is around 80 million workers. In the 2010 census, Brazil's total population had reached 191 million inhabitants.

TABLE 4   Strike distribution in the public and private spheres, Brazil – 2004 to 2012

Year	Sphere	Total public	Public *Public servers*	Public *State companies*	Private	Public and private*	Total
2004	Nº	185	*158*	*27*	114	3	302
	%	61.3	*52.3*	*8.9*	47.7	1	100
2005	Nº	162	*138*	*24*	135	2	299
	%	54.2	*46.2*	*8*	45.2	0.7	100
2006	Nº	165	*145*	*20*	151	4	320
	%	51.6	*45.3*	*6.3*	47.2	1.3	100
2007	Nº	161	*140*	*21*	149	6	316
	%	50.9	*44.3*	*6.6*	47.2	1.9	100
2008	Nº	184	*155*	*29*	224	3	411
	%	44.8	*37.7*	*7.1*	54.5	0.7	100
2009	Nº	251	*215*	*36*	266	1	518
	%	48.5	*41.5*	*6.9*	51.4	0.2	100
2010	Nº	269	*234*	*35*	176	1	446
	%	60.3	*52.5*	*7.8*	39.5	0.2	100
2011	Nº	325	*296*	*29*	227	2	554
	%	58.7	*53.4*	*5.2*	41	0.4	100
2012	Nº	409	*380*	*28*	461	3	873
	%	46.8	*43.5*	*3.2*	52.8	0.3	100

SOURCES: DIEESE (2006, 2009B, 2012 AND 2013B)

in the form of a wage increase, or of labor protection clauses and employee benefits (such as, for example, longer rest periods, food assistance, etc.) That is to say that the strikes stopped being predominantly about avoiding losses or recovering from them, as they had been in the 1990s (see Tables 3 and 4 below). The most constant demands in this new cycle were for actual wage gains, for achieving and expanding the profit sharing program called Participation in Profits and Results (PLR),[14] and for establishing Job and Salary Plans that allowed career progression (both in the public and the private sphere).

---

14   The Participation in Profits and Results (PLR) was an annual bonus paid by the companies to the workers. Prescribed by law, this form of variable, non-mandatory remuneration was usually negotiated via unions.

TABLE 5   Strike distribution by type of demands, Brazil – 2004 to 2012

Type	2004		2005		2006		2007		2008	
	Nº	%	Nº	%	Nº	%	Nº	%	Nº	%
Offensive	197	65.2	207	69.2	217	67.8	209	66.1	284	69.1
Defensive	161	53.3	135	45.2	168	52.5	146	46.2	171	41.6
Maintenance of current conditions	*54*	*17.9*	*72*	*24.1*	*110*	*34.4*	*61*	*19.3*	*72*	*17.5*
Noncompliance with rights	*107*	*35.4*	*70*	*23.4*	*87*	*27.2*	*101*	*32*	*118*	*28.7*
Protest	28	9.3	50	16.7	49	15.3	48	15.2	53	12.9
Solidarity	2	0.7	2	0.7	2	0.6	1	0.3	1	0.2
No information	0	–	2	0.7	0	–	0	–	0	–
Total strikes	302	–	299	–	320	–	316	–	411	–

Type	2009		2010		2011		2012	
	Nº	%	Nº	%	Nº	%	Nº	%
Offensive	349	67.4	353	79.1	421	76	561	64.3
Defensive	253	48.8	203	45.5	339	61.2	589	67.5
Maintenance of current conditions	*124*	*23.9*	*87*	*19.5*	*216*	*39*	*310*	*35.5*
Noncompliance with rights	*156*	*30.1*	*137*	*30.7*	*178*	*32.1*	*412*	*47.2*
Protest	55	10.6	52	11.7	81	14.6	110	12.6
Solidarity	2	0.4	0	–	–	–	1	0.1
No information	0	–	0	–	–	–	–	–
Total strikes	518	–	446	–	554	–	873	–

SOURCES: DIEESE (2007, 2009, 2012, AND 2013), MODIFIED. OBS.: 1) THE LAST ROW OF THIS TABLE REPRESENTS THE TOTAL NUMBER OF STRIKES IN EACH YEAR. IT DOES NOT REPRESENT THE SUM OF THE COLUMNS, SINCE ONE SINGLE STRIKE CAN MAKE MORE THAN ONE TYPE OF DEMAND; 2) THE PERCENTAGES ARE CALCULATED OVER THE TOTAL NUMBER OF STRIKES IN THEIR RESPECTIVE YEAR

As we can see in Table 5, there was a reduction in the number of defensive strikes – for the payment of late wages, for already existing rights to be respected, etc. The frequency of offensive activity was not the same in all sectors. In the private sector, for instance, this type of activity was more common among industry workers, while the shutdowns in the service sector were notably defensive during most of this period. Between 2004 and 2012, the offensive demands were present in most strikes; in the average of the nine years studied, in 69.3% of them. This tendency was contrary to what had been observed in the 1990s, when, although there were more strikes, most of them had defensive demands: 71% of the strikes that took place during both terms of Fernando Henrique Cardoso's presidency (1995–2002) presented demands that concerned maintaining current conditions or fighting noncompliance with laws and previous agreements. In other words, in the 1990s, workers apparently had to run fast to remain in the same spot, while in the 2000s, with less effort – i.e. with fewer strikes – they managed to advance to reach new goals.

In addition to a quantitative difference between the 1990s and the 2000s-2010s, what we have here is a qualitative difference in terms of the achievements of Brazilian unionized workers. The last years of the Fernando Henrique Cardoso government were especially difficult for workers: the number of strikes reached 298 in 2002; in 64.8% of them there were defensive demands. In the same year, only 25.8% of the agreements signed between workers and employers obtained wage readjustments above the inflation rate (See Chart 2).

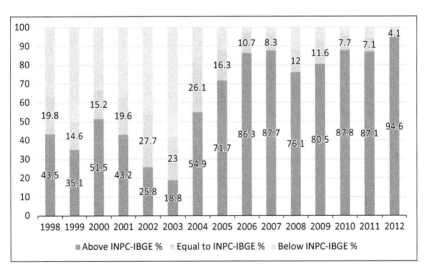

CHART 3   Readjustment distribution balance of collective negotiations (1998–2012)
SOURCE: DIEESE. COMPOSITION: CESIT (CENTER OF UNION STUDIES AND
LABOR ECONOMY OF CAMPINAS STATE UNIVERSITY – UNICAMP).
Note: INPC = National consumer price index

We can state that workers have made new achievements since 2004. The strikes were more ambitious and managed to have their demands met, either in total or in part. The data regarding wage readjustment are also very significant. They appear in Chart 3 and cover a longer period, allowing us to draw some comparisons.

We can see that it was precisely in 2004, the year we consider as the beginning of the strike cycle in discussion, that the number of wage agreements with readjustment above the National Consumer Price Index (INPC) increased considerably, jumping from 18% to 54% of the agreements. Since then, this amount continued to grow, reaching the impressive percentage of 95% of the agreements with readjustment above inflation in 2012.

4   Final Considerations

The data concerning the increase in strikes and their achievements in those nine years under the Workers' Party government should not be taken hastily as evidence of the unions' strength, which they actually lacked. Brazil was not, as some sections of the country's mainstream press had argued, a "unionist republic."

When it comes to organization, Brazilian unionism continued to have its ability to organize hindered by the maintenance of the state's corporative union structure, which kept the unions dependent on the state both in the financial and legal aspects, and discouraged organization in the workplace. The union structure also hindered the organization of unregistered workers, which formed half of the Brazilian workforce.

As for the unions' achievements, if, on the one hand, workers obtained wage increases and the expansion of employee benefits through the vast majority of the collective agreements they reached thanks to the category strikes, on the other hand, the union movement's general demands were systematically blocked, as we have already established. Given that the improvement of life conditions and the facilitation of union organization and struggle were propitiated, to a certain extent, by the PT governments' policies, the union movement, in order to avoid wearing out the image of the PT governments or aggravating contradictions with allied forces, accepted quite passively the fact that the government ignored some of unionism's historical banners such as the automatic inflation replacement, which would have significantly favored non-unionized workers and workers affiliated to unions with less leverage.

This new phase of Brazilian unionism, facilitated by the workers' struggle in the new conditions created by the neodevelopmentalist policy, can be characterized as a phase that introduced, at once, a strong, victorious activity in the field of demand struggle, and a moderate political orientation at the union movement's leadership. That allows us to say that unionism's participation in the neodevelopmentalist political front brought positive results to the workers, but also limitations to their struggle.

PART 2

The Nature and Dynamics of the Crisis that Led to the Impeachment

∵

CHAPTER 7

The Political Crisis of Neodevelopmentalism and the Instability of Democracy

1   The Political Crisis

The political crisis to which we refer here is that of Dilma Rousseff's neodevelopmentalist government.[1] Contradictions already present in Brazil's political process escalated, new ones emerged, and an organized political force with the capacity to overthrow the government was consolidated. The crisis was fundamentally triggered by the strong offensive seeking to restore the orthodox neoliberal camp that intended to unleash a new wave of neoliberal reforms in Brazil (Saad-Filho & Boito Jr., 2016). This point is important: the crisis was not provoked by labor and popular struggle. Although this struggle was an important component of the political crisis, it was far from being the main one. Only the orthodox neoliberal camp would be able to seize governmental power if the president were ousted.

The neodevelopmentalist camp and the orthodox neoliberal camp were not groupings with random social composition, and their belief in rival economic doctrines was not their main cohesion factor. The neodevelopmentalist platform contemplates primarily the interests of the big internal bourgeoisie, while the neoliberal proposal contemplates the demands of international capital and the fraction of the Brazilian bourgeoisie associated with it. Each of these big bourgeois fractions had recruited allies among the dominated classes. The neodevelopmentalist policy of the big internal bourgeoisie contemplated, in a peripheral way, some claims of segments of the working class, the lower middle class, the rural workers in family agriculture, and the marginal mass of workers, segments with which it had formed a broad, heterogeneous and contradictory polyclassist political grouping that we call the neodevelopmentalist front. This front vied for the control of economic, social, and foreign policies with the camp formed by big international capital, the bourgeois fraction associated with it, and the upper middle class, which constituted the orthodox neoliberal camp (Boito Jr. & Berringer, 2013). The governments supported by the Workers' Party (PT) represented the neodevelopmentalist camp in the same way that

---

1   This chapter was written in October/November 2015.

the governments supported by the Brazilian Social Democracy Party (PSDB) represented the orthodox neoliberal camp.

The political crisis of 2015 blurred the line dividing the camps, a line that had prevailed in recent times of Brazilian politics. The dividing line setting classes and their fractions in the neodevelopmentalist camp on one side and fractions aligned in the orthodox neoliberal camp on the other had never been straight and rigid. With the crisis, though, it became more winding and malleable than ever, and this change increased the strength of the neoliberal orthodox camp. At the top of the neodevelopmentalist front, the conflict between national banking capital and national productive capital had always remained alive; and on the front as a whole, the conflict between the demands of the working masses – salary, labor rights, and land – and the interests of various segments of the big internal bourgeoisie had also remained active. However, until then, the unity of the neodevelopmentalist front had clearly prevailed over its internal conflicts. In the crisis, such unity was undermined.

We should not suppose that the other camp was free of contradictions. The upper middle class hardly felt at home in the orthodox neoliberal front. The orthodox fiscal policy, characterized by pure and hard neoliberalism, also harmed the upper middle class – directly affecting high-ranking civil servants, an important segment of this class fraction. Similarly to the insertion of the popular classes in the neodevelopmentalist political front, the insertion of the upper middle class in the orthodox neoliberal camp was largely due to the characteristics of the ideological context and the demands of the political correlation of forces.

However, the internal contradictions of the neodevelopmentalist front became exacerbated during the crisis, while the orthodox neoliberal front preserved its unity and gained new adepts. Indeed, as a result of the degradation of the economic situation (which can be blamed on the government in charge at the time, irrespective of considerations of merit), as a result of the offensive to restore international capital, and also as a result of the withdrawal of the economic and social policy by the Rousseff administration, segments of the top and bottom of the neodevelopmentalist camp began to waver politically, were neutralized, or flocked to the orthodox neoliberal camp. Important corporate associations of the big internal bourgeoisie, such as the Federation of Industries of the State of São Paulo (Fiesp), the National Syndicate of the Naval Industry and Offshore Construction and Repair (Sinaval), the Brazilian Association of Infrastructure and Basic Industries (Abidb), the Brazilian Machinery Builders' Association (Abimaq), the Brazilian Chemical Industry Association (Abiquim), and others took an ambiguous position: they admitted

the need for some fiscal adjustment while protesting against adjustment measures; important sectors of the union movement, such as the Força Sindical
central, protested against the adjustment and, at the same time, sought to
become closer to the neoliberal opposition; in Congress, parties that had
formed the government's support base split or sided with the opposition. Thus,
the support of the Rousseff government became undermined.

2   The Neoliberal Bourgeois Offensive

Some Brazilian political analysts pointed out that the first two years of
Rousseff's first term were characterized by an offensive of neodevelopmentalist policy. André Singer recently devoted an instructive study to this offensive
(Singer, 2015). The Rousseff administration did not eliminate the pillars of
the neoliberal capitalist model that prevented the implementation of a strict
developmentalist policy, but, like its predecessor, took steps to mitigate the
negative effects of this model on economic growth. In fact, the economic and
social policy during 2011 and 2012 was marked by measures to stimulate economic growth through state intervention in the economy: reduction of Special
Clearance and Escrow System tax (Selic tax), reduction in banking spread,
devaluation of the Brazilian real, expansion of the policy of local content,
tax exemptions for productive capital, and others. The then Finance Minister
Guido Mantega summarized this new orientation by coining the expression
"new economic policy matrix."

It seems reasonable to sustain the thesis that this new matrix represented
not only a radicalization of the neodevelopmentalist policy, but also a change
within it: an attempt to benefit the productive segment of the big internal
bourgeoisie to the detriment of the interests of its banking segment. In other
words, this policy deepened a conflict that had always been present in the big
internal bourgeoisie and, at the same time, aroused the reaction of international capital and the fraction of the Brazilian bourgeoisie associated with
it. Such forces waged an offensive against the Rousseff government in early
2013. International agencies, risk assessment agencies, the conservative press
in Europe and the United States, the great local media, bourgeois opposition
parties, the upper middle class, and some of the state institutions that housed
this social segment entered the struggle against the finance minister's policy.
Much of this struggle focused on the superlative denunciation of inflation and
the attack on corruption at Petrobras, the state-owned energy company – i.e.,
it tried to wave flags that could attract popular support.

3   The Participation of the Upper Middle Class

An important chapter of the political offensive for restoration and the resulting crisis is the political action of the upper middle class. First, this action
provided a broad and active mass base for the offensive to restore the internationalized bourgeoisie. Hundreds of thousands of demonstrators gathered in
the main cities of Brazil in February, March, April, and August 2015. The protests converged on the demand for President Rousseff's impeachment. There
were also countless pot-banging protests. All available information on these
protests proved that they were mainly actions of the wealthy middle class. Such
actions were not controlled by the internationalized bourgeoisie and, precisely
for this reason, they maintained a difficult relationship with the leadership of
the PSDB; however, they operated as the main instrument of legitimization of
the bourgeois offensive for restoration.

    Second, the upper middle class also acted through important state institu-
tions against the ruling party and the neodevelopmentalist government itself.
The upper middle class held a strategic position in the Judiciary, the Public
Prosecutor's Office, and the Federal Police. The officials at the top of these
institutions – judges, prosecutors, public defenders, appellate judges, delegates, and others – enjoyed wages and working conditions unmatched in the
Brazilian public sector. Moreover, we must consider the role of such institutions within the state. They represented what Pierre Bourdieu called "the right
hand" of the state (Bordieu, 1998), i.e., the branch of the state charged with
maintaining the law and the capitalist order. Due either to their class member-
ship or their positioning in this branch of the state bureaucracy, the officials
who led such institutions took a militant position against the social policy of
neodevelopmentalism. The PT, following the same path as other parties with a
social-democratic profile, engaged in the practice of nepotism and corruption,
with the main objective of privately and illegally financing election campaigns
and winning support in congress. Senior officials of the Public Prosecutor's
Office, the Federal Police, and the Judiciary took advantage of this corrupt
practice to unilaterally denounce, investigate, and judge almost exclusively the
corruption practices committed by the PT and its allies.

    It is true that the neodevelopmentalist governments increased the number
of civil service positions, expanded the autonomy of the Public Prosecutor's
Office, and did not restrict the privileges of any of these high-ranking officials.
However, the main aspects of the neodevelopmentalist social policy were
against the economic interests and values of the upper middle class as a whole,
both in the public and private sectors, and thus were perceived by its members as a threat. Cash transfer programs for the underprivileged population,

racial and social quotas in universities and public service, extension of labor rights to both male and female household servants, appreciation of the minimum wage, among other measures, were seen by the upper middle class as a bill they would have to foot through taxes. These measures would also pose a threat to the advantages their children enjoyed in the most coveted courses at the country's most prestigious universities and in higher civil service positions, and present an affront to the values of meritocracy, so dear to professionals with university degrees. The neodevelopmentalist policy measures seemed like an intrusion into the authoritarian and paternalistic relationship that middle-class families entertained with their household employees. They were considered undesirable for allowing spaces and institutions previously reserved for the upper middle class to be "invaded" by individuals coming from popular sectors.

The public order policy enforced by the PT administrations also bothered the upper middle class. It fell short of the harshness that delegates, prosecutors, and judges, as public order officials, would have liked to see implemented. The Lula and Rousseff governments maintained the capitalist order and the repression of the popular struggle. However, in comparison with the repressive policy enforced by the orthodox neoliberal front's governments, the public order policy of the PT governments seemed too tolerant for the upper middle class.

4   The Presence of the Working Classes

The popular struggle also contributed to the emergence of the crisis, despite playing in it a secondary role when compared to the neoliberal offensive for restoration. Using Mao Zedong's well-known concept, the main contradiction that determined the crisis was the one that set the entire orthodox neoliberal camp against the neodevelopmentalist political front. The contradiction between the working classes and the bourgeoisie had a secondary role in the crisis – not because it concerned disputes of lesser importance for the lives of millions of Brazilians – but because the labor and popular struggle was still segmented and mainly economic in character.

The neoliberal offensive for restoration began before the demonstrations of June 2013, but, unlike these, it had always shown political clarity and enough strength to target the conquest of government power. Consequently, after a brief initial hesitation, the offensive for restoration of the orthodox neoliberal camp began to stimulate street demonstrations in order to direct them toward the goal of defeating the Rousseff government electorally. The heterogeneity and lack of leadership of the demonstrations facilitated this work of reaction. In 2014, the year of the presidential election, the great press started again to encourage the demonstrations, now directing them against the Football World Cup. Very symptomatically, the press did not take on this approach in 2015 in the face of a similar event: the Rio de Janeiro Olympics. The June 2013 demonstrations were a component of the crisis because they warded off a large part of the lower middle class, which had benefited from the strong expansion of university education promoted by the neodevelopmentalist government itself. In fact, research indicates that these manifestations were dominated by young people, with higher education and middle or lower income, who felt disappointed with the low-quality employment that the economy offered them even though they had earned a college degree (Ridenti, 2013).

The trade union movement grew strong at the time when the neodevelopmentalist policy prevailed. Two very simple indicators attest to this fact: in 2003 there were about 300 strikes and, a decade later, following a regular growth, there were more than 2,000 strikes per year. Also in 2003, only 18% of collective agreements and conventions reached real wage increases while, ten years later, no less than 95% of such agreements and conventions reached increases above inflation. However, such increases did not lead to the union movement's political growth. The struggle remained on a strictly demanding level, and segmented by categories. As the unions' gains increased the companies' spending with wages, they were not welcomed by the big internal bourgeoisie; however, there is no evidence that such gains have imploded the neodevelopmentalist political front. Clearly, what happened instead was the defection of part of the union movement from the neodevelopmentalist front. The workers' dissatisfaction came from the fact that the neodevelopmentalist policy had ignored historical demands of the union movement: reduction to a 40-hour workweek, strict regulation of outsourcing, end of the welfare factor, among others. Mostly, those who had defected were attracted by the orthodox neoliberal camp.

5   The Instability of Democracy

The crisis of the Brazilian government was associated with the instability in Brazilian presidentialism and in bourgeois democracy itself. Both the situation of instability and the state of crisis are characterized by the emergence of important obstacles to the reproduction of a given political structure or institution, such as a state, a political regime, or a government. However, unlike what occurs in a crisis, in an unstable situation there is no organized political force *willing and able* to replace the institution whose continuity seems to be faltering. Thus, the situation of instability falls short of the state of crisis.

The federal executive, in what we could call an authoritarian presidential regime, was in control of the legislative activity (Torre, 1996; Saes, 2001). This control ceased to exist when the Rousseff administration was defeated in the election for the presidency of the House of Representatives. This institutional instability was linked to the offensive for restoration of the orthodox neoliberal camp, but it meant something more than merely its institutional facet. The Brazilian Congress's insubordination was promoted, of course, by neoliberal forces, but also by a group that resisted the fiscal adjustment and by the Evangelical caucus in its declared war on the feminist and LGBT movements.

We have also witnessed a situation of instability in the bourgeois democracy in Brazil, since it is a limited democracy. We have already referred to the authoritarian presidentialism that empties the legislative and representative functions of the National Congress. To this we should add the precariousness of democratic freedoms: lack of freedom of union organization, the state's repressive apparatuses, and even private militias acting on their own against the working population in low-income neighborhoods and rural regions, not to mention the existence of an extremely concentrated and deregulated media. The instability in Brazil's democracy became visible in a conjuncture of successive attempts to revoke the verdict of the ballot boxes in October 2014. There were several legal actions with many different arguments, procedures and instances, whose only common points were the contempt for the democratic rule of the will of the majority and the goal of deposing the government, both indicating the bourgeois opposition's disregard for democratic institutions and values. At the time of writing this, a crisis of democracy has not yet erupted because the proposal to establish a dictatorial regime is pretty weak in the opposition front, a situation that differs from that of 1964, when the military coup took place.

6   The Government's Reaction and the Popular Movement

In the face of the political offensive for restoration of the forces of the orthodox neoliberal front, the Rousseff administration opted for a policy of retreat rather than of resistance. Indeed, it applied the fiscal adjustment, an important part of the program of the bourgeois neoliberal opposition, and did not take the initiative to mobilize popular sectors, not even to defend its mandate.

Thus, the socialist and popular camp would have first to engage in a defensive struggle. Such struggle would have two goals, related to one another in a complex and even contradictory way. On the one hand, it would have to resist the government's policy of fiscal adjustment. On the other hand, it should also defend democracy and, therefore, the mandate earned at the polls. If the socialist and popular movement, fearing to favor reaction, decided to remain neutral regarding the fiscal adjustment, it would fail to defend elementary interests of the popular classes. Conversely, if, in view of the conservative retreat of the Rousseff government, it proposed to fight for the constitution of a popular power right there and then, the only practical result would be the advance of the reaction, given the correlation of forces at that moment. It is certain, however, that the defense of the mandate had its own limitations. If the government was to stick to the instruction of defending itself in the impeachment process only within state institutions while maintaining the policy of fiscal adjustment, the defense of the president's mandate may be undermined.

Furthermore, the socialist and popular camp would need to present its proposal to face the situation of instability affecting Brazil's limited democracy and authoritarian presidentialism. It would be necessary to advertise and develop a proposal leading to an offensive. The exclusive and sovereign constituent assembly for the reform of the political system is an ideal that, if pursued and victorious, could strengthen Brazil's democracy, unblocking the path to the reforms demanded by the popular movement.

CHAPTER 8

State, State Institutions, and Political Power in Brazil

Conflicts of classes and class fractions affected the Brazilian state substantially during the PT administrations, particularly during the 2014–2015 crisis.[1] Several state bureaucracy institutions were captured by different classes and class fractions that fought for conflicting policies and functioned, in some cases, as centers for the implementation of the policy of hegemonic sectors, and in others as non-hegemonic centers of resistance to these policies. Such conflicts may appear to have been only institutional, but, in reality, they expressed class conflicts in a specific way.

Let us make two clarifications. Firstly, we have not witnessed a fragmentation of the state, that is, we have seen neither a separation of its institutions among all classes and class fractions present and active, nor its disfiguration as an institution endowed with unity and a unique class nature. No party, organization, or socialist movement was in control of any institution of the Brazilian state. More than that, even the labor movement, the peasant movement, and other popular movements that struggled for reforms within capitalism were able to, at most, participate in one or another institution that were peripheral to the state's decision-making process and, consequently, influenced them very modestly. Examples of such institutions were the Labor Justice, the Public Ministry of Labor, the National Institute for Colonization and Agrarian Reform (Incra), the National Indian Foundation (Funai), and advisory boards for the implementation of public policies. In fact, the institutions of the Brazilian state were controlled by rival bourgeois fractions, and also by the middle class, or, to be more precise, by the upper fraction of the middle class that was associated with one of the bourgeois fractions that disputed political hegemony within the bloc in power.

Secondly, neither did the contradictions within the government lead to an emergence of a zigzagging and contradictory state policy in Brazil, except during the short periods of severe political crisis. This stemmed from the fact that the result of the dispute between rival bourgeois fractions that controlled

---

1 This chapter written in coauthorship with Alfredo Saad-Filho during the second term of the Dilma Rousseff government.

different state institutions was determined by the dominant institutions – those that made up the Federal Executive, for starters – and only partially incorporated in its search for a balanced compromise the policies pursued by the fractions occupying subordinate institutions.

The phenomenon of appropriation of state institutions by different fractions of the ruling class – and even by fractions of dominated classes integrated with capitalism and that can serve as allies of the competing bourgeois fractions – is very present in capitalist states. In a country like Brazil, whose authoritarian presidential political regime controlled a decision-making process that relegated the Legislative branch and the political parties to a secondary place, the dispute for control over the institutions of the Executive and Judiciary branches was strong. These are topics duly addressed by the renewed Marxist theory of the capitalist state (Poulantzas, 1968) and by Brazilian and Latin American political science – suffice it to remember the concept of bureaucratic ring originated in Chilean political science. Nevertheless, it is certain that in exceptional situations, when contradictions of classes and class fractions are exacerbated to the point of generating political crises, there may be an escalation in the conflict among state institutions and even a subversion of the hierarchy established by the governmental policy and/or by the current political regime.[2]

This is exactly what has happened in Brazil during the 2014 election campaign and the subsequent period: both authoritarian presidentialism and the Dilma Rousseff government reached a crisis point. The Legislative and the Judiciary powers, the Public Prosecutor's Office, the Federal Court of Accounts, all of these institutions, supported by the action of the Federal Police – which, in theory, should be subordinated to the Executive power – acted against institutions that were strategic for the Federal Executive branch's social, economic, and foreign policies – Brazilian Petroleum Corporation (Petrobras),

---

2   Our argumentation is grounded on Nicos Poulantzas's book titled *Political Power and Social Classes*, published in French in 1968. In this work, institutional conflicts within the state refer to conflicts among bourgeois fractions present in the bloc in power, sometimes between their allies, but always within the limits established by the unified institutional structure of the capitalist state. Ten years later, in 1978, Poulantzas published the book *L'État, le Pouvoir, le Socialisme,* in which he broke with numerous theses from the previous book (Poulantzas, 1978). In the 1978 book, Poulantzas revised his treatment of conflicts among state institutions, considering them now as indicators that these institutions represented mere "condensations of force relations," with unlimited malleability. As such, we add, their nature resembled that of a changing class, and they were able to pursue objectives that transcended the capitalist order. In this case, the class and institutional unity of the state would disappear even during periods of stability.

the Brazilian Development Bank (BNDES), the Ministry of Foreign Affairs (Itamaraty), and the Federal Executive's leadership itself. As we will see, each group of conflicting institutions represented, in a specific and complex way, one of the bourgeois fractions that disputed the hegemony of the bloc in power.

We can then say that, if it is true that the Brazilian state at the time organized the domination of the capitalist class, it is also certain that this was done in a complex way that did not exclude contentious political disputes. This situation offers elements with which we can draw some reflections on the Brazilian capitalist state and an assessment of the strategy of the political and electoral action adopted by the left and center-left parties in that period. The last section of this chapter will be devoted to such reflections. First, we will investigate a) how the Brazilian bloc in power was organized; and b) how conflicts within this bloc in power became conflicts among different state institutions, though they seemed to be mere institutional conflicts.

1   The Bloc in Power and Class Alliances

We have argued in other works (Saad-Filho & Boito Jr., 2016)[3] that it is not enough to acknowledge that the Brazilian state under governments led by the PT coalition maintained the domination of the bourgeois class. This statement is correct, but it serves only as a starting point. If we stop there, we will not be able to explain the complexity and multiplicity of conflicts that made up the Brazilian political process in that period. In fact, the Brazilian bloc in power admitted many different rival bourgeois fractions, some of them being organized as social forces and in condition to fight for political hegemony.

First, we have big capital. Since the beginning of the military dictatorship, Brazilian economic and foreign policies have been prioritizing the interest of this fraction, to the detriment of medium capital. The latter is made up an ample set of small and medium businesses with reduced economic power and political influence; during the PT coalition governments, these businesses did not act as a distinct social force, that is, they did not have their own political organization and program. Big capital, in turn, is subdivided into two fractions or subfractions: the first is the big internal bourgeoisie (Nicos Poulantzas 1974; 1976), which intends to maintain and improve its position in Brazilian dependent capitalism and keeps a relationship both of cooperation and conflict with international capital. The second is the associated, integrated, or

---

3   See also Chapters 2 and 3 of this book.

internationalized fraction of the Brazilian bourgeoisie, whose interests coincide with those of international financial and productive capital. The competition between the big internal bourgeoisie and the associated bourgeoisie has been the main dispute within the bloc in power since the beginning of the coalition governments led by the PT.[4]

The big internal bourgeoisie was formed by big businesses controlled by national capital and was allocated in different economic sectors – shipbuilding, heavy construction, agribusiness, processing companies, and also by national bank capital. The latter was the sector of the big internal bourgeoisie that was closer to international capital, but it demanded from the state – with successful results – a specific and protective action, so that national banks could control the Brazilian banking sector. This control had been threatened during the Fernando Henrique Cardoso governments in the 1990s but was strengthened by the policy enforced by the Lula da Silva and Dilma Rousseff administrations in the 2000s and 2010s. The fraction we here call the associated or integrated bourgeoisie was made up of economic groups based in Brazil but owned by international capital companies, and also of national capital companies with a direct dependency relationship with these groups. Just as it happened with the internal bourgeoisie, the associated bourgeoisie was present in various economic sectors. The foreign capital-owned processing companies, which

---

4   Here we have to add two conceptual and terminological clarifications that the reader might find somewhat boring. 1. The term *internal bourgeoisie* serves to distinguish, in dependent countries, a bourgeois fraction that is less ambitious than the old *national bourgeoisie* – the latter having sometimes assumed anti-imperialist positions – but that is not a mere extension of the interests of foreign capital in the country's inland areas where its accumulation base is located. Jacob Gorender, to express this same idea, used the term *Brazilian bourgeoisie* – aiming to indicate an intermediate position between national and foreign (Gorender, 1981). We do not use this term because it might give the impression of referring to the whole of the bourgeoisie – the Brazilian bourgeoisie – and not to just a fraction of that social class. 2. As for the fraction of the bourgeoisie perfectly integrated with imperialism, the Communist International called it the comprador bourgeoisie, a concept and denomination widely used in the analyzes and resolutions of the International for dependent countries. We have retained the idea of a fraction of the bourgeoisie whose interests are complementary to the interests of foreign capital within the dependent country, but have abandoned the term "comprador" because it was pertinent to the period of the old international division of labor, when the large commercial importing and exporting companies located in dependent countries were the most powerful segment of the bourgeois fraction integrated with imperialism. Today, the segments of the integrated bourgeoisie are different and more diversified, hence our decision to employ the adjectives "associated" or "integrated." The term "internationalized," which we have already used, may lead to confusion because the Brazilian internal bourgeoisie itself has internationalized its business, taking advantage of the trade liberalization and the stimuli implemented by the PT governments.

represented a large part of the consumer durables industry in Brazil, might move, depending on the economic political policies being considered, in the opposite direction from that of national bank capital, and side with the big internal bourgeoisie. This occurred, for instance, when Lula's and Rousseff's governments implemented tariff and non-tariff protection measures to favor the Brazilian automotive industry.

It is clear that the divisions within the bourgeoisie were complex. There was no straight, rigid line separating the different bourgeois fractions, which in turn were not homogeneous blocs devoid of contradictions. Firstly, as we can infer from the examples above, different fractioning systems intersected: industrial and banking capital, national and foreign capital, big and medium capital, among others were elements that might create conflicting tensions within a single company (Farias, 2009). Due to this very intersection, the line dividing the fractions was winding and flexible. Ergo, in some situations, national banks, because they were banks, grew close to their foreign counterparts, despite being national. By the same token, a foreign industry based in Brazil, because it was an industry, might get close to the national industrial sector, despite being foreign. Secondly, there were contradictions within one and the same fraction – for example, the contradiction within the big internal bourgeoisie between the industrial and bank sectors regarding interest rates. These contradictions have remained secondary in the face of the opposition that divided the two main bourgeois fractions, but they might eventually cause the defection of one or other sector in specific circumstances. The sugar and alcohol sector, after having supported the Lula da Silva governments and Dilma Rousseff's candidacy in 2010, moved away from the Rousseff government due to the energy and price policy measures that led ethanol to lose market share.

These considerations lead us to conclude that it is possible to detect, in each of the two most important fractions of the bourgeoisie, some segments that made up a more consistent core, and others that integrated, say, a gelatinous periphery. However, broadly speaking, the orthodox neoliberal capitalist strategy of development adopted in the 1990s and the neodevelopmentalist strategy adopted by the PT governments in the 2000s and 2010s affected these bourgeois fractions in very different ways. Each of them created affiliations according to more or less stable interests – the associated bourgeoisie and international capital identified with orthodox neoliberalism, while the big internal bourgeoisie identified with the neodevelopmentalism of the PT-led coalition governments.

In the 1990s, during the two governments of the improperly named Brazilian Social Democracy Party (PSDB), the state's socioeconomic policy primarily served the interests of the associated fraction of the Brazilian bourgeoisie and international financial and productive capital. The policy that expressed this arrangement of power was orthodox neoliberalism, which implemented, as in all of Latin America, the reduction of social and labor rights, the privatization and sale of public companies, an ample trade liberalization, and financial deregulation.

Lula da Silva's rise from the Workers' Party to the Federal Executive in the 2002 election changed this picture. The capitalist development strategy began to combine heterogeneous elements drawn from neoliberalism and the old developmentalism (Morais & Saad-Filho, 2012). The neoliberal capitalist model persisted, but developmentalist elements were incorporated into it through economic policy measures. The ample trade liberalization initiated by the government of Fernando Collor de Mello (1990–1992) and increased by Fernando Henrique Cardoso was maintained, but the PT administrations guaranteed the preference for local companies in purchases of goods and services by the government and by state-owned companies that had not been privatized – the so-called local content policy. Privatizations were not revoked, but the PT governments strengthened the remaining state-owned companies, starting with Petrobras, the giant state-owned oil company. The policy of high interest rates continued, but the PT governments strengthened and expanded the big state investment bank (BNDES), offering subsidized interest rates to big Brazilian companies. These economic policy measures improved the position of the big internal bourgeoisie in the bloc in power, had the support of big Brazilian companies, and earned increasing hostility from international financial and productive capital.

The big internal bourgeoisie never aspired to more than a modification or reform in the neoliberal model so that its interests could prosper within it. This fraction is financially, politically, and technologically dependent on imperialism, and it has no intention of breaking with it. It only intends to moderate the elements of the neoliberal capitalist model that directly harm its interests – the trade liberalization that reached several sectors of the Brazilian industry, and the high interest rates that inhibited the growth of national companies. Given the big internal bourgeoisie's limited aspiration, we can affirm that the economic policy of the PT governments, even without breaking with the neoliberal capitalist model, raised it to the position of hegemonic fraction within the bloc in power, a position that belonged to the associated bourgeoisie and international capital in the 1990s.

Each of these powerful fractions of the bourgeoisie established alliances and found support outside the ruling bloc. The big internal bourgeoisie formed a political front that sustained the PT governments for several years and included the lower middle class, workers' unionism, a significant part of the peasant movement, and a large portion of the marginal mass of workers. While prioritizing the interests of the big internal bourgeoisie, the PT governments offered each of these social sectors something that allowed them to improve their working and living conditions: a great increase of the number of openings in vocational and higher education, racial and social quotas for universities and for the public service, minimum wage appreciation policy, popular housing construction program, financing and market reserve for small family-based agriculture, cash transfer policies for those in extreme poverty, and others. The marginalized workers, who are the beneficiaries of the two major income transfer programs – "Family Grant" (*Bolsa Família*), and "Continuous Benefit Program" (APC) – constitute the social sector that votes more massively and consistently for the PT presidential candidates. In the 2014 election, when some social sectors wavered or withdrew from the neodevelopmentalist front, the workers of the marginal mass were the ones to guarantee Dilma Rousseff's victory.

The associated bourgeoisie, in turn, established an alliance with the urban upper middle class. This fraction of the middle class was PSDB's most active and faithful electoral base. The upper middle class considered the social policy of the PT-led coalition governments an affront to its economic interests and a threat to the social prestige it enjoys in Brazilian society. This upper middle class is comprised of workers with very high wages – both by Brazilian and international standards – allocated in the public and private sectors, and also of economically successful self-employed professionals, such as administrators, economists, engineers, doctors, lawyers, university professors, architects, and other workers in similar occupations and professions. However, only workers who are economically successful in these professions belong to the upper middle class. There are many doctors, university professors, lawyers, and journalists who have not found a good position in the job market, thus belonging to a lower strata of the urban middle class. Also part of the upper middle class are career civil servants, such as judges, prosecutors, attorneys, officers of the Armed Forces and the federal police, among others.

The support provided by the lower middle class, the working class, the peasantry, and the marginal mass of workers to the governments of the big internal bourgeoisie of Lula and Rousseff was critical and fraught with conflict, involving desertions and moments of crisis. By the same token, the support provided by the upper middle class to the PSDB and the orthodox neoliberalism of the big associated bourgeoisie was not unconditional. We will discuss this further ahead.

2   The Political Regime and the Contradictions within the State
        Bureaucracy

As we have seen, in the Brazilian state, the bloc in power was shared among
different segments of big capital, that is, among very restricted segments of
the bourgeoisie, which is itself a minority class. To this restricted power con-
dominium there was a corresponding closed political regime with decision-
making power strongly concentrated in the Federal Executive branch. The
president of the Republic, as the head of the federal bureaucracy, took center
stage, personalizing the political game. In Brazilian democracy, the decision-
making process was authoritarian. Some authors talk about hyperpresidentialism, and others go even further, talking about civilian authoritarianism
(Saes, 2001).

The National Congress occupied a subordinate position in the formulation
and implementation of the state policy. The Presidency of the Republic took
over the legislative functions by instituting the provisional measures,[5] and by
gaining control of the agenda and voting sessions in the National Congress,
through tactics such as the concentration of power in the presidencies of
the Chamber of Representatives and the Senate, the voting of projects by the
college of party leaders, the so-called emergency regime, and the exchange
of political favors for votes from senators and representatives. No wonder
an important symptom of the political crisis in Dilma Rousseff government
in 2015 was precisely the atypical situation created by the more autonomous
activity of the presidents of the Senate and the Chamber of Representatives in
relation to the Federal Executive branch.

Political parties, performing primarily in the arena of the National Congress,
were marginalized from government activity. In Brazil, there was no party government, but government parties (Poulantzas, 1978). During the Fernando
Henrique Cardoso administrations, the PSDB had the role of securing congressional approval for government decisions, about which the party was not even
consulted. This very same procedure was followed during the Lula da Silva
and Dilma Rousseff administrations. The PT had emerged in the 1980s as a
mass party, linked to unionism and popular movements. Its passive, subordinate position in the administration of governments elected by the party itself
illustrated the strength of the authoritarian presidential regime. It was definitely better to hold positions at the higher levels of state bureaucracy and at

---

5   A provisional measure is a legal act in Brazil through which the President of the Republic can
    enact laws effective for a maximum of 60 days (they may be renewed only once for the same
    period), without approval from the National Congress.

different government institutions than to win seats in Congress. The National Congress – then with 32 political parties, at least six of which with considerable influence and representation, and made up of 513 representatives and 81 senators – was a politically heterogeneous environment. It maintained ties with very diverse social sectors and was therefore not suitable as a center for organizing the political hegemony of such a restricted fraction of the bourgeoisie as big capital.

The regularity of the polarization between the PT and the PSDB in 20 years of presidential elections emphasized the consolidation of a multiparty system polarized by these two major parties. Each of them had their preferred party alliances and also had a large number of small and medium parties available for various political arrangements. These are political parties whose sole objective is – as long as the capitalist order is ensured – to obtain positions and financial advantages for their members. We can use Max Weber's nomenclature and call them "patronage parties," as long as we bear in mind that they are not, contrary to what Weber's typology supposes, parties devoid of ideology (Weber, 1946). Both the Workers' Party and the PSDB bought the support of numerous patronage parties, particularly during Lula da Silva's first term. The behavior of these parties, which together amounted to the expressive number of about 200 representatives in the Federal Chamber, contributed to the political emptying of Congress and its subordination to the Executive.

The concentration of the decision-making process at the top of the federal bureaucracy turned the institutions of the state bureaucracy into a privileged target in the political struggle. The various bourgeois fractions in dispute worked to capture bureaucratic institutions from the Federal Executive to there establish their centers of power and their trenches of resistance to specific policies and to the governments they opposed. The capture of institutions by one or another fraction in dispute did not happen at random. It depended on countless factors – the relationship between these institutions and the Presidency of the Republic, the economic and political function of the institution, the social composition of the staff that occupied it, the correlation of forces, and the country's recent political trajectory.

We will now set aside the core of the Federal Executive, which consisted of the Presidency and some key ministries that conceived, directed, and implemented the country's development strategy. Our focus is to highlight state institutions that, despite not being the center of power, were of great strategic importance, either to implement state policy or to resist it. It will not be possible here to carry out an in-depth analysis of the vast group of state institutions that actively participated in the struggle for fractional hegemony. We will consider only a few that have played an important role in this struggle. Giant state-owned enterprises were centers of power for the big internal bourgeoisie. The Brazilian Development Bank (BNDES), Petrobras, and Banco do Brasil stood out. Strategic sectors of the Judiciary, the Public Prosecutor's Office, and the Federal Police were centers of resistance to the policy of the hegemonic fraction, giving voice, directly or indirectly and for various reasons, to the interests of the associated bourgeoisie and the upper middle class. The conflict between these institutions was greater during the PT governments and was a thorough demonstration of the disputes between bourgeois fractions within the very heart of the Brazilian state.

3   BNDES, Petrobras, and the Big Internal Bourgeoisie

In this section, we will first demonstrate the importance of the policy of the BNDES and Petrobras for the big internal bourgeoisie. We will then examine the conflict that this policy unleashed and the state institutions involved in it.

As we previously asserted, the PT governments did not dispose of the macroeconomic tripod implanted in Brazil under the second Fernando Henrique Cardoso government: a floating, appreciated exchange rate, which makes it possible to contain inflation to the detriment of local production of manufactured goods; high interest rates, which make investments more expensive; and the creation of primary surplus for the rollover of the public debt. The PT governments, however, made this tripod more flexible and, above all, created mechanisms to moderate its inhibitory effects on local production and investment. Two institutions were of major importance to implement this policy: BNDES and Petrobras.

In 2007, Lula da Silva appointed Luciano Coutinho to chair the BNDES. Coutinho is a developmental economist who remained in office until Rousseff's impeachment – he was the longest-serving president of the institution, with ten years as chair. Through this bank, possibly the largest public development bank in the South Hemisphere, the Lula and Rousseff governments started offering negative, subsidized interest rates to big national companies. The long-term interest rate (TJLP) offered by the BNDES was equivalent, at the beginning of the second Dilma government, to less than half of the basic interest rate and was below the inflation rate. The BNDES budget increased tenfold during the PT governments and, during his second term, Lula implemented the so-called "national champions" policy, which aimed at taking big national companies to leadership positions in their fields on a global scale (Bugiato, 2014). In the food business – and the meat field more specifically – the BNDES was able, through huge subsidized loans, to transform Friboi into the world's largest company in the processed meat sector. Always with the support of the BNDES, the company purchased processing plants on four continents, standing as a successful example of the PT neodevelopmentalist industrial policy. In addition to huge and subsidized loans, the BNDES supported big national companies in capital formation. The bank created BNDESPar and joined as a shareholder in companies it intended to promote. Loans and shareholding became possible thanks to large transfers from the National Treasury to the state bank.

The Lula government also supported the "national champions" through diplomatic agreements. Southern countries, particularly those in Latin America, were favored by the Brazilian diplomacy, obtaining loans from the BNDES for the construction of roads, hydroelectric plants, railroads, and other infrastructure works, under the condition that they hired big Brazilian construction companies to perform these services. Hence the PT administrations established a foreign policy that served the interests of the big internal bourgeoisie (Berringer, 2015). Another good example is the construction of the Port of Mariel in Cuba, which aroused much criticism from the PSDB, the representative of the bourgeoisie associated with international capital. This port was built, fundamentally, by the Odebrecht group, one of the major Brazilian construction companies. But the construction involved more than 300 Brazilian companies from the most diverse segments. The celebration of the completion of the first part of the work, in January 2014, was a political event that brought together several progressive heads of state from Latin America, including Evo Morales and Nicolás Maduro. The BNDES' strong financing policy meant a huge increase in public spending, hampering the production of primary surplus for the rollover of public debt – a fundamental element to understand international capital's opposition to the bank policy.

Petrobras, the state oil giant, was another lever of the PT neodevelopmentalist policy. While BNDES aimed at circumventing the financing bottleneck, given that private banks in Brazil were reluctant to finance production and did so at very high interest rates, Petrobras changed its purchasing policy to moderate the effects of trade liberalization on local production, resuming the classic route of import substitution. In his 2002 presidential campaign, Lula da Silva had announced that Petrobras would change its purchasing policy, ceasing to import both small and large ships, platforms for oil exploration in deep waters, drilling rigs, and other equipment, starting instead to buy them in Brazil in order to stimulate local production. This was an item of the campaign program that Lula da Silva actually delivered. The shipyards carried out a strong recovery. The sector had faced a deep crisis in the 1990s. The Fernando Henrique Cardoso government had implemented a policy that encouraged Petrobras to import goods, services, and the equipment necessary for oil production, and reduced the sources of financing for ship production. In 2003, the shipbuilding industry employed only about 4,000 workers. With the policy change implemented by the Lula government, the supply of jobs grew, reaching around 100,000 in 2014. With new orders and the return of financing, old shipyards in the state of Rio de Janeiro were reopened and, in the Northeast and South regions, new shipyards were created (Gomes, 2015).

Lula da Silva appointed Sergio Gabrielli president of Petrobras. An engineer aligned with neodevelopmentalism, Gabrielli presided over the company from 2005 to 2012. In addition to the new purchasing policy, Gabrielli increased and diversified the company's investments and started to invest more in prospecting and research. Some Petrobras administrators claim that the company had been converted, in the 1990s, into a kind to financial institution for the oil sector and that the new policy brought it back to its original functions. An important result of this policy was the discovery of deep-water oil reserve in the pre-salt layer. Lula da Silva, in his second term, changed the regulations for oil exploration, replacing the so-called concession regime created by Fernando Henrique Cardoso – which encouraged the participation of foreign companies in oil extraction operations – by a sharing regime. This new regime greatly increased the participation of the state in the income from the oil extracted, made it mandatory for Petrobras to participate as an operator in all oilfields, and created the Pre-Salt Social Fund, which should allocate its resources for health and education.

The growth of the shipbuilding sector can be considered one of the great successes of the industrial policy of the PT governments. It became a rather large and diversified chain, comprising both shipyards and the heavy construction industry (Sabença, 2014). It brought together the interests of big national companies, the national scientific and technological community, and a relevant part of trade unions. This was typical of the polyclassist political front that sustained neodevelopmentalism. In other sectors, however, the result was not the same. In the traditional manufacturing industry – textiles, footwear, clothing – local production was affected by imports from Asia, notably from China. In the electrical and electronic sectors, which are focused on products with a higher technological density – automobiles, computers, household appliances, and electronic goods – foreign capital became predominant, while companies occupying these chains' intermediate links, where local capital had greater participation, lost market due to trade liberalization.

4   Judicial Institutions, the Associated Bourgeoisie, and the Upper
      Middle Class

The PSDB consistently criticized the BNDES' and Petrobras' policies. Fernando
Henrique Cardoso, José Serra, and other party leaders published several articles in the press in which they listed arguments against these two centers of
power of the big internal bourgeoisie. In the name of the balance of public
accounts, they criticized the BNDES financing operations for burdening the
National Treasury and, in the name of democracy and transparency, argued
that the BNDES determined the companies that could have access to large
loans based on criteria that were not technical, but strictly political. In the case
of Petrobras, they argued that the ambitious investment program was unre-
alistic and irresponsible, and that the mandatory participation of the state
company in all oilfields warded off foreign investments, hampering access to
the wealth of the pre-salt. The local content policy, which obliged Petrobras
to purchase at least 65% of its inputs from Brazilian companies, was seen as
outdated protectionism and denounced as an anachronistic market reserve
strategy. In those party leaders' opinion, this policy raised Petrobras' costs and
inhibited technological development.

      These disputes over BNDES and Petrobras clearly illustrate the general the-
sis presented above that the Brazilian political process revolved around a conflict between two fractions of the bourgeoisie and that this conflict drove the
ideologies and discourse of the main political parties. It may seem odd that the
PSDB, a bourgeois party, was opposed to policies that served vigorously and
undeniably the interests of big national companies in the shipbuilding, construction, engineering, food, and steel sectors, among others. The party's proposals were linked to alternative measures that would clearly harm big national
companies and serve the interests of international capital and the local companies integrated with that capital – for example, import houses. Within the
Marxist problematic, there is only one way to understand this fact: through
the concept of bourgeois fraction. The PT acted as a defender of the interests
of the big internal bourgeoisie, while the PSDB acted as a representative of
international capital. Furthermore, this same conflict appeared in a specific
way in the ideological dispute: the PT governments, while defending the policies of the BNDES and Petrobras, triggered a neodevelopmentalist discourse;
the PSDB, while criticizing these policies, resumed the discourse of hard-line
neoliberalism of the 1990s. In other words, neoliberalism and neodevelopmentalism, as ideas, expressed the interests of rival bourgeois fractions.

      Let us see how this conflict developed. While the economy grew and the
political situation was favorable to the PT governments, the PSDB leaders

found themselves isolated. However, when the Brazilian economy started to decline, as new political conflicts arose and old conflicts were exacerbated, the PSDB found in the institutions of the Judiciary and of the Public Prosecutor's Office a powerful instrument to resist the policies of the PT governments. Three important characteristics of the Judiciary and the Public Prosecutor's Office predisposed them to function as trenches in the struggle of the big bourgeoisie associated with international capital and the upper middle class, which is their ally against the socioeconomic policy of the PT administrations.

The first characteristic is that employees of judicial institutions are the most highly paid civil servants in Brazil – they occupy the top of the upper middle class. In all, they amount to about 40,000 judges, prosecutors, attorneys, and public defenders. The starting salary of a public prosecutor varies between 29 and 38 times the monthly minimum wage for a workweek of 25 hours. What goes beyond this meager journey is computed as regularly paid overtime, increasing the earnings of this layer of state bureaucracy. The situation of the judges is similar. A judge's salary is around 40 times the minimum wage, and these professionals are entitled to countless benefits, such as meal allowances and the so-called housing allowance – the latter adds a monthly gain of around five times the minimum wage to the earnings of all magistrates, including, strangely enough, even those who reside in their own home. According to news reports, in 2015 the judges of the states of Minas Gerais and São Paulo received between 117 and 235 times the minimum wage. It is true that BNDES' and Petrobras' top employees are also well paid, but their wages are lower than the wages of the Judiciary and, more importantly, the Presidency of the Republic does not control judicial institutions, unlike what happens in the public bank and the oil company. This is precisely the second peculiar characteristic of these institutions: the Judiciary and the Public Prosecutor's office enjoy, according to the Federal Constitution, full administrative and financial autonomy: Judges and prosecutors can even set their own salaries. The third characteristic that predisposes these institutions to oppose the PT governments is the role they play within the capitalist state: the function of maintaining public order. They are what Pierre Bourdieu called "the right hand of the state" (Bourdieu, 1998). This function tends to oppose that branch of the state against governments – such as those of the PT – that facilitate the organization and struggle of popular movements, including those that resort to illegal forms of struggle: arable land occupation, roadblocks, and so on.

Since the beginning of the PT governments, the upper middle class expressed a great deal of antipathy toward their social policy. Such positioning had economic as well as ideological reasons. At the economic level, the upper middle class saw itself as a victim of excessive taxation and rebelled against the high expenses the state devoted to social programs aimed at the low-income population. At the ideological level, the upper middle class saw in the social policies of the PT governments a threat to the social apartheid that it intended to maintain in Brazil.

At the inception of the PT government cycle, a cash transfer program called "Family Grant" (*Bolsa Família*) was implemented. Members of the upper middle class always tended to be against this program, believing that their privileged social position derived from their personal effort and individual merits. They regarded low-income workers as being unskilled and lazy people who therefore deserved to live as badly as they did. In their opinion, the cash transfer would encourage laziness and be unfair to those who worked and had merits. Resistance to the "Family Grant" program was widespread but diffuse.

After the "Family Grant" program, there were measures that attacked, albeit superficially, the consolidated positions of the upper middle-class families: racial and social quotas in universities and in the public service. In this case, in addition to a diffuse reaction, an organized and active resistance began, for example, at the University of Brasilia: students and professors campaigned fiercely against the quotas program, and the case was taken to the Supreme Federal Court, which considered the quotas constitutional.

More recently, the extension of labor rights to domestic workers was approved, and finally, so was the health care program "More Doctors" (*Mais Médicos*). The labor rights of domestic servants increased the costs of the upper middle class, in addition to threatening the authoritarian, paternalistic relationship that its members maintained with their domestic workers – wealthy families employed at least one permanent, multipurpose domestic worker, if not an entire entourage of cooks, drivers, babysitters, doorkeepers, and night watchmen. The "More Doctors" program mobilized the opposition of all medical associations in the country with a racist, anti-communist discourse against Cuban doctors brought by the government to treat the lower class population, which lacked ample access to primary health care.

We should add that the minimum wage appreciation policy of the PT governments and the successful cycle of strikes that were underway in Brazil since the mid-2000s greatly improved the earnings of workers at the base of the wage pyramid. The lower class' increased income caused environments and institutions that had previously been frequented exclusively by the wealthy and the white middle class – such as airports, medical clinics, and high-end bars and restaurants – to be "invaded" by black and low-income workers. Social networks are full of expressions of discomfort and revolt from the rich and white regarding this racial and social mingling.

Judges, prosecutors, attorneys, and federal police agents joined the PSDB leadership in order to erode the neodevelopmentalist policy and the PT governments. In at least two instances, the action of the Federal Police, the Attorney General's Office, and the Judiciary, combined with a broad, biased, and detailed coverage of events by the mainstream media and with the parliamentary pressure of the PSDB, succeeded in producing political crises that threatened Lula da Silva's mandate in 2005 (Martuscelli, 2015) and Rousseff's mandate in 2015. The targets were the key institutions of the neodevelopmentalist policy: the BNDES and Petrobras. The work of such agents and institutions was largely facilitated by the passive and even subservient attitude of the Workers' Party and its governments towards judicial institutions. The PT and its administrations, to avoid exacerbating political conflicts or challenging the Judiciary, refused to mobilize their social base to oppose the partial, unequal, and illegal treatment they received from these institutions. Let us illustrate this situation with the Petrobras scandal.

In 2014, it was revealed that a cartel of construction companies had bribed a small number of politically appointed Petrobras directors to secure a virtual monopoly of oil-related contracts. The Brazilian construction sector is heavily concentrated around 15 large (mostly family-owned) firms that emerged in the late 1950s during the construction of the new capital, Brasília. Those firms expanded rapidly during the military dictatorship (1964–1985), and they currently dominate the market for public works (Sabença, 2014). Bribes allegedly allowed those companies to capture and allocate hundreds of contracts to cartel members; in turn, corrupt directors at Petrobras channeled part of those funds to the political parties that supported the government in the National Congress. On the one hand, the local content policy favored some companies through a market reserve system. On the other hand, a parliamentary base was created for the government.

It is important to note that the agents of the Attorney General's Office, helped by the Judiciary, made ostensible political use of the investigation. They neglected clues that indicated the PSDB's involvement in similar cases, selectively leaked classified or misleading information to competing media organizations, made the timing of the revelations coincide with crucial moments of the 2014 electoral process, and so on. When the situation came to a boil, the mainstream press started to claim that there was one way to get rid of the corruption at Petrobras: suspending the mandatory participation of the state company in the exploration of all oilfields and eliminating the policy that established preference for local production in input purchases. Immediately after that, the PSDB presented bills in the Chamber of Representatives and the Senate to alter the entire Petrobras policy to address the interests of oil companies, shipyards, and key European, American, and Asian construction companies.

Concerning the heavy construction sector specifically, the European capital pursues a similar objective. In an article published in the newspaper *O Estado de São Paulo*, the European Union Trade Commissioner Cecilia Malmström, after quick moral considerations about the spread of corruption in the Brazilian public works market, stated that the European Union would close a trade agreement with Mercosur only if its companies had greater access to this market. Significantly, she said nothing about the European companies Siemens and Alstom, both having pleaded guilty at a process that investigated the practice of corruption in the São Paulo train and metro system under the PSDB governments. What truly matters is that in 2013 the turnover of the public works market in Brazil was higher than the Indian and Argentine markets combined. If the Judiciary declared the largest domestic construction companies were ineligible for public contracts, irrespective of the intentions involved, the effect would favor international capital over the interests of the big internal bourgeoisie.

The real objectives of international capital and the fraction of the Brazilian bourgeoisie associated with it remain hidden most of the time. Those objectives are detrimental not only to the big internal bourgeoisie but also to workers employed at Petrobras' production chain. The action of the orthodox neoliberal opposition focuses on the discourse against corruption, whose ideological function is to cover up the real motives of the bourgeoisie integrated with international capital and the upper middle class. The discourse and the effective action against corruption are selective: they only address institutions and parties that are aligned with the neodevelopmentalist trend, which indicates that their main target is neodevelopmentalism, not corruption. The rhetorical objectives do not coincide with the real ones because, in bourgeois democracies, minority interests also need popular support to thrive. Should the neoliberal campaign admit that its goals are to weaken Petrobras and eliminate the local content policy, it would have no future. The neoliberal revolt against corruption allows the internationalized bourgeoisie and the upper middle class to hijack popular revulsion against white-collar crime so it will serve as the basis for a policy that, in reality, is contrary to popular interests.

5   Final Considerations

Under the PT governments, the Brazilian political process has revolved around a conflict between two fractions of the big internal bourgeoisie. Admittedly, this struggle also matters to the popular classes, since the neodevelopmentalist policies of the big internal bourgeoisie support limited income and employment gains for the majority and help to improve the conditions for further struggle. However, on both sides, the main conflict is driven by bourgeois sectors.

This exceedingly limited social field is linked to a backward and authoritarian bourgeois democracy. The Workers' Party, instead of deepening, expanding, and radicalizing democracy to reinforce its claim to power, became entangled in the capitalist state institutions and distanced itself from its original social base. It also believed that, by appropriating some bureaucratic institutions of the state, it would be able to govern with tranquility, without any disrespect to order and other institutions. That was not the case. The Judiciary, this penultimate trench of the conservative forces – the ultimate being the Armed Forces – had turned against the PT's center-left policy.

The question remains whether it would be possible, once the rules of the authoritarian, conservative, and corrupt political system in force in Brazil were accepted, to do something different than what the PT governments did.

CHAPTER 9

Operation Car Wash, the Middle Class, and State Bureaucracy

The Operation Car Wash is a complex, multidetermined phenomenon.[1] Its analysis requires us to resort to subtleties of the theory of the capitalist state and social classes, and to be knowledgeable about the agencies of the Brazilian capitalist state and about the social classes that influence contemporary Brazilian politics. In this chapter, which is partly an essay, we will attempt to demonstrate that those directing Operation Car Wash acted, at the same time, as members and representatives of the upper fraction of the middle class, and also as state bureaucrats inserted in a specific branch of this apparatus whose particular function was to maintain the capitalist order.

1 The State's Social Function, Social Classes, and Bureaucracy

In the Marxist theory, the capitalist state is defined by its social function: to organize the domination of the bourgeois class. However, one should not assume that the combination of the state's social, economic, cultural, and foreign policies matches the bourgeois class's demands. In addition to the bourgeoisie and the working class, we find in modern capitalist societies – in larger or smaller numbers, depending on the society in question – other social classes: the small bourgeoisie, the middle class, and the peasantry. Furthermore, these classes are segmented in layers or fractions: internal bourgeoisie and associated bourgeoisie; upper, intermediary, and lower fraction of the middle class and of the peasantry; and workers that fail to find stability in the specifically capitalist production and that we call marginal mass of workers – a segment that has grown considerably under the neoliberal capitalist model. In various manners, it is possible to contemplate the interests of these different classes and fractions through the capitalist state policy without having to deny its bourgeois nature. In reality, the capitalist state implements a policy that moderates class conflict, stabilizing the bourgeois domination for that very reason.

---

1 This chapter was written in 2016.

In the case of the middle class, many of its members are, at the same time, state employees, some of them even occupying positions of command in the civilian and military bureaucratic apparatus. Their action is determined, firstly, by the demands of the bureaucratic system: their position is ruled by the norm of law, and the employee occupies a specific position in the hierarchic chain, with the duty to obey his or her superior. Secondly, however, this employee is also an individual from the middle class, thus demonstrating interests and ideology that are typical of this social class. Well, there is no antagonistic contradiction between bureaucratic determination and class determination in the action of these agents; the middle class is not interested in overcoming capitalism. However, a) the corporative demands of the middle class may clash with the economic interests of the bourgeoisie or of the hegemonic bourgeois fraction in the bloc in power at a given period; and b) the class to which the state agents belong may lead them to establish political goals that might jar with the goals of the hegemonic bourgeois fraction in the bloc in power.

In the Brazilian Tenentista movement, bureaucratic and class determination resulted in a political movement that had a decisive role when the 1930 Revolution wiped out the hegemony of the big agro and mercantile bourgeoisie. The *tenentes* (lieutenants) aimed, as members both of the National Army and of the middle class, at policies to strengthen the state and develop Brazilian capitalism. We can say that, in the *tenentes'* actions, class determination prevailed over the bureaucratic determination: in a critical situation, the *tenentes*, albeit inspired by military values, defied the norms of the military institution and rebelled against their superiors. They acted as a sort of "middle class party," representing the class to which they belonged, not in an organized manner, but from above, i. e. acting in its name. This complex political relationship between a branch of the state bureaucracy and the middle class is not exclusive to Brazil; other capitalist countries have witnessed similar phenomena. In the case of Operation Car Wash, whose goal had nothing to do with those sought by the *tenentes'* struggle, we notice a situation that is, in formal terms, very analogous.[2]

2   Operation Car Wash and the Middle Class

The capitalist state bureaucracy performs various functions: education, health, social assistance, public services, order maintenance, and others. Each of these

---

2 The denouncement and uproar against corruption also had an important role in the Tenentista movement (Sodré, 1979).

functions can create specific ideological dispositions in different bureaucratic branches. The state agents involved in Operation Car Wash are responsible for the task of maintaining the capitalist order, and that imbues them with an elitist, authoritarian disposition. These same agents are part of public service's highest paid tier. Judges and prosecutors receive an initial salary that may vary between 29 and 38 times the minimum wage, and they enjoy, thanks to the way the Brazilian political system works, the capacity to establish their own remuneration, vacations that may last up to two months, and often shorter workweeks, lifetime job stability, and countless benefits in addition to their salaries – such as housing, clothing, education, and others – that allow their gains to extrapolate considerably the constitutional wage ceiling. They constitute an actual caste encrusted in the state. Federal Police chiefs do not receive those advantages, but they do occupy a rather privileged position in the public service. All of them – judges, prosecutors, and chiefs of the federal police – are members of the upper middle class. Either as bureaucrats or as members of the upper fraction of the middle class, these agents had an interest in putting an end to the cycle of PT administrations.

Operation Car Wash served like a sort of upper middle-class party. In consonance with the position of most of the rich middle class, it aligned itself with imperialism and the Brazilian bourgeois fraction linked to the latter in order to promote President Dilma Rousseff's impeachment. It contributed enormously to the restoration of the pure, hard neoliberalism, a policy that, in the 1990s, expressed the hegemony of big international capital and the fraction of the Brazilian bourgeoisie associated with it. Nonetheless, this did not necessarily mean that Operation Car Wash represented imperialism or the bourgeoisie. From the moment President Rousseff was removed from power until the writing of this article in June 2016, the bureaucracy of Operation Car Wash has shown signs that it can acquire autonomy and complicate the consolidation of the Temer government. As it was revealed in Romero Jucá's publicized confession, the members of the present government staff feel Operation Car Wash should have been concluded already. There is evidence that Operation Car Wash counted on information offered by U.S. intelligence agencies, and the mainstream media as a whole has practically been part of the operation: it has worked on public persuasion, giving legitimacy to the instances when those being interrogated had their rights trampled, and has supported the investigation's selective nature. In other words, imperialism and the bourgeoisie encouraged the operation and saw in it an endeavor that served their interests. They were not mistaken. The interim government under Temer has already started, through interim minister José Serra, to replace the South-South foreign policy with a policy of passive alignment with the United States, and already threatens the protection of the national economy, starting with the oil reserves in the pre-salt layer of the Brazilian coast. However, it would be a mistake to assume that Operation Car Wash is, for that reason, a representative of imperialism and the bourgeoisie, a mere instrument of these forces that, in the end, gained the most with the coup d'état. Yes, Operation Car Wash was used by a bourgeois fraction – international capital and the associate bourgeoisie – to fight the rival fraction – the big internal bourgeoisie.[3] Nevertheless, it is a fact that there are more classes and class fractions at play in these circumstances besides the bourgeoisie and the working class, and the bourgeoisie cannot control the actions of all the branches of the capitalist state apparatus.

The economy "dream team" led by Henrique Meirelles, who represents imperialist and bourgeois interests, had its work disturbed by the actions – unexpected for many – of Operation Car Wash and the Attorney General of the Republic. Senators and congressmen with prominent roles in the interim government were arrested, and there were threats against dozens of congressmen whose task was precisely to approve the plans of the interim minister of economy. As we write this, the press has divulged that the accusations that resulted from Sérgio Machado's plea bargain involve the interim president Michel Temer. The latter then felt the need to defend himself in a public release. There is no doubt that Operation Car Wash's actions are selective and have three main targets: the Workers' Party (PT), the heavy construction industry, and Petrobras (which form the main segment of the big internal bourgeoisie), and also the state agencies that became a privileged power center for this bourgeois fraction. However, the persecution against the PT and the lenience – up until recently – towards the PSDB and the PMDB may have reflected a tactical calculation conceived at a previous stage of the crisis. The upper middle class picked the PT and its governments as their main enemy. But the discourse against corruption is not a mere pretext. In reality, it represents one of the motivations for the battle against the PT governments, even though that is not the main reason – which actually is combating the social policy created by the PT administrations, as the affluent upper class perceives it as a threat. It is important to remember that the FHC government needed an attorney general to put away all the charges to contain the action of the Public Ministry,

---

3 Peter Bratsis published an article with ample information on the systematic use imperialism has made of the so-called campaigns "against corruption" to harass dependent economies, progressive governments, and local bourgeoisies (Bratsis, 2014). I published a short article analyzing the links between imperialism and Operation Car Wash (Boito Jr., 2014). Since then, there have been several detailed revelations about the participation of the U.S. Department of Justice in this operation.

and the press – including the right-wing *Veja* magazine – had also denounced the PSDB government's corruption. The ideological operation, which makes it possible to neutralize the adversaries or attract allies for the battle against the PT governments, consists in turning the main goal into a secondary one when it comes to discourse. In the new stage of the crisis, represented by the constitution of the Temer interim government, it seems like Operation Car Wash is escaping the control of the bourgeoisie and imperialism.[4]

3   The Middle Class and Corruption

Let us try to align some elements to explain why the war against corruption has a larger audience among the middle class. According to common sense, corruption is supra-historical and repudiated by anyone with the slightest sense of justice. This instinctive, spontaneous perception is being implicitly and surreptitiously smuggled into the field of socialist thinking. If a material or immaterial good belongs to or originates from a public institution, it is inadmissible, according to "our sense of justice," that this good should be the object of private appropriation or manipulation. Well, the very idea of corruption is an ideological creation of the capitalist state.

Unlike the pre-capitalist states, where positions were occupied only by individuals belonging to the ruling class and where material resources meshed with the property resources of the individuals who performed the functions of state, the capitalist state is formally open to individuals from all social classes and its material resources are property resources of the state itself – they are public resources, formally separate from private resources. In the pre-capitalist states, even the idea of corruption in the sense we understand it today was inconceivable. The ships that democratic, slave-owning Athens mobilized to the war were built with resources from the great lords of the city – the trierarchs – who, moreover, commanded the boats they built – the triremes; the regiments of the absolutist state's feudal army were property of the big aristocrats that passed them along to their offspring as inheritance, just as it happened with the positions in civilian administration; closer to us, and now

---

4   Another important theme is the repercussion of the struggle between bourgeois fractions in the relationship among the Brazilian state agencies. Some of those agencies can be converted into centers of power for this or that struggling bourgeois fraction. BNDES and Petrobras have become, during the PT administrations, centers of power for the big internal bourgeoisie, and the Central Bank turned into a center of power for the financial capital. See Chapter 8 of this book.

already addressing the pre-capitalist traits of the subordinate spheres of an already capitalist state, the election in small towns in Brazil was conducted, back in the days of the Old Republic, at the private residence of the locally dominant oligarch, known as a *coronel* (colonel) (Boito Jr., 2007; Mossé, 1979; Telarolli, 1982). The capitalist state establishes a formal distinction between public resources and private resources, and the idea of corruption is born from that distinction. However, in practical terms, the state resources are in the service of the capitalist class, and that is why we understand that such separation is formal. In other words, the idea of corruption must be treated with the good old concept of ideology: an unconscious, deformed, and interested representation of reality.

Let us try – in essay style, fundamentally through theoretical deduction, and relying on non-systematic information – to indicate some elements of the relations between social classes and the state agents' corruption. Corruption is an element of the bourgeois ideology of state, but the bourgeoisie maintains an ambivalent relationship with the practice of corruption. That is so, no matter if we consider how each capitalist's private interests relate with corruption, or if we take in consideration the behavior of the bourgeois class. In the world of capitalist competition, each bourgeois wishes all his competitors to be honest while he alone is allowed the prerogative of corrupting. As a class, the bourgeoisie fears the accusation of corruption and the fight against this practice because it fears they may contribute to reveal the class nature of the capitalist state to the eyes of the working class. However, in its fraction struggle, which we could call a fratricide battle, a bourgeois fraction may wage the war against corruption to fight the hegemony of a rival bourgeois class. That is what we have been observing in Brazil with Operation Car Wash: imperialism and the bourgeois fraction associated with it make a political use of corruption in order to destroy the hegemony that the big Brazilian internal bourgeoisie obtained during the PT governments. Of course, while doing that, international capital and the associated bourgeoisie accept the risk of opening the eyes of the working class, betraying the largest joint interests of the bourgeois class. The interest of a fraction may blind and betray the interest of the class as a whole.

The working class tends to reject corruption for reasons and in a manner that are specifically connected to labor. It judges corruption from the perspective of both the producer and the consumer. Corrupt actors, be they active or passive, do not produce anything; they are perceived as parasites; and their actions must be countered because they also increase the inequality in wealth distribution. Other specificity is that the working class tends to see corruption as one of the "evils" that exist in society and in the capitalist state, and not necessarily as the worst of them. The concentration of property, the concentration of wealth, the exploitation of labor, and the very condition of the bureaucrats and of the professional bourgeois politicians, which are considered to be "natural" practices by other social classes, are perceived by the working class as causes of the workers' poor life conditions. Judges of law earning an initial remuneration that corresponds to 30 times the minimum wage and being able to reach throughout their career a monthly gain of around 140 times the minimum wage, as it was reported by *Caros Amigos* magazine in 2015, is a legal situation, but it is perceived as something as revolting as the corrupted practices by the directors of Petrobras; the same could be said about the benefits that the state awards legally to big capitalists. They are legal, but they demonstrate that the separation between public patrimony and private property, which is typical of the capitalist state, is a relative separation that causes as much revulsion as corruption itself.

The social class that firmly rejects the corruption perceived as capitalist society's absolute evil is the middle class. It is the absolute evil that admits only one legal and moral correction. Such stance comes from the economic condition and meritocratic ideology that characterize it. For the middle class, the capitalist social organization only needs one repair: the individual merit criterion should rule always. Meritocracy is an ideology that values non-manual labor and stigmatizes manual labor. The social differences are conceived, in this ideological setting, as a result of the individual differences in each person's gifts and merits. Non-manual labor would be the prerogative of those whose long, successful educational path proves their superiority and merits. It is an ideology that introduces a deformed vision of social inequality, deformed to such an extent that it justifies the upper-class workers' social and wage advantages – deforming and justifying are the overall functions of the bourgeois and petit bourgeois ideology. Well, this ideology has a particular, privileged area of realization: the capitalist state.

The state bureaucracy has a formal organization based on the competence required for each position and role in the state hierarchy, and its institutions are a privileged workplace for the middle class. Recruitment for state positions, unlike what happened in pre-capitalist states, is conducted through public exams with merit evaluation. The formally public nature of the capitalist state agencies is an icon for the middle-class bureaucrats and cannot be tainted by the economic power, a field where otherwise those belonging to the middle class see themselves in disadvantage in relation to the capitalists. How to legitimize the judges and prosecutors' incredibly high earnings, both to Brazilian and international standards, if the rules of meritocracy and bureaucracy were violated by practices such as nepotism, cronyism, and quid pro quo? For the middle class, the evil is not in the state's rules of bureaucratic organization that create parasitic, privileged segments, but in the violation of these rules through corruption. Of course, a middle-class citizen may gladly accept a well paid public job offered by a political sponsor, just as a bourgeois will not hesitate before violating someone else's property to increase his own. For the rest, in corrupted practices we find usually a middle-class employee breaking the state norms and a bourgeois violating someone else's property somehow. But what we have there are individual interests of class members clashing with the interests and ideology of the class to which these individuals belong. Such facts do not deny that the middle class has an interest in the rules of bureaucracy just the bourgeois has an interest in the norms that protect private property.

∴

In regard to the present circumstances, it will be possible to adjudicate the question of whom Operation Car Wash represents if we observe and analyze what is to come. Will judges, prosecutors, and chiefs of police truly challenge the members of the interim president's governmental staff?

As for the complex matter of the relationship between political struggle and protests against corruption, so frequent in Brazilian history (Martuscelli, 2015), our reflections are preliminary. However, if our hypotheses prove to be correct, we have some indications to understand why the middle class is so prone to mobilizing against corruption, and we also have indications to reflect about how specifically, from the perspective of the working class, one must battle corruption, which is an ever-present practice in the capitalist state.

CHAPTER 10

The Crisis of Neodevelopmentalism and the Dilma Rousseff Government

The successive administrations linked to the Workers' Party (PT) implemented, with variations according to circumstances, a policy that was much closer to the old Brazilian developmentalism than to the state welfare reformism.[1] It was a policy that we can call neodevelopmentalist, closer to the lineage initiated by Getúlio Vargas than to the one produced by European social democracy. Neodevelopmentalism was in force in the 2000s and 2010s not only in Lula da Silva and Dilma Rousseff's Brazil, but also in Nestor and Cristina Kirchner's Argentina.

In order to understand that policy, it is necessary to distinguish between the notion of economic *model*, which indicates a whole formed by an economic apparatus with a specific profile and to which legal norms and institutions are coherently bound, and the notion of economic *policy*. In the latter, we have a set of governmental measures that establish a more or less coherent capitalist development strategy, measures that affect distinct areas such as credit, taxes, tributes, salaries, foreign trade, among others. Well, the same economic model may encompass, within certain boundaries, important variations in the economic policy. Here is an example. The developmentalist economic model enforced in Brazil between the 1930s and the 1970s comprised Getúlio Vargas's economic policy – with the expansion of labor rights and economic nationalism –, Juscelino Kubitschek's liberalization policy to foreign capital, and the military governments' policy of downgrading social rights.

Within the neoliberal capitalist model, governments may implement an orthodox, moderate, or even neodevelopmentalist neoliberal policy. To offer the reader an initial, synthetic definition of the neodevelopmentalist policy, we shall say that *this policy is the form of developmentalism that is possible within the boundaries imposed by the neoliberal capitalist model.* Brazilian and Argentinean neodevelopmentalist governments maintained the model inherited from their predecessors, but they encouraged economic growth by resorting to the state's intervention in the economy – as the old developmentalism

---

1 This chapter was written in 2016, while Dilma Rousseff was temporarily suspended from office to stand trial in the Brazilian Senate.

used to do – thus moving away from the ideology and practices of a minimum state. However, this interventionism and the growth it was expected to generate stumbled on, among other things, the limitations imposed by fundamental elements of the neoliberal capitalist model. Here we refer to legal, economic, and institutional elements that reduce the state's investment capacities, discourage private productive investment, and diminish the market for the national production – elements such as high interest policy, huge spending in rolling over the public debt, trade liberalization, the Central Bank's effective autonomy, privatizations, financial deregulation, and others.

Neodevelopmentalism was bound to meet a crisis at some point. It depended, as many have observed, on a favorable situation at the international market, and, we should add, on a very heterogeneous political front whose unity was precarious[2]. In 2005, neodevelopmentalism faced its first political crisis, the corruption scandal that the mainstream press called "*Mensalão*" (Martuscelli, 2015). Many analysts claimed that the crisis that began in 2014 would be its ultimate crisis, putting an end to the neodevelopmentalist cycle. There were countless facts that really seemed to point in that direction: the crisis within the Workers' Party, which was the political instrument of this development cycle; the small room for maneuver that the neoliberal capitalist model allowed the economic growth policies; the falling price of commodities in the global market; the big bourgeoisie's frail, ephemeral support to the neodevelopmentalist policy. We will not enter the territory of prospective analysis – to find out whether that represented indeed the ultimate crisis for neodevelopmentalism. On this subject, everything is too uncertain, and peremptory prognostics reveal more ignorance of the historical process's complexity than anything else. What we can say is that these circumstances revealed a track where Brazil and a good portion of Latin America, after marching to the beat of its own drum for over a decade, was now being bullied to keep in step with Europe's austerity.

In this chapter, we will examine the social bases of the neodevelopmentalist policy in Brazil, the interests it served, its opponents, the conflicts it triggered, and the crisis that victimized it during Dilma Rousseff's second term. We will begin with a brief controversy regarding the bibliography, taking as a starting point some considerations about this political crisis itself.

---

2   We have analyzed the contradictions of neodevelopmentalism and of the political front that backed it, as well as the possibility of a resulting political crises in a short text titled "The Contradictions of the Developmentalist Front" (Boito Jr., 2012a). Also in 2012 we gave a long interview to the newspaper *Brasil de Fato,* where we approached the issue of a possible neodevelopmentalist political crisis in broader terms.

1   A Couple of Things to Learn from the Crisis

The political crisis in the Dilma Rousseff government, which led to her deposition, in spite of its new and recent contradictions, stemmed mainly from the
exacerbation of the contradictions that were already at play in Brazil's political
process since the beginning of the cycle of the PT administrations. That is precisely why this crisis, in highlighting these contradictions, casts in hindsight a
new light upon these governments. It thus leaves us with a few lessons.

The first lesson, contrary to what part of the bibliography and left-wing
organizations have claimed, is that the governments linked to the Workers'
Party were very different from the 1990s governments linked to the PSDB.[3]
Various works with disparate theses and argumentations have actually identified such governments or minimized the differences between them. Lula da
Silva would have been the continuation of FHC or, at best, introduced very
marginal differences in comparison to his predecessor. Following that line
of analysis, we could recall here the works of Francisco de Oliveira, Leda
Paulani, Luiz Filgueiras, Reinado Gonçalves, Valério Arcary, and others. Even
I, despite always having stressed that the governments linked to the PT represented a fraction of the Brazilian bourgeoisie that had been marginalized
in the FHC era, underestimated up until the mid-2000s the impact of this
change in Brazil's political process (Oliveira F., 2010; Paulani, 2008; Filgueiras
& Gonçalves, 2007; Arcary, 2011; Boito Jr., 2005b). It is a fact that part of this
bibliography was produced during Lula da Silva's first term, when the differences between his administration and the FHC government were less visible.
Nevertheless, a critical reference to this bibliography may be instructive. By
the way, it is important to remember that up to the end of 2015 several critical intellectuals and left-wing organizations still claimed, precisely because
they underestimated the differences between the PT and the PSDB, that the
campaign to impeach Rousseff was a mere smokescreen with which the opposition planned to blackmail the government. Well, the political crisis that led
to the deposition of President Rousseff was a major factor indicating, as we

---

3   We are not employing here the terms "PT governments" or "PSDB governments," but instead
    "governments linked to the PT" or "linked to the PSDB." In Brazil, we have government parties,
    but not party governments. Just like the FHC governments were not, strictly speaking, PSDB
    governments or coalition governments led by this party, the Lula da Silva and Dilma Rousseff
    governments were not PT governments or led by the PT. The PSDB was the FHC government
    party in the same way that the PT was the Lula da Silva government party and the Dilma
    Rousseff government party. Neither the PSDB nor the PT determined the path of the govern-
    ments they backed and helped to staff.

understand it, that all these analyses need to be revisited and reconsidered. If the governments linked to the PT were identical or very similar to those linked to the PSDB, how can we explain the deep, prolonged crisis faced by Brazilian politics and – take notice – the absence of any conciliation proposal coming from either of the parties involved in the conflict?

The second lesson is that the crisis's prolonged aspect suggests that what was at stake was very important to the parties involved: class interests. We did not witness a conflict between the working class and the bourgeoisie about choosing between capitalism and socialism – a conflict that we could have properly called a *class struggle*. Instead, we witnessed a class conflict with a comparatively smaller scope that set a confrontation – in a complex, intricate system of alliances and oppositions – between different segments of the capitalist class and of the dominated classes that disputed the appropriation of wealth and income. The distributive class conflict was at the base of this political crisis. It was not the crisis's only engine. The conflicts around demands from the women's, black, and LGBT movements – which maintain various, complex relations with the distributive class conflict – were also part of the crisis. That was evident in the action and influence of the "Bible Bench" – a group of Evangelical parliamentarians – during the impeachment process in the Chamber of Representatives. But the main conflict was the distributive class conflict. In the political dissimulation game, Michel Temer felt the need to publically deny several times that he intended to extinguish labor and social rights, but he did not feel the need to deny that his government might reverse the rights of women, black citizens, and members of the LGBT community, even though it was well known that such reversal was one of the goals of the forces participating in the parliamentary coup d'état.

Evidently, a class conflict is neither a conflict between political personalities – Dilma Rousseff, Aécio Neves (then national president of the PSDB), Eduardo Cunha (then president of the Chamber of Representatives), Lula da Silva, Michel Temer – nor a conflict between opinion trends. We will not criticize here the personalist explanation of the political process – it does not seem wise to believe that a handful of individuals pursuing their own interests would have the power to shake an entire country. We will, however, say a few words about the explanation of the crisis as a conflict between opinion trends or doctrines – neodevelopmentalism and neoliberalism – conceived separately from the class conflict.

The explanation that focuses on the contention between opinion trends, without questioning how such trends are linked to the class conflict, makes an idealistic mistake, and, knowingly or not, sticks strictly to the liberal tradition that can be traced back to John Stuart Mill and reaches John Rawls and Jürgen Habermas. This kind of concept assumes the existence of a public space where there is the free formation of different opinion trends that are all of them subject to the citizens' free, conscious scrutiny. A left-wing version of this same approach sees Brazilian politics as a dispute between political projects that may occasionally be introduced as "class projects," but merely in an allusive, ancillary way.[4] For certain, there are political and economic projects – the neodevelopmentalist and neoliberal currents are real and active – but they are only a superficial dimension of something more profound and important that is often disguised by the political discourse. In the same way that in 2015 Dilma Rousseff's neodevelopmentalist government put aside its beliefs and campaign promises and began to enforce a neoliberal adjustment program, the neoliberal bourgeois opposition betrayed the market principles it had always preached and voted, at the National Congress, against the adjustment measures proposed by the government. Such developments would have been inexplicable if we, in analyzing the political struggle, stuck to the dispute between projects – neodevelopmentalism and neoliberalism.

Firstly, it is important to question the reasons that allowed neodevelopmentalists and neoliberals, and not other currents or projects, to occupy center stage and polarize the political conflict in Brazil. There was a sociopolitical filter, delineated by the interests of class and class fraction, and by their balance of forces, which protected some currents or doctrines, and marginalized others in the political process. Secondly, it is necessary to keep in mind that the attachment to this or that project was *not strictly* free and individual, or in other words, it was not socially random. Considering the ruling class, it is possible to demonstrate that the bourgeois segment that supported, at least until 2014, the neodevelopmentalist policy was different from the one that defended, at that same period and even more fiercely later during the political crisis, the return to the neoliberal policy. Considering the camp of the working classes, we must remember, for a quick example, that the organized movements of peasants and the marginal mass of workers – the Landless Workers' Movement (MST), the Homeless Workers' Movement (MTST), the Movement of People Affected by Dams (MAB), the Popular Movements Central (CMP), and others – maintained their distance from the neoliberal camp or even challenged it openly and militantly. In the case of the union movement, there was a more complex

---

4   Examples of this kind of analysis can be found in the book organized by Emir Sader titled *Lula e Dilma: 10 Anos de Governos Pós-Neoliberais no Brasil* (Sader, 2013). I highlight Sader's own article, titled "A Construção da Hegemonia Pós-Neoliberal," in which the project struggle, detached from class conflicts, is conceived as the engine of the entire Brazilian political process.

situation because this movement was divided: part of the union movement swung between the neodevelopmentalist and the neoliberal camps. However, even this division was socially established, that is, not explained by workers' and unionists' free ideological options. Surveys on the subject of unionism show that union centrals rested on social bases that displayed important differences in income and education level, in the relative weight of workers from the public and private sectors, and in the power of union pressure, and indicate that such differences influenced the political option of union leaders (Galvão, Marcelino & Trópia, 2015).

Among the authors that used the idea of conflict or even of class conflict to explain the crisis, we find two characteristic and opposing – but equally problematic – positions. We had the analysis that assumed that the governments linked to the PT represented the workers, while the other, in contrast, maintained that such governments represented the bourgeoisie.

The latter appears, for instance, in the already mentioned book by Valério Arcary: the PT would be a government not of workers, but of the bourgeoisie as a whole (Arcary, 2011). In this case, the political crisis could only be explained as the moment when the bourgeoisie (as a whole), after having backed the PT administrations, joined the opposition when it came to the conclusion that the PT had lost the ability to manage the new situation created by the economic crisis. This idea was defended by intellectuals close to the United Socialists Workers' Party (PSTU) in public debates about the crisis. It is important to remember, however, that a key portion of the bourgeoisie was fighting against the PT governments even before the crisis, during a period when there was considerable economic growth. What else did the PSDB's organized opposition do besides expressing its bourgeois dissatisfaction?

As for the opposing thesis, which claims that the PT administrations represented the workers, it is defended by the PT intellectuals and leaders. During the political crisis, the Rousseff government would have been challenged by the bourgeoisie and by the "elites" precisely because it represented the workers. The political crisis would have been a rebellion of the bourgeoisie or "the elites" against a popular government. Valter Pomar defends this thesis in an article about the political crisis in Brazil (Pomar, 2016). The problem facing this kind of analysis is that, even though they did not represent the entire bourgeoisie, the PT governments did represent, both objectively and subjectively, a portion – or fraction – of Brazil's bourgeoisie. The economic policy measures of these administrations focused on the interests of the Brazilian big internal bourgeoisie – shipbuilding, heavy construction, agribusiness, mining, national banks – and only secondarily contemplated the interests of the popular classes. The publications of the business associations in the period before the political crisis revealed the systematic support of this big business fraction to the Lula and Rousseff administrations (Berringer, 2015; Sabença, 2014; Gomes, 2015).

The two class analyses above defend opposing positions but originate from a common idea: they treat the bourgeoisie as a unified, fracture-free class, ignoring that the capitalist class can be, and usually is, divided into fractions with different economic interests. In fact, the PT governments represented the hegemony of one Brazilian bourgeois fraction in detriment of another. That is what keeps us from speaking of the bourgeoisie in general terms when we analyze the PT administrations, and that is what we will attempt to demonstrate next.

2   The Bloc in Power and Class Alliances

We have argued that the bloc in power in Brazil encompassed countless bourgeois fractions. Firstly, we had big capital, which, in turn, was divided in two fractions or subfractions: a fraction we could call, according to Nicos Poulantzas (1974), the big internal bourgeoisie, which intended to maintain and improve its position in Brazilian dependent capitalism and keep a relationship of cooperation and competition with international capital; and a fraction we could call the internationalized or associated fraction of Brazilian bourgeoisie, acting in alliance with big international financial and productive capital. Secondly, we had a vast amount of small and medium companies with reduced economic power and political influence that did not act as a distinct social force, i.e., they lacked organization and a political program of their own in these circumstances. During the PT governments, the main dispute within the bloc in power occurred between the big internal bourgeoisie and the internationalized or associated bourgeoisie. Between 2003 and 2014, these two bourgeois fractions held different positions in national politics: the big internal bourgeoisie, mostly since 2008, took over the hegemony inside the bloc in power, while the internationalized or associated bourgeoisie occupied a subordinate position inside this bloc and found itself in the opposition.

With the political and economic crisis, the big internal bourgeoisie was attracted to the political camp of the associated bourgeoisie, and, in the worst-case scenario, it might dissolve as an autonomous class fraction.[5] The bourgeois

---

5   Aided by students André Barbosa, Julia Nunes, and Rosylli Oliveira, we conducted a survey about the position of the big internal bourgeoisie during the crisis. We consulted documents from the Federation of Industries of the State of São Paulo (Fiesp), the National Confederation of Industry (CNI), the Brazilian Agribusiness Association (Abag), the Brazilian Machinery

fractions are not a simple reflection of the profile and economic insertion of the capitalist companies; they depend on the impact of the state's economic policy on the bourgeois segments, and also on the various business segments' capacity for political organization. They are formed, they develop, and may also disappear. The outcome of the crisis will tell us what will happen with the big internal bourgeoisie as a distinct fraction of the bourgeois class. For now, let us see which segments integrated this fraction and which economic policy it defended before the crisis.

The big internal bourgeoisie was not a homogenous bourgeois fraction. It was riddled with fractioning systems that could undermine the unity that was conferred to it by the fractioning of international capital/national capital. The big internal bourgeoisie was formed by companies with predominantly national capital, and encompassed, besides the financial sector – notably the big national banks –, the productive sector and, within the latter, it was distributed into shipbuilding, heavy construction, agribusiness, processing industry, and commerce.[6] In all these segments, moreover, the fractioning between big and medium capital could cause pertinent political effects according with the circumstances and with the aspect of the economic policy being considered. The banking sector was the fraction of the big internal bourgeoisie that was closest to international capital, since the current pattern of financial accumulation in global capitalism was favorable to it. However, the national control over the banking system, a control that had always been criticized by international agencies such as the IMF, had been threatened under the FHC governments, and a reaction from Brazilian banks and the PT's rise to government were necessary to force back the foreign capital's march into the sector.

As for the bourgeois fraction that we could call "comprador," if we were to employ the terminology from the Communist International documents, or alternatively, associated or internationalized bourgeoisie – denominations more in line with the current model of imperialist domination –, it was a fraction constituted by the international economic groups operating in Brazil – be it with branches and facilities installed in the country, as suppliers of goods

---

Builders' Association (Abimaq), the Brazilian Association of Infrastructure and Basic Industries (Abidb), the National Syndicate of the Naval Industry and Offshore Construction and Repair (Sinaval), and other business associations that represent sectors of the big internal bourgeoisie. The tone of the documents of these associations is of support for the fiscal adjustment and defense of reforms that hurt the interests of public workers and employees of the private sector. They want the adjustment to be made at the expense of the workers. That was not what stood out in the previous period. Then, they defended state measures favoring economic growth, sparing the workers' interests.

6   In Chapter 8 of this book, we discuss this subject in more detail.

and services for Brazilian economy, or as mere speculative capital –, and also, we should stress, by companies of predominantly national capital that maintained a relationship of direct dependence with international capital – as, for instance, suppliers of intermediary goods for the industry of durable consumer goods, importers of goods produced abroad, etc. This bourgeois fraction was also affected by different systems of fractioning that, just as it occurred with the internal bourgeoisie, could undermine its political unity. The foreign capital-owned processing industry, which dominated the sector of durable consumer goods, could side with the big internal bourgeoisie – in a movement opposite to that national banking capital. That was what happened in the occasions when the Lula da Silva and Dilma Rousseff administrations took protectionist measures favoring the local production of motor vehicles.

Thus, the fractioning of the bourgeoisie is complex. There is no straight, stable line separating the bourgeois fractions (Farias, 2009). In some circumstances, the intersection of fractioning systems can cause national banks to grow closer to their foreign counterparts, in spite of being national; likewise, also depending on the circumstances, the foreign industry with facilities in Brazil can grow closer to the national industrial sector, in spite of being controlled by foreign capital. On top of that, there are contradictions within each of these fractions – the banks and the national productive sector face a well-known conflict regarding the definition of interest rates. If the proximity between the internal bourgeoisie and international capital becomes more stable and comprehensive, and if the contradictions at the core of each of these two fractions escalate, these conditions may lead, in the worst-case scenario, to the dissolution of each one of them as a distinct class fraction. Even if this extreme situation does not come to pass, an instability of the fractions can, at minimum, lead to the displacement of one or other sector to the rival bourgeois fraction – the sugar/ethanol sector had backed the Lula da Silva governments, but moved away from the Rousseff administration because of the losses it suffered due to the change in energy policies that relegated ethanol to the background and started prioritizing the pre-salt oil.

Should such considerations lead the researcher to abandon the concept of bourgeois fractions? We understand that is not the case. In general lines, the orthodox neoliberal capitalist development strategy that was adopted in the 1990s and the neodevelopmentalist strategy adopted by the PT governments in the 2000s and 2010s were strategies that affected rather unequally the bourgeois fractions mentioned above, and each of them formed links of representation with somewhat stable interests – the internationalized bourgeoisie recognized itself in the orthodox neoliberalism of the PSDB administrations, reborn in 2016 with the PMDB program called "Bridge for the Future," while the big internal bourgeoisie used to find its place, at least until 2015, in the neodevelopmentalism of the Workers' Party governments.

The PT administrations did not revoke the neoliberal capitalist model, but introduced in it elements of the economic policy inspired in the old developmentalism. The trade liberalization initiated by the Collor government and expanded by the FHC administrations was maintained, but Lula and Rousseff created protectionist niches for the national companies. They implemented the local content policy for the acquisition of goods and services by the state and by state companies, and, particularly during the first term of the Rousseff administration, they enforced various tariff and non tariff protection measures to favor the Brazilian automotive industry.

The privatizations were not revoked, but these same governments adopted a policy to strengthen the remaining big state companies, starting with Petrobras. The high interest policy was not interrupted either, but the overall – although not linear – trend during the PT administrations was of a drop in interest rates in relation to the 1990s, and, most importantly, the National Bank for Economic and Social Development (BNDES) budget was multiplied practically tenfold and started to offer strongly subsidized interests to big Brazilian companies. In the first term of the Rousseff administration, the interest rate for 2011–2012 suffered a sharp reduction, in a policy that was part of the so-called "new economic matrix" implemented by finance minister Guido Mantega. This policy improved considerably the position of the big internal bourgeoisie at the core of the bloc in power, relied on the open support from the big internal bourgeoisie's business associations – the Brazilian Machinery Builders´ Association (Abimaq), the Brazilian Association of Infrastructure and Basic Industries (Abidb), the National Syndicate of the Naval Industry and Offshore Construction and Repair (Sinaval) – and faced criticism and growing opposition from the international financial and productive capital.

In harmony with this new development policy, the PT governments altered their foreign policy as well.[7] They moved farther away from the United States – with the shelving of the Alca proposal; the creation of the G-20; the active, prominent participation in the Brics group – and grew closer to the South Hemisphere countries. Thus, they obtained greater room for maneuver in the international arena and managed to advance a policy to expand the big internal bourgeoisie's business in South America, Africa, and the Middle East.[8] In

---

7   See Chapter 5 of this book, as well as the groundbreaking work by Berringer (2015).

8   The neodevelopmentalist policy followed an ascending line in the 2000s and 2010s. That is why we do not agree with André Singer's analysis (see Singer, 2012), for whom the PT governments implemented a Bonapartist policy in the sense of tending to alternatively one or

spite of such novelties and of the conflicts with international capital, the big internal bourgeoisie, financially and technologically dependent on this same international capital, showed signs, as indicated above, of aspiring only to a reform of the neoliberal capitalist model, and not to a rupture with this model.

Each of the two bourgeois fractions that polarized the conflict within the bloc in power sought alliances and support outside this bloc. The big internal bourgeoisie, thanks to the initiative of the PT governments, found itself strengthened by a political front that submitted to the hegemony of its interests and that sustained those governments. The neodevelopmentalist front encompassed, during most of that period, the lower middle class, most of the labor union, the peasant movement, and most of the marginal mass of workers. Without failing to prioritize the interests of the big internal bourgeoisie, the PT governments offered something to each of these popular classes: more slots in public universities with social and racial quotas, financing for private university students, a policy to appreciate the minimum wage, cash transfer programs, financing and institutional market reserve for small family agriculture, large expansion of slots in vocational schools, a program to build popular housing, a program to build cisterns in the semiarid region, and others. The marginal mass of workers, benefited by cash transfer programs, the building of popular housing, the program to build cisterns, and the expansion of vocation schools, was the sector that displayed massive, constant turnout, at least since 2006, to vote for the PT candidates (Singer, 2012). In the 2014 presidential election, when a significant mass of voters withdrew their support to the candidate of the neodevelopmentalist front, it was the marginal mass of workers, mainly those from the rural areas of the northeast states, who ensured Dilma Rousseff's victory.

The associated bourgeoisie, in turn, established an alliance with the urban upper middle class. This fraction of the middle class has become a captive electorate for the PSDB. In the regions of Brazil where the size and influence of the upper middle class is greater, so is the PSDB's. The orthodox neoliberal program did not contemplate in all aspects the interests of the upper fraction of the middle class, but it has aligned with neoliberalism because it saw in the PT's social policy a threat to its privileged socioeconomic position in Brazilian society (Cavalcante, 2015). This social group was formed by waged workers

---

another class or class fraction due to the instability in the correlation of forces. If that were the case, it is important to clarify that we should have had a zigzagging economic policy, which is something that definitely did not happen. I have criticized this aspect of Singer's analysis in Boito Jr., 2013b and in Chapter 4 of this book.

with high salaries, both for Brazilian and international standards, allocated both in the public and the private sector, and also successful liberal professionals: administrators, economists, engineers, lawyers, medical doctors, college professors, and other professionals with a higher education degree. Taking into consideration the analysis of the political crisis faced by the Rousseff government, it is crucial to remember that judges, prosecutors, district attorneys, appellate judges, and chiefs of the Federal Police, i. e. agents of the Operation Car Wash and of the entire section of the justice system engaged in opposing the PT governments, are not only employees of the state's repressive branch, but also members of the upper middle class. That was how the forces were positioned before the political crisis was unleashed.

3   The Political Crisis

The economic divisions of class do not appear at the level of the political process in a fixed, identical manner. The line dividing the neodevelopmentalist camp, composed by the big internal bourgeoisie and its allies, from the orthodox neoliberal camp, formed by international capital and its internal supporters, was never a straight, rigid line. This dividing line, winding and flexible, suffered meaningful displacements since 2013, when the political crisis began. These displacements meant important changes in the correlation of forces between the two camps and formed the very history of the unleashing and development of the crisis.

Brazil's economy, which had grown 7.5% in 2010, remained at a plateau in 2011–2012 with a very low growth rate. The neoliberal opposition noticed the opportunity, gave up the defensive attitude, and seized back the political initiative. It chose as its nemeses the then finance minister Guido Mantega and his "new economic policy matrix." The economy sections of the great newspapers started stressing the need to reduce state costs, end fiscal exemptions, and raise the interest rate. The Special Clearance and Escrow System rate (Selic rate) had been reduced to 7.5% annually, and profit from financial investments was close to zero.

This is a key point: the crisis was caused by a political attack from the orthodox neoliberal camp, directed by international capital and the country's bourgeois fraction linked to it, and not by the popular struggle. Many display some confusion when examining this problem. The fact that polls indicated that the Rousseff administration had its image damaged – and, afterwards never recovered – due to the protests of June 2013 leads some analysts to suggest that the political crisis was caused by the rise of the popular struggle. Double mistake. Firstly, because only the first stage of the protests of June 2013 had a clear popular character. That was the stage in which the Free Fare Movement (MPL) fought against the raise in transport fares. At a second stage, the protests incorporated new social sectors, including the upper middle class; broadened their slogans, including in particular the generic discourse against corruption; and became dependent on the media, which started to drive them against the federal government. At the beginning, the struggle against the raise in transport fares was addressed to mayors and state governors, but the mainstream media federalized the protests.

What we have here is a complex articulation between two kinds of oppositions. The main one, which caused the political crisis and put the international bourgeois camp against the neodevelopmentalist front, articulated – favorably to the orthodox neoliberal camp – with the existing contradictions within the neodevelopmentalist front itself. The "Fare Revolt" gathered, as surveys show, young people from the lower middle class, workers that, in most cases, were also students. This had been the sector benefited by the PT governments' policy to expand higher education, doubling the number of Brazilian college students. As it happens, the labor market for students with a degree grew very little. Due to the reactivation of the primary-export function of Brazilian economy, the jobs created were predominantly positions that did not require high qualification and that paid low salaries (Pochmann, 2012). It was the frustration of the young people from the lower middle class that found its voice in the "Fare Revolt" and even in the second stage of the June protests (Ridenti, 2013). This frustration, however, remained politically acephalous, not surprisingly given how the Free Fare Movement (MPL) celebrated spontaneity, which allowed the protests, for that very reason, to be highjacked by the reactionaries and channeled into the growing support for neoliberal candidates in 2014.

As we have indicated, there are various contradictions at the core of the neodevelopmentalist front. The contradiction between the lower middle class youth and the front brought up something new that developed as the number of college students grew without a corresponding growth in jobs for those with a degree. However, there were contradictions that had been present since the beginning of the governments of the neodevelopmentalist front. In the camp of the popular classes, the union movement was very active in this period of strike struggle, managing to obtain a general improvement in salaries (Boito Jr.; Galvão & Marcelino, 2015). Harsh economic conflicts occurred between unions and groups of the big internal bourgeoisie. The peasant movement, in spite of social policies that benefited the settlers, always felt dissatisfied with the drastic reduction in land expropriations, or in other words, with the marginalization of camped peasants. As for the ruling classes, there were

contradictions inside the internal bourgeoisie itself. The most remarkable conflict was the one between the big national banks and the national productive
sector regarding fiscal policy and the interest rate. Between them, new contradictions also emerged. The transfer of prioritization of the energy policy
from ethanol to the pre-salt oil pushed the sugar/ethanol sector away from the
Rousseff administration.

The fact is that when the orthodox neoliberal camp initiated its offensive
for restoration, the neodevelopmentalist front was tearing itself apart. As we
have seen, the big internal bourgeoisie was beginning to side with the neoliberal opposition. It was convinced, as evidenced by the documents we have
studied, that the fiscal adjustment was the only way to resume the economic
growth; therefore, it decided to back the adjustment, and, of course, in order to
spare its own businesses, demanded adjustment measures that penalized the
workers and not the companies. These changes appeared in several developments of the political stage. The unanimous support from the big union centrals to the government was withdrawn, the PSB moved to the opposition, the
PMDB fractured and later started to organize the impeachment process in the
Congress, and a business entity as important as Fiesp went from actively backing the neodevelopmentalist governments, defending the Lula administration
even during the so-called "*Mensalão*" crisis in 2005, to a frenetic activism for
the deposition of the Rousseff government.

The offensive for restoration, headed by classes and class fractions that
formed the orthodox neoliberal camp, obtained an important victory. Michel
Temer became the interim president, and both his program, called "A Bridge
for the Future," and his first decisions evidenced the goal to return to the neoliberal platform of the 1990s. The popular movement remained at a stage of
segmented struggle for demands. There was neither a program nor a political
organization guiding or framing the working masses. The formation of a popular power did not appear under these circumstances. In this situation, the main
enemy to be fought was the parliamentary coup d'état. However, the Rousseff
government and the PT proved not to be up to the challenge. Rousseff abandoned the program she had promoted during the campaign, implemented a
heavy fiscal adjustment, and moved away from the union and popular movements. Lula only too late started participating in the protests defending the
government. He only did so after judge Sérgio Moro tried to have him arrested
and taken to Curitiba, Paraná. Dilma Rousseff only spoke in the last protest
that took place at Vale do Anhangabaú, in the city of São Paulo, in April 17, few
hours before the voting on the impeachment process started at the Federal
Chamber.

The impeachment was confirmed by the Senate in August 31. However, it is not possible to state that this will be the final crisis for neodevelopmentalism. The fate of the PT and the neodevelopmentalist program is unknown.

Why Was the Resistance to the 2016 Coup D'état so Weak?

Why, during the 2015–2016 political crisis, was President Dilma Rousseff abandoned by the social sectors that had up until then benefitted from the policies implemented by her administration?

This is a relevant question regarding, among others, the union movement, the marginal mass of workers, and also good part of Brazil's bourgeoisie. Let us try to offer some partial answers for each of these cases.[1]

We are concerned, above all, with the political dispositions present in the social segments mentioned above. We shall refer merely in passing to the strategy chosen by the Workers' Party and the Rousseff government. It is important to stress, though, that this strategy contributed to weaken the resistance to the coup d'état, for two reasons. Firstly, because the fiscal adjustment implemented by President Rousseff and by Finance Minister Joaquim Levy led to discord, of different kinds, both between the government and the workers, and between the government and the bourgeois fraction that had supported it. As mentioned before, Rousseff betrayed her campaign discourse, causing the popular and union movements to pull away from the government. It was very hard to explain to the workers that it was necessary, on the one hand, to defend the Dilma Rousseff mandate, as that meant defending democracy, and, on the other hand and at the same time, fight the socioeconomic policy enforced by that same government. Secondly, the government's strategy weakened the resistance to the coup when it chose to combat the parliamentary coup almost entirely within the state institutions, dismissing the importance of the struggle on the streets – a struggle that, ironically, the Brazilian right-wing managed to employ successfully.

1   The Internal Bourgeoisie Was Divided in the Face of the Coup

In order to obtain information on the position of the bourgeois sectors in face of the governmental policy, we can employ, with method and parsimony, the

---

1   This chapter was written in 2017.

mainstream media reports, but we should offer special attention to the big business associations' own press. Brazil's bourgeoisie is organized in official unions grouped in federations and confederations, but also in civil associations that gather more specific business segments and that play a key role in organizing and expressing their interests. We have conducted a survey of the information on the material published by the press of some important business entities during Rousseff's first term and during the years of political crisis. The survey encompassed strategic confederations, federations, unions, and civil associations of agriculture and industry – in particular the National Confederation of Industry (CNI), the Federation of Industries of the State of São Paulo (Fiesp), the National Union of the Naval and Offshore Construction and Repair Industry (Sinaval), the Brazilian Machinery Builders' Association (Abimaq), the Brazilian Association of Infrastructure and Basic Industries (Abdib), the National Confederation of Agriculture and Livestock of Brazil (CNA), and Brazilian Agribusiness Association (Abag).[2] We started off, as it was necessary and unavoidable, with some previous notions and concepts regarding the bourgeoisie and its relationship with the state.

Brazil's bourgeoisie had been maintaining varied, complex relations with international capital. There has not been a national anti-imperialist bourgeoisie in Brazil, but neither have matters ever come to a situation in which all the capitalist companies in the country were foreign or linked to international capital. There is a fraction of Brazil's bourgeoisie, the internal bourgeoisie, which, even though it antagonizes foreign capital, competes with it, disputing positions in the national economy and, to a lesser degree, in the international economy as well. The PT governments represented this bourgeois fraction, with the support of sectors of the popular classes, and the coup against the Rousseff administration was directed precisely by international capital and by the sector of Brazilian bourgeoisie associated to it, relying on the support from the upper fraction of the middle class. The remarkable, crucial fact that the Michel Temer government abandoned the (moderately) nationalist policy in favor of the oil and gas chain – a regime of exploration, refining, supply of ships, heavy equipment, etc. – serves to illustrate this thesis. Well, why did this

---

2   The survey was conducted under my guidance by scientific initiation scholarship students Rosylli Oliveira and Julia Nunes, then majoring in Economy and Earth Sciences at Unicamp, and I am thankful to both of them. The material consulted includes magazines, bulletins, and documents from the mentioned associations. See <http://www.portaldaindustria.com.br/cni>; FIESP <http://www.fiesp.com.br>; Sinaval <http://sinaval.org.br>; Abimaq <http://www.abimaq.org.br>; Abdib <https://www.abdib.org.br>; CNA <http://www.cnabrasil.org.br>; Abag <http://www.abag.com.br>.

bourgeois fraction that had been benefitted by the PT governments not come to the defense of the Rousseff administration?

The bourgeoisie and its fractions acted as pressed by specific circumstances. They did not have the clear interests, the political unity, the capacity to organize, and the freedom of action that many of the left-wing analysts assumed. In Brazil's case, the internal bourgeoisie was represented by a government organized by a political party that had not been built by the bourgeoisie itself, but that, for that very reason, had more freedom to impose some concessions upon the internal bourgeoisie, hence garnering a base of popular support. That was what made it possible for the greater interests of this fraction to prevail in face of international capital and the associated bourgeoisie. Thus was born the neodevelopmentalist political front that put an end to the hegemony enjoyed by international capital and the associated bourgeoisie in the 1990s. Reading the publications from the business associations' press allows us to see that, in the years of economic growth, when the stagnation and radical economic liberalization of the FHC governments were still a fresh memory, this bourgeois fraction accepted such concessions – appreciation of the minimum wage, cash transfer, acknowledgment of the working class's right to the demanding struggle, expansion of public service, etc. The documents from the business associations, when listing what they considered to be problems, bottlenecks, and difficulties of the Brazilian economy, did not highlight the PT governments' social policy. They accepted it, although with little enthusiasm.

The situation started to change in 2013. The relevant facts were the low economic growth, international capital's ideological offensive against the new economic policy matrix proposed by minister Guido Mantega, and, finally, the fiscal adjustment enforced during Rousseff's second term. It was in these new circumstances that the internal bourgeoisie started to see the concessions that ensured popular support to the neodevelopmentalist policy as too high a price to pay. If in 2005, during the crisis of the Lula government, the big internal bourgeoisie entered the battlefield to defend the president, the same did not happen when the Dilma Rousseff government faced its own crisis ten years later.

The researched associations linked to the industry and agriculture sectors list some demands that appeared recurrently in the course of Dilma Rousseff's entire second term and during the crisis period. Among these recurring demands, two groups stand out. The first is against the interests of international and financial capital, while the second is against those of the working class; the first prevailed in the first two years of the administration, while the second started to be highlighted by the business associations' press in 2013. In the first group of recurring demands, we have: low interest rates, depreciated exchange, public financing at subsidized interests for investments, investment in infrastructure, local content policy (protectionism), industrial policy, and others. In the second group of recurring demands, we have: social security reform, labor reform, fiscal adjustment based on the reduction of social spending and the austerity of the civil service, and others. Following the business associations' press, it becomes evident that the second group of demands gained prominence as the period of low growth and the economic crisis went on, and that the campaign of the rival bourgeois fraction for the fiscal adjustment gained strength.

The internal bourgeoisie did not move as a whole. Part of it was prosecuted in the courts, due to the fact that the articulated forces of imperialism, of the associated bourgeoisie, and of the upper middle class had used corruption as a weapon to isolate and even destroy the national companies of heavy construction and engineering; another part actively joined the coup – the most important cases are CNI and Fiesp, judging by the evidence of these associations' own press. Since 2011, the processing industry found itself in a downward path due to the influx of Chinese manufactured goods; part of the internal bourgeoisie still remained neutral in face of the crisis – that was the case of the shipbuilding industry, which, having grown by an annual rate of 19%, was reluctant to join the impeachment coup, and later campaigned against the Michel Temer government's dismantling of the local content policy.

The result, however, was a representation crisis. The represented party – the big internal bourgeoisie – no longer recognized itself in its representative – the Rousseff administration, a government that, I repeat, had been backed and cheered by this bourgeois fraction until at least 2012. The offensive for restoration of big international capital and the Brazilian bourgeois fraction associated to it, supported by the activism of the upper middle class, found then a freer path to advance.

2   The Marginal Mass of Workers Remained Passive

Brazil's dependent capitalism has always maintained a large number of workers integrated only peripherally and superficially to the strictly capitalist production. Capitalism's specific way to integrate the worker is through the payment of salaries for production and the attainment of surplus-value. Well, the peasants with little or no land, the autonomous urban workers without professional education, the street vendors, the providers of domestic service of all kinds, the underemployed, the unemployed, and others integrate Brazil's capitalism only as intermittent wage earners, as occasional autonomous vendors of goods infrequently produced by capitalist companies, or even only as consumers. They are at the fringe of the system. The neoliberal dependent capitalist model caused the marginal mass of workers to grow. Most of these workers voted for candidates from the Workers' Party to the presidency. They were the PT governments' electoral mass base.

This political relationship has nothing to do with what the liberals, their parties, and the mainstream press imagine and preach. Those workers are not citizens whose choice of vote stems from disinformation, from Lula's alleged charisma, or from cronyism. The PT governments addressed these sectors' actual interests and did it with a mass policy, and not with sporadic favors in exchange for political support, as it is typical of cronyism. Let us not forget the programs of cash transfer and supply of goods and services that benefitted the marginal mass of workers: "Family Grant," the "Continuous Benefit Program," "Light for All," "My House, My Life," "Cisterns Program" for the semiarid region, "National Program for Access to Technical Education and Employment" (Pronatec), among others. The marginal mass of workers, when offering the PT their votes, acted thus in the same way as all other classes and social groups: they voted for the candidate that addressed their interests in some way and with more or less amplitude.

In spite of this general common element, the relationship between these workers and the PT governments displayed a peculiarity. It was a populist – or to be more precise, a neopopulist – kind of relationship. We know very well that this concept is frowned upon by a good portion of left-wing intellectuals. However, let us not lose ourselves in arguments over terminology. Even though we use the word populism, we do not use the same concept (= idea) of populism employed by liberals. In their opinion, the populist politician obtains popular support by conning, deceiving, and even hypnotizing the "uneducated masses." In the populist relationship the politician must minimally address the interests of his or her social base. In Brazil's case, this interest is the income distribution that, by its popular and progressive characteristics, differentiates populism from Bonapartism, since in the latter the social base's demand is conservative.

Getúlio Vargas (1930–1945 and 1951–1954), in classic Brazilian populism, relied on the proletariat that had recently migrated from rural areas and had no organization experience – the new proletarian generation that replaced the immigrant workers of the Old Republic (1889–1930) –, amassing popular support for the developmentalist policy of industrialization. His weapon and banner was the Consolidation of Labor Laws (CLT), the legal statute that still haunts the neoliberals to this day. In the 1980s, the new unionism evidenced that the working class and other urban wage earners had more capacity for struggle and organization than the pre-1964 workers. Lula da Silva and Dilma Rousseff, to implement neopopulism, relied not on this new, more combative working class from which, ironically, Lula had come, but on the marginal mass of workers, composed by segments of working classes with low capacity to organize and exert pressure, finding then in such segments popular support to neodevelopmentalism, the policy that reformed the neoliberal capitalist model still in force in Brazil. The Brazilian populist tradition found a new seat and spoke louder than what had been initially intended by the PT's founders, who aimed, as they insistently claimed, at overcoming the Vargas era following a leftist path.

Well, the populist relation immobilizes the worker politically. A social sector with low capacity for organization, challenged from above by professional politicians or governments, becomes prisoner of what we could call a cult or fetish of the protective state. It delegates to the capitalist state, whose institutions seem to hover above the social classes, the function of "protecting the poor." It is true that a segment of the marginal mass of workers became organized and fought in movements for land and housing. This segment was indeed very active in the resistance to the coup. However, it still represented a tiny minority. Most of the marginal mass of workers was absent from the struggle and allowed the coup to happen. This group considered the state as a free, sovereign entity, which must take the initiative to protect the "poor" and whose actions should not depend on the relation of forces among social classes – and that is the reason why we also employ the expression fetish of the state.

The workers of the marginal mass were crucial to the PT candidates' victories in presidential campaigns, but these workers did not have a clear awareness of that fact. They did not realize the impact of their own vote on the national political situation; they did not understand that, if their interests depended on the PT governments, the latter in turn depended even more on the political – and not merely electoral – support from the marginal mass. And the PT displayed no interest whatsoever in changing that perception. In the moment of crisis, when the strength and (alleged) sovereignty of the PT government dissipated into thin air, the workers of the marginal mass had neither ideological conditions nor the ability to organize and move in defense of the government. The Lula and Rousseff administrations and the PT itself gave up the opportunity to organize this mass, have it overcome populism, and make it see that it should rely on its own strengths. They would not and could not seek its support in the moment of crisis.

Under classic populism, in August 1954, the political passivity of the popular segments that had been maintained under the spell of populism was transformed into its opposite and identical counterpart. Challenged by Getúlio

Vargas's poignant "will and testament" letter they erupted into the streets in great but powerless riots, and assaults against the mainstream media and U.S. consulates. Carlos Lacerda, the journalist who had headed the press campaign against Vargas, fled to Bolivia, terrified. In August 2016, Dilma Rousseff did not appeal to the people, so even this spectacle of powerless rebellion was beyond what neopopulism could offer us.

3   The Unionized Workers Were Neutralized

Three factors explain the almost absence of Brazilian unionism in the resistance to the parliamentary coup of August 31, 2016. First, Dilma Rousseff betrayed her campaign discourse. The second factor is that unionism had always occupied a subordinate position in the neodevelopmentalist political front that sustained her government. The third factor is the peculiarity of the Brazilian unionist structure and of the personnel leading the unions.

Dilma Rousseff's electoral campaign in October and November 2014 was centered in the defense of economic growth, income distribution, and criticism to the fiscal adjustment policies. The candidate did so systematically, pedagogically, and eloquently. Hers might have been the most leftist of the PT's presidential campaigns. Hence, that campaign managed to attract forces and organizations from the left – such as the Socialism and Liberty Party (PSOL) – that traditionally criticized the PT governments. As it happens, as soon as she was inaugurated, Rousseff started to implement a heavy fiscal adjustment without even bothering to offer any justification to those who had backed her candidacy. She brought into the position of finance minister an economist, Joaquim Levy, who was traditionally linked to the financial sector and who enforced cuts of all kinds, turning a situation of low growth rate into a recession. The progressive union movement started criticizing the government and pulled away from it.

The relationship between the union movement and the PT governments had never been peaceful. Its best phase was during Lula's second term (2007–2010), when the boom of commodities, the raise of the minimum wage, and the public investment advanced the economic growth. However, over the years, the PT administrations ignored historic demands made by the unions in symbolically compelling occasions, as in the case of Dilma Rousseff's rally to 40,000 unionists during the 2010 campaign at the Pacaembu Stadium, in São Paulo. These governments did not address the demand to reduce the legal workweek, to put a restrictive regulation on outsourcing, to improve the pension system for retired people, to alter brackets and percentages of the income tax, to acknowledge the public servers' right to bargain, and others. What unionism achieved was mainly an indirect victory: the economic growth and huge unemployment reduction – from 13.5% in 2003 to 4.6% in 2014 – made it possible for the union struggle at its base to become stronger and for the struggling workers to reach significant wage gains. Their direct victory, resulting from the government's deliberate actions, was the appreciation of the minimum wage, which saw an actual 75% rise between 2003 and 2012.

Finally, it is necessary to keep in mind that the Brazilian union movement is dependent on the state. This structure started to be put together during Getúlio Vargas's first term in office (1930–1934), on the same decade in which Salazar in Portugal and Franco in Spain implemented state unionism in the Iberian Peninsula. In Brazil, to this day, a union, to be recognized as such, must obtain an authorization, the "state union letter." Once that letter is obtained, the union can negotiate in name of a segment of workers that is specified in that letter. Moreover, it will do it in a regime of legal monopoly of representation – union unicity – and will have access to the forbidden fruit that every union covets: the abundant financial resources from the mandatory contribution from all workers, unionized or not, that flow regularly into the official union coffers.

Thanks to this structure, the government can intervene meticulously and systematically in the union life: it hands out union letters according to its own interests, controls the use of the unions' finances and elections, and interferes through the courts, deposing or suspending union directors. The political results are important: Brazil has an increasingly growing number of increasingly smaller unions; a large percentage of union leaders are actually state agents at the core of the working class' demanding movement – such leaders are popularly called *pelegos*, which is a layer of lamb skin that gauchos traditionally place over the saddle to offer more comfort to the horse rider –, and there is a huge distance between the leaderships, castled in this system, and the base. At the moment of the coup, we saw all sorts of things: *pelegos'* union centrals supporting the parliamentary coup, leaders of progressive union centrals afraid to suffer interference from the state if they politically mobilized their bases against the coup, and progressive unionists displaying surprise at the bases' negative reaction when they were asked to mobilize. The overall result was disastrous to the left wing. The leadership of three progressive union centrals – the Unified Workers' Central (CUT), the Men and Women Workers' Central of Brazil (CTB), and Intersindical – mobilized against the parliamentary coup. This leadership supplied the resistance with financial resources, logistical support, and means of communication. However, the base unions remained silent, did not show up, neither did they mobilize the workers. In the protests against the parliamentary coup, we had the student movement, some popular movements – such those demanding land and housing –, and progressive sectors of the middle class, but we did not see oil workers, metalworkers, bank clerks, civil construction workers, in short, we did not see there any strong, active sector of the union movement.

The right wing won the street struggle by a landslide. Their protests for Rousseff's impeachment displayed a far superior number of people than those present in the demonstrations defending the elected president's mandate.

4   After the Coup

Having consummated the coup in August 31, 2016, when president Dilma Rousseff, suspended from office since April 17, was irrevocably deposed, these same actors started to display specific complaints about or open opposition to the Michel Temer government.

The businesspersons from the productive sector, through their associations, began to criticize the fiscal adjustment, the reduction and increase in price of credit, the new wave of trade liberalization, and even started to escalate the controversy to a doctrinaire level, criticizing the administration's "ultraliberalism." Both the president and the vice-president of Fiesp, an entity that had championed the coup campaign, published successive articles on the mainstream media condemning the economic policy of the Temer government, particularly the end of the local content policy. None of that meant they had moved to the opposition, though.

The unionists, facing the deep, broad policy to remove their rights – the projects for labor reform and social security reform of the Michel Temer government – began to mobilize. With the popular movements' essential collaboration, they managed to organize a meaningful general strike on April 28, 2017. But it was too late by then. The labor reform, which revoked pillars of Brazilian labor laws, was approved. Moreover, neither the union movement nor the popular movement managed, up to the moment when we write this, to demonstrate enough strength to resist the reactionary policy displayed by the whole of the Temer administration.

What about the workers of the marginal mass? These received a "visit" from Lula. It was the "Lula's Caravan for Brazil," with which the former president traveled through the nine states of the Northeast region. There, Lula was embraced by the crowds, offered speeches promising better days, and terrified all the reactionaries by showing off his enormous popularity. He practiced neopopulism, which relies on the workers of the marginal mass, unlike Getúlio

Vargas's populism, which relied on the young working class that had just migrated from the rural areas. In all polls, he was then the favorite candidate to win the 2018 presidential election. Only the legal persecution of which he had been victim could prevent him from becoming the only progressive candidate with good chances to win the runoff.

Afterword

Bolsonaro and the Rise of Neofascism

The current political situation in Brazil is very peculiar if compared to that of the other Latin American countries, and this peculiarity refers to the right-wing radicalism of the Bolsonaro government.[1] The president and his entourage openly defend the implementation of a dictatorship in Brazil, the use of torture as a method to repress left-wing supporters, the perpetuation of women and black people in a subordinate position in Brazilian society, and traditional sexual morality. The Bolsonaro government combines this concept, which, as we will discuss ahead, we characterize as fascist, with radicalized neoliberalism, thus creating a situation that, while not unique in the world, is unusual when we consider Brazil's recent political history.

Since the mid-2010s, Latin America has seen the rise of conservative, neoliberal, authoritarian governments, with different combinations of these traits according to the country in question. While in Chile and Argentina the neoliberals and conservatives came to power through popular vote, in Brazil this occurred through a coup d'état that deposed Dilma Rousseff in 2016, during the first half of her second term. As many are aware, it was a coup that met the new standard, as it had happened with Paraguayan President Fernando Lugo in 2012, i. e. a plot that formally followed some legal rules and procedures while, in terms of content, disrespected them either openly or covertly. The entire impeachment process against Dilma Rousseff was based on an unusual, extravagant interpretation of the Fiscal Responsibility Law, which is part of the legislation that seeks to perpetuate the neoliberalist socioeconomic policy. Such interpretation of the law allowed the framing as a crime of responsibility – punishable with impeachment – of a trivial accounting procedure of the Rousseff administration and, more importantly, a procedure that the presidents that preceded her, not to mention several state governors, had adopted without being bothered by the Legislative branch.

This coup d'état, due to its consequences and the dynamics that made it possible, changed the Brazilian political process profoundly. It put in motion conservative, antidemocratic forces so far dormant, robbed the popular vote of its credibility, prompted the return of the military as prominent political

---

1   This afterword to the English edition is a modified version of an article I wrote in November 2020 for the magazine published by the Latin American and Caribbean Observatory (OLAC) of the Institute of Latin American and Caribbean Studies (IEALC).

actors, led to an extreme judicialization of political conflicts, encouraged
dissension between state branches and institutions, and discredited democracy. It was the professional bourgeois politicians in the Legislative and state
Executive branches who took the initiative to discredit the popular vote when
they nullified the results of the presidential election of October 2014, won by
Dilma Rousseff. By discrediting the source of their own legitimacy, the professional bourgeois politicians opened the doors so that the civil bureaucracy –
particularly the Judiciary bureaucracy – and the military bureaucracy – mainly
the Army – could become prominent political actors. These political parties
lost ground in Brazilian politics.

   The current president, Jair Bolsonaro, was elected via a micro party previously devoid of any relevance in national politics and, until June 2020, he
antagonized the National Congress and showed no interest whatsoever in organizing a support base for his government among senators and representatives.
He surrounded himself with the military – today, it is estimated that around
nine thousand Armed Forces officials occupy first- and second-tier positions in
Bolsonaro's cabinet. During the first semester of 2020, the president repeatedly
threatened the National Congress and the Federal Supreme Court (STF), even
speaking several times at street demonstrations organized by far-right-wing
groups that demanded both institutions to be shut down. None of that was
considered a crime of responsibility by the National Congress. Representative
Rodrigo Maia, president of Congress and member of Democrats (DEM) – a
party born from the former political wing of the military dictatorship –, halted
the proceedings of countless requests for Bolsonaro's impeachment, requests
based on the fact that the president was publicly and blatantly threatening the
democratic institutions in flagrant disrespect for the Brazilian Constitution. In
turn, the Legislative branch and STF pressured the president to obtain a conciliation pact, an endeavor in which they were successful. Cornered and defeated,
the popular, democratic movement merely observes the development of the
situation.

   We shall see by the end of this chapter the evolution of the Brazilian political situation, which moved from the escalation of the conflict between the
fascist right and the traditional right to a conciliation pact between these two
forces. Before that, we shall explain why we characterize Bolsonarism as a variation of fascism, whose interests the Bolsonaro government represents, and
how a neofascist group managed to rise to power. In this journey, we will alter-
nate between two movements. On the one hand, we will analyze the Brazilian
political situation, trying to contribute to the understanding of this current
moment in Brazil and Latin America. On the other hand, though, we will also
help to develop the concept of fascism, employing, in this case, the Brazilian

circumstances as our main example. Hence this afterword has two distinct goals, and we hope this duality will not confuse the reader.

1   When Can We Speak of Fascism?

We will present a few controversial statements to clarify our position to the reader. Many authors refuse to employ the concept of fascism to characterize any present-day far-right line of thought. This refusal stems from motivations and arguments that vary according to each author and each theory tradition.

In this debate, there is the empirical, historicist refusal to employ the concept of fascism to current days. Emilio Gentile, a renowned historian who has studied Italian fascism, believes fascism is a movement and a political regime that occurred in Italy between 1919 – when the fascist movement was created – and 1945 – when this regime was overthrown for good. Gentile is an empiricist. He denies the distinction between concept and historical phenomenon. He states that the concept of fascism is the very history of fascism, which had no predecessors in the nineteenth century, neither will it be replicated in the twenty-first century (Gentile, 2019).[2] If we were to accept the full identification between concept and historical fact contained in this statement, that would keep us from using other concepts like, for instance, democracy and dictatorship in characterizing different democracies and dictatorships that we have known through history. Political science would become impossible. Another empiricist variation of the refusal to employ the concept of fascism to describe any present-day far-right line of thought is found in authors like Enzo Traverso (2019a and 2019b). Traverso speaks of "post-fascism," selecting a few characteristics of the original fascism and discussing whether these are present in the present-day extreme right. He draws a positive conclusion for some of these characteristics and a negative one for others. This procedure, if conceived as a baseline and a mere tool to identify a problem, might be somewhat useful, but it is erroneous if conceived as the very process of characterizing the studied phenomenon. To select traits of the fascist political phenomenon, we do not begin with historical facts in the raw, as it would be impossible to do so. We always begin with historical data and, at the same time, with some generalities or a systematic theory. Therefore, what we select, the relation between different selected traits, which is primary and which is secondary – all of that

---

2   "The definition of fascism is its history. (...) a twentieth-century phenomenon, which had no predecessors, neither will it be replicated in the future." (Gentile, 2019, our translation.).

also depends on the theory we employ. Traverso, conversely, makes a sort of accounting operation: he claims that the current far-right would have a larger or smaller portion of fascist characteristics and that other parts would be new. Next, he presents the would-be solution of resorting to the term "post-fascism" – a term that means strictly nothing. The reader might make the effort to analyze the results to which this method would lead if applied by Biology in identifying and characterizing species.

Let us focus now on the field of Marxism. There we also find authors who refuse to apply the concept of fascism to the current reality. Here we restrict ourselves to the incorrect thesis, for reasons we shall indicate, to speak of fascism in dependent countries. To our way of thinking, the misconception here consists of blending form of state, political regime, and bloc in power. We must distinguish these three concepts to address this matter properly. Now consider the concepts of form of state and political regime. The former refers to dictatorship and democracy, while the latter refers to the characteristics of the institutions and of the political process inside a certain form of state – presidentialist democracy, parliamentarist democracy, military dictatorship, fascist dictatorship, etc. Thus, both refer to the institutional organization of the state and the political game. The concept of bloc in power, in turn, refers to the classes and class fractions that wield the power of the state in a certain form of state or in any political regime. The proof that the institutional organization of power – form of state and the political regime – and the forces that wield the power – bloc in power, political hegemony – are two dimensions that must be considered separately, each in its specificity, and in its relative autonomy in face of the other, is that such dimensions allow variable combinations, even though they are not random combinations. The same kind of dictatorship – for example, the military dictatorship – or of democracy – such as a parliamentarist democracy based on a non-polarized multiparty system – can comprise various blocs in power and various hegemonic bourgeois fractions.

Fascism must be considered, first and foremost, as a particular sort of dictatorship, that is, a specific dictatorial regime. Implicitly or explicitly, the vast majority of those who study fascism agree with this idea. Well, within certain limits, the bloc in power and the hegemonic fraction in this sort of dictatorship may vary.[3] In the original fascism, the hegemonic bourgeois fraction was the big imperialist bourgeoisie; in a dependent country, fascism may, on the contrary,

---

3   We say "within certain limits" because, in the case of fascism, it is a dictatorship born from a reactionary mass movement that, for this very reason, will always be an anti-popular regime. The same does not necessarily occur with the military dictatorships. There were progressive military dictatorships during the bourgeois revolutions in all continents (Boito Jr., 2020).

organize the hegemony of the imperialist foreign capital and of the associated fraction of the local bourgeoisie subordinated to this capital.[4] Ergo, neoliberalism, the political program that extends the opening of dependent economies to imperialist capital, and fascism, a particular sort of dictatorship, are not, in spite of what some authors claim, mutually exclusive phenomena. As we intend to show, the Bolsonaro government is both neofascist and neoliberal.

The Marxist authors who accepted the task of building a general, theoretical concept of fascism, and on whose works we sought inspiration, are Palmiro Togliatti (2019 [1970]), Leon Trotsky (1968), Dimitrov (1935), Gramsci (1978), Daniel Guérin (1965 [1936]), and Nicos Poulantzas (1970). We chose not to reproduce exactly the concept of any of them. This way, we work with a concept of fascism that comprises the form of the state (dictatorship), the political regime (the organized mass base), and a particular aspect of the social composition of the bloc in power (its anti-popular character). In Palmiro Togliatti's polished formula, fascism is "a reactionary regime of the mass." Starting with this precious realization, we shall see why the Bolsonaro administration must be considered a fascist government.

2   Bolsonarism Is One of the Species of the Fascism Genre

Fascism is a particular sort of bourgeois dictatorship as well as the movement and ideology that defend and justify this dictatorship. The Bolsonarist movement in Brazil is a fascist movement that occupies a dominant position in the current government. What we still lack in Brazil is a fascist dictatorship. We have a bourgeois democracy facing crisis and decay.

---

4 We thus disagree with Atilio Boron, who, in an important article published in the 1970s during the great Latin American debate about military dictatorships, cited the fact that Latin American countries are devoid of an imperialist bourgeoisie as one of the reasons why one could not speak of fascism when referring to such countries. Just like João Quartim de Moraes, who also spoke in that historical debate, Boron offered decisive arguments that allowed the characterization of such dictatorships as a political phenomenon of a new sort: a) the control of the state by the Armed Forces, and b) the merely passive, diffuse support from part of the working classes to the dictatorial regime, instead of an active, organized support. However, the argument concerning the formation of the bloc in power seems, for the reasons we have mentioned, unfounded (Boron, 2003 [1974]), (Moraes, 1971). Boron and Moraes debated the issue with authors such as Cueva (1977) and Santos (1977), both of whom sustained that the Southern Cone dictatorships of the 1970s were fascist dictatorships. A brief overview of this debate can be found in Trindade (1982).

The fascist movement is a reactionary movement based on the petit-bourgeoisie and the middle class. The Bolsonarist movement was born as a mass movement from the large street demonstrations that took over the country in 2015 and 2016 calling for Dilma Rousseff's deposition. It is a reactionary movement of the middle class and, more precisely, of the upper fraction of the middle class. It also comprises small owners – the very organized segment of autonomous truck drivers was fascist right from its inception. Isabela Kalil, an anthropologist who for three years has been researching the right-wing protestors in Brazil based on interviews conducted during street demonstrations, tallied 11 key elements present in the discourse of Jair Bolsonaro and his supporters: 1. anti-corruption, 2. anti-communism, 3. anti-PT, 4. anti-left, 5. anti-feminism, 6. anti-politicians, 7. anti-parties, 8. anti-abortion, 9. anti-homosexuality, 10. anti-privileges, 11. anti-system. (Kalil, 2019). These are typical themes of the fascist discourse, both of the original fascism and the current one, once taken into consideration, obviously, the particularities of each one. For example, anti-feminism and prejudice against the LGBT population are more pronounced in the current fascism, given that nowadays the feminist and LGBT struggle is stronger than at the beginning of the twentieth century. Also, in its form, this discourse is, just like in the original fascism, a contrarian discourse, in which a negative dimension prevails – a characteristic that Norberto Bobbio claims to be standard in the fascist ideology discourse (Bobbio, 1997).

It is true that during the 2018 campaign, Jair Bolsonaro's candidacy gathered support from popular sectors, due to various reasons: the passionate support from Pentecostal and Neopentecostal churches, motivated by conservative customs, as numbers show that it was the Evangelical vote that led to the far-right candidate's victory (Ronaldo Almeida, 2019); the feeling of insecurity of those living in the outskirts neighborhoods, frequent victims of the organized crime; the long, intense, conservative political manipulation of the corruption in the Brazilian state; the exploitation by the far-right of the anti-system discourse, which had been abandoned by most of the Brazilian left. However, that support was moderate and limited to the campaign. Bolsonarism's true core remained in the middle class and among small owners (Prandi, 2019; Cavalcante, 2020), which is what characterizes the fascist mass movement.[5] Through its political leaderships, hundreds of digital influencers, and the

---

5   "Still in July 2016, when Lula had 22% of the intended votes, Bolsonaro (then still a member of the PSC) appeared in fourth in the polls, with 7%. However, he was already in first place (19%) among those receiving between 5 and 10 times the minimum wage (MWs) and those receiving more than 10 MWs (16%). Although with a high rejection rate among the same tiers, in September 2018 Bolsonaro led Haddad (PT), 40% to 15% in both segments, and 34% to 14% among voters with a college degree. On the eve of the runoff (October 27, 2018), vote intentions (Bolsonaro vs Haddad) by segments were: 55% to 37% (men), 41% to

organized groups that constitute it, such as the group called "Brazil's Three Hundred," this movement openly states that its main enemy is communism – or Bolivarianism – and sets for itself the goal of eliminating the left from the national political process. Bolsonaro himself, already as a candidate in 2018, announced in a public, insistent, threatening manner that in his administration the left would either be sent to jail or to exile.

Another observation regarding the issue of the fascist ideology: it is a petit-bourgeois ideology, as classical Marxist authors have argued. Most often, though, these authors highlight a few petit-bourgeois elements of this ideology but do not attempt to detect its fundamental characteristic, leaving a lot to be desired when they relate it to the kind of political crisis and social base that generates fascism. About this subject, we resort to a non-Marxist author that obviously examines the issues from the perspective of a different theory, but who provides a hypothesis that, if rectified, can be seized in a Marxist analysis of fascism. I refer to the above-mentioned thesis by Norberto Bobbio about the fundamentally negative, destructive character of the fascist ideology (Bobbio, 1997).

> Firstly, that fascism, more than anti-ideological, as it chose to present itself right from the start, has been the bearer of a negative or destructive ideology, in which hate is more prominent than love, negation abounds more than affirmation, so much so that Mussolini himself was led to state that in its early years fascism was not a party but an "anti-party," and this has been reiterated several times, as well as proven in several occasions.
>
> BOBBIO, 1997, 3, our translation

∴

> Fascism is received, evaluated, and judged not so much for the few, confusing, and frequently contradictory positive solutions that it proposed, but for its countless "no's" to this or that aspect of society, politics, economics, and the mentality of those days.
>
> BOBBIO, 1997, quoting DE FELICE, 1966, 18, our translation

42% (women), 35% to 49% (up to 2 MW s), 54% to 34% (between 2 and 5 MW s), 63% to 28% (between 5 and 10 MW s); 62% to 31% (over 10 MW s), and 55% to 34% (college degree). In August 2019, the income segments that most approve of the president's performance (excellent and good) remain being those between 5 and 10 MW s (39%) and over 10 MW s (37%). All data are from Datafolha electoral polls." (Cavalcante, 2020).

According to our analysis, the negative character of the fascist ideology results from the hegemonic inability of the petit-bourgeoisie and the middle class in the circumstances in which fascism is born – and, by saying so, we already rectify the hypothesis we imported from Bobbio to apply it in the Marxist camp. Hegemonic inability? How to characterize it? We are not saying that both the aforementioned social classes are congenitally incapable of conducting any political process. We are only asserting that these classes, given their socioeconomic insertion, have more difficulty to occupy a hegemonic position, and that this difficulty appears as a clear hegemonic inability in the circumstances in which the fascist movements are born. That is why the petit-bourgeois fascist movement never succeeded in taking over the government or enforcing a dictatorial regime without previously wielding control to the bourgeoisie, or, in other words, without previously being politically co-opted by the bourgeoisie. The fascist social movement is petit-bourgeois and of the middle class, but the government and the fascist dictatorship are bourgeois.[6]

And how to characterize this hegemonic inability? Precisely by the fact that the fascist movement is very clear and sure in defining its enemies – communism understood in a vast sense, the bourgeois democracy, feminism –, but, at the same time, is rather vague and confusing in defining what it intends to put in their place. And why? Because what it intends to put in their place is a reactionary, inviable utopia, and the fascists sense this inviability. They long for a capitalist society with no organized labor or popular movements, having women return to the confinement of domestic work, making the LGBT community become invisible once more, and so on. Hence its irrationalism and negationism. Who aspires to the impossible needs to deny reality and objective knowledge. The negationism of the current federal government is flagrant in its attitude toward the Covid-19 pandemic, the ludicrous theses suggesting the Earth is flat, and others. Those are tormented petit-bourgeois and middle-class workers – understanding the term "tormented" or "desperate" as a practical notion indicating the following sociopolitical situation: they feel a social malaise, but do not understand its causes and, moreover, they do not know how to overcome it. They are easy prey to the co-optation by the bourgeoisie. A fascist government or dictatorship does not meet the social or economic interests of fascism's support base, but the interests of the bourgeoisie and particularly of

---

6 The Italian Social Republic, better known as the Republic of Salò, is an exception that confirms the rule. In this last stage of the already weakened and territorially mutilated Italian fascist regime, the petit-bourgeois fascist movement became mostly free of the Italian bourgeois authority, but that was only achieved because it submitted to the authority of Hitler's occupying troops (De Vito, 2020).

the hegemonic bourgeois fraction in the bloc in power. As Poulantzas observed, the petit bourgeoisie is one of the first victims of the fascist socioeconomic policy and starts "living off ideologies" (Poulantzas, 1970). In our attempt to analyze the fascist ideology, the causal chain works as follows: petit-bourgeois and middle-class malaise as they perceive the threat of socioeconomic decline and destructuring of the patriarchal ideology with which they organized their social universe; utopian reactionary restoration aspirations; irrationalism and negationism of (adverse) reality to hide to their own eyes the inviability of their ambitions – the fascist irrationalism –; and, as a result of such negationism, the prevailing negative, destructive attitude.

The current Brazilian fascist movement does not have a mass party. Brazil lacks this tradition. The Brazilian Integralist Action (AIB) in the 1930s, the Communist Party in the 1940s, and the Workers' Party in the 1980s started on a journey in that direction, but soon deviated or were forced to deviate from that path – the PCB was declared illegal in 1947, as soon as the Cold War began. What present-day fascism in Brazil does have is a mobilized reactionary social base, thus displaying the key element that defines the fascist phenomenon. This social base is mobilized through digital media, particularly social media (Filgueiras & Druck, 2020). Bolsonarism has hundreds of digital influencers and follows an ideologue, the author Olavo de Carvalho, indisputably the movement's main intellectual. He lives in the United States, but, through online courses teaching philosophy and politics, he has mentored thousands of intellectuals and activists of the movement. His work goes back to the 1990s. In 2002, he created the *Mídia sem Máscara* (Unmasked Media) website, which has since then been a permanent, well-known source of fascist indoctrination (Patschiki, 2012). Other institutions, like the Borborema Institute, offer conservative and/or fascist education courses.

This network of organization and ideological education debates the paths taken by the government and successfully pressures Bolsonaro into taking certain political decisions, managing even to get ministers appointed or deposed. All of this is a regular part of the routine of the Bolsonaro administration and is followed attentively by the mainstream press. As we write this, Bolsonaro has just created a great political conflict, involving even the military group in his government, in order to meet the interests of his social base. Pressured by this base through social media, he nullified an agreement his administration had made with the state of São Paulo for the production and distribution in Brazil of a vaccine against the new coronavirus. The campaign against the agreement stemmed from the fact that it involved a Chinese lab, which has created the vaccine and holds its patent. The Bolsonarists believe the virus was produced at a lab in China as part of a communist plan to dominate the world. They do not wish China to profit now from the evil it allegedly caused. The fascist intellectual Percival Puggina addressed the issue in an article titled "*Vacina chinesa, não*" ("No to the Chinese vaccine") on the *Mídia sem Máscara* website (Puggina, 2020). Many also believe that the Chinese vaccine is the second stage of their plan: the vaccine would insert in people's bodies a microchip implant that would allow China to control the population of the world." It has become commonplace for the Bolsonaro administration to withdraw from a previously made decision due to pressure from the base through social media. The government's communication with its base through social media is thus a method to mobilize politics and the government that has been employed systematically by Bolsonaro. Even without a mass party, the fascist movement is active and influential on political decisions.

3   The Bolsonaro Government and the Originating Political Crisis

Since his inauguration as president in 2019, Bolsonaro has made sure to form a government with neofascist leaders. This fascist group not only held the presidency of the Republic, but also controlled the Ministries of Foreign Relations, Education, Citizenship, and Environment. These offices were handed to Olavo de Carvalho's former students, conservative Evangelicals, and members of the right that migrated to the fascist movement. Next to them, there is the military group at the government's top levels, most of them from the Army, reformed, and ranked as generals. They are from the extremist wing of the military dictatorship – its so-called "hard line." The fascists and the military form a top tier of the government, do not hide their anti-democratic opinions, and openly defend the dictatorship and the torturers of the old dictatorial regime. Both president Bolsonaro and vice-president General Mourão have defended on several occasions, both verbally and through writings in the mainstream press, one of the main figures responsible for the torture system implemented in Brazil: General Brilhante Ustra, a torturer himself. Bolsonaro assigned for the Ministry of Finance Paulo Guedes, a banker and ultraliberal economist with a PhD from the University of Chicago, where he studied under Milton Fredman. Hence, there we have a composite governmental cabinet: fascists, military, and neoliberals connected to the traditional right. It is important to emphasize that this heterogeneity of the governmental cabinet does not pull the Bolsonaro administration from the pattern of fascist governments. These were never "full-blooded fascist" governments. They always relied on the participation of the traditional right (Paxton, 2004). And this heterogeneous composition is part, in a manner of speaking, of the fascist governments' DNA: fascism as a movement is different from fascism in government, and it is precisely this metamorphosis that demands a political composition. Let us study this further.

Just like the original fascism, Brazilian fascism is, as we have mentioned, a petit-bourgeois and middle-class movement. In order to rise to the government, this movement depended, just like the original fascism did, on an external, superior force to pave the way for its arrival. In Germany and Italy in the first decades of the twentieth century, this force was those countries' monopolist, imperialist fraction of the bourgeoisie. In terms of the economy, the monopolist capital had already prevailed in face of the middle capital of the competitive period; as for the politics, however, the monopolist capital had not yet succeeded in controlling the social, economic, and foreign policy of the state, that is, still had not obtained the political hegemony inside the bloc in power. It rose to the condition of hegemonic fraction when it co-opted the fascist petit-bourgeois movement and turned it into a tool of its hegemony. We should add that it was never a completely passive tool. Young Gramsci called attention to this fact, and Nicos Poulantzas qualified it theoretically by stating that the petit-bourgeoisie is pushed away from the status of driving force of the fascist movement to a position of subordinate but active force, merely as a support-class of such regimes.[7] In Brazil during the second half of the 2010s, the external, superior force that co-opted the fascist petit-bourgeois and middle-class movement was the imperialist capital and the Brazilian bourgeoisie fraction integrated into it, the associated bourgeoisie.

The alliance between imperialism and this bourgeois fraction had been the hegemonic force in the bloc in power in the 1990s under the Fernando Henrique Cardoso administrations (1995–2002). Its program was the instauration in Brazil of the neoliberal capitalist economic model that already predominated in the main countries of Latin America: trade liberalization, financial deregulation, privatizations, withdrawing of labor rights. In terms of political parties, the so-called Brazilian Social Democracy Party (PSDB), Cardoso's party, which, we should inform the foreign readers, never had anything to do with social-democratic parties, was the vanguard of this program in Brazil. There was a bourgeois fraction that competed with the associated bourgeoisie. It was the fraction that we have called the big internal bourgeoisie, freely employing a concept advanced by Nicos Poulantzas (1974). It was composed

---

7   Young Gramsci wrote an article titled "La caduta del fascismo" and published in *L'Ordine Nuovo* of November 15, 1924: "At the base of everything is the problem of fascism itself, a movement that the bourgeoisie considered a simple 'tool' of reaction in its hands and that, instead, once evoked and unleashed, is worse than the devil and allows no one to master it, forging ahead by its own volition." (Gramsci, 1978, 264, our translation).

of big companies, mostly national ones, from the banking, industrial, agricultural, and commercial segments that, although united to imperialist, also competed with it. This big internal bourgeoisie occupied, under the Cardoso administrations, a subordinate position in the bloc in power. In the course of the 1990s, the conflicts of the big internal bourgeoisie regarding key aspects of the neoliberal platform were exacerbated. This process occurred *pari passu* with another process that was taking place outside the bloc in power.

The Workers' Party, which had a program of structural reforms for the Brazilian society and economy, after being defeated in two consecutive presidential elections, gradually weakened this program until it was converted, in the second half of the 1990s, into a moderate developmentalist program. The big internal bourgeoisie, from the right, and the PT, from the left, both stepped towards the center, and ended up finding themselves in close positions at the end of the 1990s and beginning of the 2000s. The PT then managed to constitute the governments we call neodevelopmentalist – the developmentalist policy that is possible within the boundaries of the neoliberal capitalist model that the PT governments decided to maintain. This path chosen by the PT displeased the left, but it displeased much more imperialism and the associated bourgeoisie whose hegemony was gradually replaced by the hegemony of the big internal bourgeoisie. That is the setting behind the coup that had Dilma Rousseff impeached in 2016. This coup was the last act of a long political offensive to restore the associated bourgeoisie and imperialism, and against the PT's neodevelopmentalist governments.

With the Michel Temer administration (2016–2018) began an aggressive neoliberal policy whose objective was to dismantle what had been built during the Lula (2003–2010) and Rousseff (2011–2016) governments. He approved a labor reform that mutilated labor rights in Brazil (Krein, 2018) and a constitutional amendment that froze for twenty years and in concrete terms the state's spending in social investment and policies. It was the end of the cycle of the PT's neodevelopmentalist governments, the end of the hegemony of the big internal bourgeoisie, and the end of the neodevelopmentalist political front that the PT administrations had built by engaging the popular classes and that had led to improvements in the living conditions of its various segments.

However, the associated bourgeoisie, having risen to power through the 2016 coup d'état, had a serious problem ahead: it lacked a competitive candidate for the 2018 presidential election. The big bourgeois press, thus far very excited about the neoliberal reforms implemented by the Temer government – such as the approval of the labor reform and the constitutional amendment that limits state spending (except for the refinancing of the public debt) –, published countless alarmist articles about the risk that the 2018 presidential election might represent to the continuation of the neoliberal economic pol-icy. In other words, the bourgeoisie started to perceive democracy as a burden and danger. When the Judiciary and the Armed Forces jointly condemned Lula without proof and kept him from running for president, they sought out a solu-tion for the troubling problem of the popular vote that frightened the bour-geoisie so dreadfully. This was the first step. The big bourgeoisie would take the second and decisive step by its own volition. It made a point of getting rid of its own candidates. A few months before the election, it had become clear that neither Geraldo Alckmin (PSDB) nor Henrique Meirelles (MDB), the candi-dates of the most important and traditional bourgeois parties, had any chance of winning. The official vote count would confirm the polls. Put together, the votes for Geraldo Alckmin and Henrique Meirelles did not surpass 6% of the total in the first round of the 2018 elections. The situation was quite similar to the sort of political crisis that precedes the rise of fascist governments.

In reality, the most important elements of the Brazilian political crisis repro-duced, in new historical conditions, the sort of political crisis that, according to Poulantzas's description, generates fascist governments (Poulantzas, 1970). Firstly, circumstances marked by a series of defeats for the labor and popu-lar movement and by this movement's resulting defensive attitude. The orig-inal fascism was not a direct, immediate response to the threat of revolution (Guérin, 1965); it was set in power in the wake of conservative governments that preceded it and paved the way for its ascension. In Brazil, this series of defeats was represented by the deposition of the Rousseff government, the legal persecution against Lula, his arrest, and the invalidation of his presiden-tial candidacy, all of it accomplished in the clearest lawfare style, while the popular movement lacked the strength to fight back accordingly. Secondly, the upsurge of a petit-bourgeois and middle-class reactionary, conservative (in terms of customs), anti-communist mass movement – the fascist movement itself. Thirdly, the escalation of quarrels within the bloc in power, which, in Brazil, was represented by the political offensive for restoration by the asso-ciated bourgeoisie, which did not hesitate to break with democracy to depose the government that represented first and foremost, even though not exclu-sively, the interests of its rival bourgeois fraction. Fourthly, an element partic-ularly stressed by Poulantzas, the crisis of representativeness and the electoral decline of the traditional bourgeois parties. We have already spoken of the latter. As for representativeness, a big businessman has perhaps encapsulated the general sentiment of his peers: "We need a fighter pilot; not Alckmin, who is a mere passenger plane pilot." The fighter pilot they sought was called Jair Bolsonaro.

Only in face of the situation presented above – in which the traditional parties are no longer useful and there is a reactionary mass movement marked
by a notorious hegemonic inability – do one or more fractions need and are
able to accomplish the complex political operation, not without its risks, of
co-opting the fascist movement to impose or recover the previously lost political hegemony. In this situation, they decide to "summon the devil," as young
Gramsci wrote.

The imperialist capital and the big associated bourgeoisie plunged into this
risky political operation in 2018. They have been successful up to now. The
Minister of Finance Paulo Guedes has maintained and radicalized the neoliberal socioeconomic policy inherited from the Temer government (Bastos,
2019). He has imposed a new neoliberal reform of social welfare and opened
the national economy even further. He has not managed to move as far as he
had intended in the process to privatize the remaining state companies. In
terms of foreign policy, the Bolsonaro government remains passive and subordinate to U.S. policy (Berringer, Carneiro, Soprijo, Souza & Barros, 2020). The
Bolsonaro administration is so intent on pleasing Trump that it does not hesitate in antagonizing China, the main commercial partner of Brazilian capitalism. The big internal bourgeoisie, now subordinate in the bloc in power, levels
occasional criticisms against a few political measures of the government, but
its support prevails: the Bolsonaro administration, aside from reforming social
welfare, is revoking labor rights in quick succession. In the current phase, it is
the unity of the bourgeois camp that has predominated.

4 Fascism and Bourgeoisie: Unity, Conflicts, and Conciliation

Bolsonaro's neofascist government is bourgeois and neoliberal, but its active
social support base is petit-bourgeois and of the middle class. Unlike the bourgeoisie, these intermediate layers of society do not have a solid commitment
to neoliberalism. In reality, they have other priorities, and that upsets the
bourgeoisie's control over the government, given that it was these social layers'
movement that made it possible for imperialism and the associated bourgeoisie to regain control over the Federal Executive branch. The Bolsonaro administration is thus marked by a characteristic set of conflicts. These are the four
most prevalent: a) the conflict between the big bourgeoisie, which prioritizes
new and deeper neoliberal reforms, and the fascist group within the government, which has other priorities; b) the conflict between the fascist group
within the government, which understands that the big bourgeoisie's support
is key to remain in power, and the social base of the fascist movements, which

does not easily accept some of the measures the government has taken to meet the interests of the big bourgeoisie; c) the conflicts between the government and democratic institutions; d) the conflicts within the governmental staff which partly express the previously mentioned conflicts and partly represent the difference between the fascist and the military groups, the latter being anti-democratic, but also averse to mass mobilization and the so-called cultural war waged by the fascists. The popular and democratic movement, having been defeated and assuming now a defensive stance, does not have any relevant participation in the main political conflicts in the current circumstances. It is important to note that the landscape of conflicts described above is similar to the typical landscape of a fascist government, a landscape that must be understood as an integral part of the very concept of fascism.

Let us examine how these relationships and conflicts have developed in the Brazilian situation. Although it is but a temporary situation, a reflection about it may transcend the current moment. It can contribute much to display basic characteristics of fascism in general and this particular brand of fascism in power in Brazil.

The social welfare reform was, in the course of 2019, the bourgeoisie's main goal. The mainstream press and all the bourgeois parties were committed to getting the reform approved, but the president was not. Minister of Finance Paulo Guedes and his staff devised the reform project, president Bolsonaro sent it to the National Congress and, afterward, washed his hands off it. The press started to denounce the president's political omission. The president of the Chamber of Representatives took for himself, publically and ostensively, the command of the struggle for the approval of this new measure against the workers. As for Bolsonaro, he devoted the year to other concerns and objectives.[8]

He chose the fight against communism, conceived in rather broad and gross terms, as his main concern. He started to promote the political and ideological turn of the Brazilian state in the international setting, a turn that includes

---

8   Another reform that the big bourgeoisie demands from the government is the administrative reform. Bolsonaro postponed this project as much as he could. Eventually, under considerable pressure, he ended up sending to the National Congress a project the press considered too timid. Remember that Bolsonaro, during most of the years in which he served as a federal representative, defended state companies and was very distant from the concept of a neoliberal economic policy. In the 2018 campaign, he had to name Paulo Guedes in advance for the Ministry of Finance in order to obtain the support of the big bourgeoisie, which did not – and still does not – trust his conversion to neoliberalism. At least in one key aspect of the neoliberal policy Bolsonaro has shown to be a believer and acts accordingly: the social policy of suppressing labor rights.

measures that do not please a large portion of the Brazilian bourgeoisie. He and his Minister of Foreign Relations Ernesto Araújo, a disciple of Olavo de Carvalho's, started to antagonize systematically and ostensibly the Chinese state, following Donald Trump's initiative, often in even more aggressive ways. However, China is by far Brazil's largest grain importer. The big agribusiness bourgeoisie publicly expressed its displeasure with the attitude displayed by the Bolsonaro administration. We understand that the big landowners did not move toward a break with the government because the latter was fulfilling the campaign promises it had offered this fraction of the ruling class: a) the promise to allow big landowners to arm themselves to intimidate and confront the peasant, indigenous, and *quilombola* (descendants of Afro-Brazilian slaves who escaped from slave plantations) movements; b) the promise to license them to use dozens of new pesticides; and c) the promise to loosen the monitoring against deforestation (Forlini, 2020). Still in the international ambit, the Bolsonaro government antagonized Cuba and Venezuela, considered moving the Brazilian embassy in Israel to Jerusalem – which pleased both the Trump administration and the theological predictions of the Pentecostal churches that support him –, and criticized "globalism" and multilateral agencies.

Along with this aggressive performance in the international landscape, in 2019 Bolsonaro made a point of fulfilling other campaign promises that are dear to his support base. The big bourgeois press saw in the president's activity something that moved the government away from what was important – for the big bourgeoisie, of course – and chastised the president, but Bolsonaro forged ahead. He took measures related to loosening restrictions on purchasing and carrying arms, relaxing the legislation and inspection regulations concerning vehicle traffic in cities and roads, and aggressively antagonized the press. He was fulfilling his campaign promises. The Minister of Women, Family, and Human Rights, the Evangelical pastor Damares Alves, set out to fight the so-called "gender ideology" and what little exists of the right to abortion in Brazil, ensured only in rather exceptional cases. These were not topics that most of the bourgeoisie took very seriously, as one can gather from reading the mainstream press.

For an outside observer, it might seem preposterous, even infantile, the relevance the president assigns to some of the ideas and measures listed above. One example is the way the president focused on relaxing inspection regulations of vehicle traffic. But the focus on these measures can be explained if we keep in mind what we have already asserted about the fascist ideology: the lack of any clear programmatic proposals – particularly in the economic field –, the importance of authoritarianism (pressuring the mainstream press, facilitating the purchase and licensing to carry arms, defending patriarchal values), and the emphasis on ideology understood as distinct social symbols of the middle class – about the traffic laws that, Bolsonaro never tired of repeating that they robbed drivers of the pleasure of driving and only served to feed the "industry of fines." Furthermore, the social welfare reform hurt the Bolsonarist middle class as well, but they were engrossed in the matters of purchasing guns and looser traffic regulations.

The same priority divergence between fascism and the bourgeoisie would appear in 2020, when the entire leadership of the Ministry of Finance, which Minister Paulo Guedes had brought in from the private initiative, resigned to protest the sluggishness of the privatization process. Guedes spoke of a "scattering" in his ministry and used that to pressure the president. However, at this point, it was not the acceleration of the privatization process that worried Bolsonaro. What he had in mind, as we shall see ahead, was his confrontation against the Supreme Federal Court and the National Congress.

Part of the Bolsonarist base, though, was not pleased with the president's performance. They expected a firmer stance from the government. In the game of unity and struggle among the fascist government, the big bourgeoisie, and the petit-bourgeois social base of fascism, one relationship impacts the others. The disgruntled criticized the way the neoliberal economic reforms were prioritized to the detriment of the fight against corruption and the so-called "old politics," which is the pejorative term with which Bolsonarism refers to parliamentary democracy and expresses its longing for an authoritarian government. Given the typical history of fascist governments, which are bourgeois governments born of the co-optation of non-bourgeois reactionary movements, all those governments face, particularly in their first stages, what those who have studied the original fascism call "desertions among its plebeian base" (Guérin, 1965; Poulantzas, 1970; Togliatti, 1970). In the case of the Brazilian neofascism, important digital influencers, initial supporters of the Bolsonarist movement, abandoned the Bolsonaro government – Artur Duval, Nando Moura, Marcelo Brigadeiro, and others. Senators and representatives of the Social Liberal Party (PSL), the party to which Bolsonaro belonged when elected, also broke with the president, who ended up leaving PSL. Today, he remains unaffiliated to any party. The greatest ideologue of Brazilian fascism, Olavo de Carvalho, increased his criticisms of the government. The idea was that 2019 should not have been the year for important economic measures, but for political measures, starting with broadening the occupation of state posts by intellectuals and political figures of the fascist movement itself. An emblematic case of the conflict between the fascist base and the fascist government was the truck driver movement. Autonomous truck drivers had participated in demonstrations since 2015 to demand the ousting of Dilma Rousseff; later, in 2018, they supported Jair Bolsonaro's candidacy; in 2019, the truck drivers had to swallow Petrobras's price policy, which was against their historical demands, privileging international investors instead.

By 2019, the Bolsonaro administration's intention to impose drastic restrictions on the democratic regime had become clear. In October, representative Eduardo Bolsonaro, son of the president, announced that the government would issue an institutional act to establish an authoritarian regime – making reference to the Institutional Act Number Five (AI-5) issued by the Brazilian military dictatorship in December 1968. Eduardo Bolsonaro aimed this statement at the Supreme Federal Court (STF), which was investigating the use of systematic production and divulgation of fake news as a political weapon. This investigation threatened the core of Bolsonarism and involved the group at its leadership and the president's own family. A lawsuit that might nullify the election of Jair Bolsonaro and his vice-president General Hamilton Mourão was being processed at the Superior Electoral Court (TSE). In Rio de Janeiro, another son of the president was the target of an investigation concerning misuse of public money, and again the entire family of the president, including his wife, seemed to be engaged in corruption. The signs pointed to the president's growing isolation in face of the attack of the Judiciary leadership. At the beginning of 2020, Bolsonaro decided to respond with an authoritarian offensive that pointed to a coup d'état.

The president started to participate in street demonstrations of far-right groups, where he would make speeches threatening the STF, the TSE, and the National Congress. The Covid-19 pandemic did not demobilize the far-right groups. They owned the streets and Bolsonaro spoke to his supporters in increasingly threatening tones. Bolsonarist groups, including armed groups, organized protests in front of the buildings holding the National Congress and the STF, demanding these institutions to be shut down. At the government, Bolsonaro assumed the risk of firing, against the military group's wishes, Minister of Justice Sergio Moro and Minister of Health Henrique Mandetta, both of them very popular with the middle class. These two ministers stood in the way of some of his political goals. Moro had hindered Bolsonaro's intervention in the Federal Police investigations; and Mandetta, to contain the pandemic, had defended social distancing measures, which the president opposed. In sum, fascism was active in the streets and gaining strength inside the governmental staff – both Mandetta and Moro were replaced by ministers who proved to be meek to the president's will. Shortly afterward, documents surfaced revealing that: a) the president wanted to interfere in the Federal Police to halt the corruption investigations involving his son and the rest of his family; b) he publicly declared to be in favor of arming the population in order to fight state governors and mayors that had decreed restrictive measures to contain the spread of the new coronavirus; c) Bolsonaro actually discussed shutting down the Supreme Federal Court with the military leadership of his government – who rejected the proposal just because most of the military understood that "it was not a favorable moment" for such measure.

On June 18, 2020, something happened that changed the game. Fabrício Queiroz, manager of the Bolsonaro family's shady, illegal businesses, was arrested. That was when the president decided to back out. That decision revealed that Bolsonaro had chosen to be confrontational without having the strength for it. The STF, most of the National Congress, and all the mainstream press resisted his pro-coup offensive. It was the traditional right, organic representative of the big bourgeoisie, that defeated the authoritarian offensive, not the popular, democratic movement – some soccer fan clubs and left-wing activists organized small demonstrations in defense of democracy, but these gathered no more than a few dozen people, and that was all.[9]

5   Final Considerations

The use of the concept of fascism to characterize the Bolsonaro government is not a mere sorting exercise deprived of greater consequences. It alerts us to the danger that threatens us: the implementation of a dictatorship with a mass base that would not only suppress the democratic bourgeoisie's typical liberties but also form a massive siege against the left, isolating it. We must value the formulation inferred from Togliatti's analysis: a reactionary dictatorship with a mass base. The use of this concept of fascism also contributes to the comprehension of the political process's dynamics in Brazil nowadays. A fascist government, even when acting within a democratic regime like in Brazil's case, relies on an active mass base, to which the government owes some satisfaction, even though it must fundamentally meet the demands of the big bourgeoisie, the force that allowed the fascist movement the rise to power. These

---

9   The difficulties for the left are huge. Surveys have shown a shift in Bolsonaro's electoral base – we do not mean the engaged base. Since he instituted the emergency aid through which about 60 million impoverished Brazilians started to receive in average the equivalent of half the minimum wage every month, Bolsonaro's popularity grew among popular communities, including in Lulism's most traditional stronghold: the Northeast region of the country. Conversely, Bolsonaro's support among the upper middle class has decreased due to the dismissals of Sergio Moro and Henrique Mandetta, and to the denialist policy in face of the Covid-19 pandemic.

relationships, which were detected and clarified by the Marxist concept of fascism, generate a typical political process that the left needs to know so it can intervene with clarity and efficiency.

The big bourgeoisie is mostly satisfied with the fascist government, but reluctant to accept the shift to a dictatorial regime, which was the goal pursued by the fascist movement's key leaders, starting by the president himself. With the labor and popular movement defeated and on defense mode, the big bourgeoisie prefers to maintain the restrained bourgeois democracy outlined in Brazil since August 2016, with the coup d'état that deposed Dilma Rousseff. By all appearances, the result was that the traditional right established an agreement with the fascist right. The STF, TSE, and the common law courts all have halted the lawsuits against Bolsonaro and his family, ensuring the president's term until 2022, and Bolsonaro, in turn, has suspended his attack on the institutions of the bourgeois democracy. For a while, part of the Brazilian left deluded itself by imagining that the conflict between the fascist and the traditional right was deeper than it truly is. The big bourgeoisie and the traditional right are satisfied with the administration's neoliberalism.

Time will tell whether this agreement has a solid foundation. As long as the popular, democratic movement is as weak as it is today, the odds that the agreement will last are great. However, just like in any truce, the agreement has not kept quarrels between the two adversaries/partners from arising.

Bibliography

Almeida, Mansueto (2010). Desafios da Real Política Industrial Brasileira no Século XXI. *Retrato do Brasil 30*.

Almeida, Maria Hermínia Tavares de (1996). *Crise Econômica e Interesses Organizados: O Sindicalismo no Brasil nos Anos 80*. São Paulo: Edusp.

Almeida, Ronaldo (2019). Bolsonaro Presidente. Conservadorismo, Evangelismo e a Crise Brasileira. *Novos Estudos Cebrap* 38(1):185–213. Available (checked 30 January 2021) at: https://www.scielo.br/scielo.php?pid=S0101-33002019000100010&script=sci_abstract&tlng=pt.

Amorim, Elaine R. A. (2012). Particularidades dos Movimentos de Desempregados no Brasil, na França e na Argentina." *In*: Boito Jr., Armando; Galvão, Andréia (orgs.). *Política e Classes Sociais no Brasil dos Anos 2000*. São Paulo: Alameda.

Arcary, Valério (2011). *Um Reformismo Quase sem Reformas*. São Paulo: Sundermann.

Bandeira, Luis Alberto Muniz (2004). *As relações Perigosas: Brasil-Estados Unidos (Collor a Lula, 1990–2004)*. Rio de Janeiro: Civilização Brasileira.

Bastos, Pedro Paulo (2019). O Programa Econômico de Bolsonaro e Paulo Guedes é um Grande Salto para a Recessão. *Fundação Lauro Campos e Marielle Franco*. Available (ckecked 31 January 2021) at: http://www.laurocampos.org.br/2019/07/05/o-programa-economico-de-bolsonaro-e-guedes-e-um-grande-salto-para-a-recessao/.

Berringer, Tatiana (2015). *A Burguesia Brasileira e a Política Externa nos Governos FHC e Lula*. Curitiba: Appris.

Berringer, Tatiana; Carneiro, Gabriel; Soprijo, Gabriel; Souza, Leonardo; Barros, Larissa. (2020). Governo Bolsonaro e os Estados Unidos: O Nacionalismo às Avessas. *Observatório da Política Externa e da Inserção Internacional do Brasil*. Available (checked 31 January 2021) at: http://opeb.org/2019/06/21/governo-bolsonaro-e-os-eua-o-nacionalismo-as-avessas/.

Bianchi, Alvaro (2004). O Ministério dos Industriais – A Federação das Indústrias do Estado de São Paulo na Crise das Décadas de 1980 e 1990. PhD Thesis. Univesidade Estadual de Campinas. Available (checked 15 December 2020) at: http://repositorio.unicamp.br/jspui/handle/REPOSIP/279956.

Bielschowsky, Ricardo; Stumpo, Giovanni (1995). Empresas Transnacionales y Cambios Estructurales en la Industria de Argentina, Brasil, Chile e México. *Revista de la Cepal* 55: 139–164. Available (checked 15 December 2020) at: https://repositorio.cepal.org/handle/11362/11980.

Bluche, Frédéric (1981). *Le Bonapartisme*. Paris: Presses Universitaires de France.

Bobbio, Norberto (1997). *Dal Fascismo alla Democrazia: i Regimi, le Ideologie, le Figure e le Culture Politiche*. A cura di Michelangelo Bovero. Milano: Baldini & Castoldi.

Boito Jr., Armando (1982). *O Golpe de 1954 – A Burguesia Contra o Populismo*. São Paulo: Brasiliense.

Boito Jr., Armando (1991). *O Sindicalismo de Estado no Brasil – Uma Análise Crítica da Estrutura Sindical*. Campinas: Editora da Unicamp/São Paulo: Hucitec. Available (checked 29 December 2020) at: https://www.researchgate.net/publication/329 947136_ARMANDO_BOITO_JR-O_SINDICALISMO_DE_ESTADO_NO_BRASIL/ link/5c24f26c92851c22a34962ab/download.

Boito Jr., Armando (1997). Politique Néoliberale et Syndicalisme au Brésil. *Lusotopie*. Available (checked 5 November 2020) at: http://www.lusotopie.sciencespoborde aux.fr/somma97.html.

Boito Jr., Armando (2002a). *Política Neoliberal e Sindicalismo no Brasil*. 2. ed. São Paulo: Xamã.

Boito Jr., Armando (2002b). "Neoliberalismo e Relações de Classe no Brasil." *In*: Boito Jr., Armando (org.). Dossiê: "Neoliberalismo e Lutas Sociais no Brasil." *Revista Ideias* 9 (1): 13–48. Campinas: IFCH-Unicamp. Available (checked 17 December 2020) at: https://www.ifch.unicamp.br/publicacoes/pf-publicacoes/ideias_9-1.pdf.

Boito Jr., Armando (2003). A Hegemonia Neoliberal no Governo Lula. *Crítica Marxista* 17: 9–35. Available (checked 9 August 2020) at: https://www.google.com/url?sa= t&rct=j&q=&esrc=s&source=web&cd=&ved=2ahUKEwiksqpuo7rAhVIHrkGH R_oCCUQFjABegQIARAB&url=https%3A%2F%2Fwww.ifch.unicamp.br%2Fcrit icamarxista%2Farquivos_biblioteca%2Fcritica17-Aboito.pdf&usg=AOvVaw3nP UFbM4mUoSFh2gknuHCU>.

Boito Jr., Armando (2005a). O Populismo no Brasil: Natureza, Formas de Manifestação e Raízes Sociais. *O Sindicalismo na Política Brasileira*. Campinas: IFCH-Unicamp.

Boito Jr., Armando (2005b). A Burguesia no Governo Lula. *Crítica Marxista* 21: 52–76. Available (checked 10 September 2020) at: https://www.ifch.unicamp.br/criticam arxista/sumario.php?id_revista=21&numero_revista=21.

Boito Jr., Armando (2007). Estado e Transição ao Capitalismo: Feudalismo, Absolutismo e Revolução Política Burguesa. *Estado, Política e Classes Sociais*. São Paulo: Editora Unesp.

Boito Jr., Armando (2012a). As Contradições da Frente Neodesenvolvimentista. Blog *Viomundo*, March 3. Available (checked 30 Dezember 2020) at: https://www.viomu ndo.com.br/politica/armando-boito-jr-as-contradicoes-da-frente-neodesenvolvim entista.html.

Boito Jr., Armando (2012b). A economia Capitalista Está em Crise e as Contradições Tendem a se Aguçar. Interview with newspaper *Brasil de Fato*, March. Available (checked 30 December 2020) at: https://se.cut.org.br/noticias/a-economia-capitali sta-esta-em-crise-e-as-contradicoes-tendem-a-se-agucar-59b4.

Boito Jr., Armando (2013a). Emancipação e Revolução: Crítica à Leitura Lukacsiana do Jovem Marx. *Crítica Marxista* 36: 43–54. Available (checked 10 August

2020) at: https://document.onl/documents/emancipacao-e-revolucao-critica-a-leit
ura-lukacsiana-do-emancipacao.html.

Boito Jr., Armando (2013b) O Lulismo é um Tipo de Bonapartismo? Uma Crítica às
Teses de André Singer. *Crítica Marxista* 37: 171–182. Available (checked 12 August
2020) at: https://www.ifch.unicamp.br/criticamarxista/sumario.php?id_revista=
48&numero_revista=37.

Boito Jr., Armando (2014). Quem é Contra a Corrupção? *Revista Fórum*. Available
(checked 14 November 2020) at: https://revistaforum.com.br/blogs/rodrigovianna/
brodrigovianna-armando-boito-quem-e-contra-corrupcao-de-verdade/.

Boito Jr., Armando (2017). A Burguesia Brasileira no Golpe do *Impeachment. Portal
Brasil de Fato*. Available (checked 13 August 2020) at: https://www.brasildefato.com
.br/2017/01/06/a-burguesia-brasileira-no-golpe-do-impeachment.

Boito Jr., Armando (2020). Por Que Caracterizar o Bolsonarismo como Fascismo. *Crítica
Marxista* 50: 111–119. Available (checked 30 January 2021) at: https://www.ifch.unic
amp.br/criticamarxista/arquivos_biblioteca/dossie2020_05_26_14_12_19.pdf.

Boito Jr., Armando; Ceceña, Ana Esther, Almerya, Guillermo; Coutinho, Carlos Nelson
(2007). Luttes Sociales et Perspectives Politiques en Amérique Latine. *Actuel Marx,*
42(2):10–24. Available (checked 10 November 2020) at: https://www.cairn.info/
revue-actuel-marx-2007-2.htm].

Boito Jr., Armando; Marcelino, Paula (2010). O Sindicalismo Deixou a Crise para Trás?
Um Novo Ciclo de Greves na Década de 2000. *Cadernos do CRH,* 23(59): 323–338.
Available (checked 26 September 2020) at: https://www.scielo.br/scielo.php?pid=
S0103497920100000200008&script=sci_abstract&tlng=pt.

Boito Jr., Armando ; Marcelino, Paula (2011). Decline in Unionism? An Analysis of the
New Wave of Strikes in Brazil. *Latin American Perspectives,* 38(5): 62–73. Available
(checked 20 October 20 2020) at: https://journals.sagepub.com/ action/doSearch?
filterOption=thisJournal&SeriesKey=lapa&AllField=decline+in+unionism.

Boito Jr., Armando; Galvão, Andréia; Marcelino, Paula (2015). La Nouvelle Phase du
Syndicalisme Brésilien (2003–2013). *Cahiers des Amériques Latines,* 80:145–164.
Available (checked 17 November 2020) at: https://journals.openedition.org/cal/4184.

Boito Jr., Armando; Berringer, Tatiana (2013). Brasil: Classes Sociais,
Neodesenvolvimentismo e Política Externa nos Governos Lula e Dilma. *Revista
de Sociologia e Política* 21(47): 31–38. Available (checked 30 December 2020) at:
https://www.scielo.br/scielo.php?pid=S0104-44782013000300004&script=sci_abstr
act&tlng=pt.

Boron, Atilio (2003). El Fascismo como Categoria Histórica: en Torno al Problema de las
Dictaduras en América Latina. *In*: Boron, Atilio: *Estado, Capitalismo y Democracia
en America Latina.* Buenos Aires: Clacso, Consejo Latinoamericano de Ciencias
Sociales. Available (checked 30 January 2021) at: http://www.clacso.org/wwwcla
cso/espanol/html/libros/estado/estado.html.

Bourdieu, Pierre (1998). *Contre-Feux. Propos pour Servir à la Résistance Contre l'Invasion Néo-Libérale*. Paris: Raisons d'Agir.

Bratsis, Peter (2014). Political Corruption in the Age of Transnational Capitalism. *Historical Materialism* 22(1): 105–128.

Bresser-Pereira, Luís Carlos (2006). Estratégia Nacional de Desenvolvimento. *Revista de Economia Política*, vol. 26(2): 203–230. Availble (26 checked September 2020) at: https://www.scielo.br/scielo.php?script=sci_arttext&pid=S0101315720 0600020003&lng=pt&nrm=iso&tlng=pt.

Bresser-Pereira, Luís Carlos (2012). Um Novo Pacto Social para o Desenvolvimento? Curitiba: UFPR. VIII Encontro Empresas, Empresário e Sociedade.

Bruno, Regina (2009). *Um Brasil Ambivalente. Agronegócio, Ruralismo e Relações de Poder*. Rio de Janeiro: Edur.

Bugiato, Caio (2012). O Papel do BNDES na Expansão dos Negócios da Burguesia Interna Brasileira. Curitiba: UFPR. Paper presented at the VIII Encontro Empresas, Empresário e Sociedade. Available (checked 26 September 2012) at: https://portal .anpocs.org/index.php/encontros/papers/37-encontro-anual-daanpocs/st/st39/ 8672-o-papel-do-bndes-no-financiamento-dos-negocios-da-burguesia-interna -brasileira.

Bugiato, Caio (2014). A Política de Financiamento do BNDES e a Burguesia Brasileira. *Cadernos do Desenvolvimento* 9(14)1: 83–103. Available (checked 5 October 2021) at: http://www.cadernosdodesenvolvimento.org.br/ojs-2.4.8/index.php/cdes/issue/ view/10

Bugiato, Caio (2016). *A Política de Financiamento do BNDES e a Burguesia Brasileira*. PhD Dissertation, Universidade Estadual de Campinas. Available (checked 12 August 2020) at: http://repositorio.unicamp.br/handle/REPOSIP/305078.

Cano, Wilson (2012). A Desindustrialização no Brasil. *Economia e Sociedade* 21: 831–851. Available (checked 26 September 2020) at: https://www.scielo.br/scielo.php?pid= S0104-06182012000400006&script=sci_abstract&tlng=pt.

Cardoso, Fernando Henrique (1966). *Empresários de Desenvolvimento*. São Paulo: Difel.

Carneiro, Ricardo (2002). *Desenvolvimento em Crise – a Economia Brasileira no Último Quarto do Século XX*. São Paulo: Editora Unesp.

Cavalcante, Sávio (2012). Estado, Capital Estrangeiro e Burguesia Interna no Setor de Telecomunicações nos Governos FHC e Lula. *In*: Boito Jr., Armando; Galvão, Andréia (orgs.). *Política e Classes Sociais no Brasil dos Anos 2000*. São Paulo: Alameda.

Cavalcante, Sávio (2015). Classe Média e Conservadorismo Liberal. *In*: Velasco e Cruz, Sebastião *et al. Direita, Volver! O Retorno da Direita e o Ciclo Político Brasileiro*. São Paulo: Fundação Perseu Abramo.

Cavalcante, Sávio (2020). Classe Média e Ameaça Neofascista no Brasil de Bolsonaro. *Crítica Marxista* 50: 121–130. Available (checked 30 January 2021) at: https://www .ifch.unicamp.br/criticamarxista/sumario.php?id_revista=67&numero_revista=50.

Chesnais, François (1997). *La Mondialisation du Capital*. Paris: Syros.

Codato, Adriano Nervo (1997). *Sistema Estatal e Política Econômica no Brasil Pós-64*. São Paulo: Hucitec/Anpocs. Curitiba: Editora da UFPR.

Coletti, Claudinei (2002). Ascensão e Refluxo do MST e da Luta pela Terra na Década Neoliberal. *In*: BOITO Jr., Armando (org.). Dossiê: "Neoliberalismo e Lutas Sociais no Brasil." *Revista Ideias*, n. 9 (1). Campinas, IFCH-Unicamp.

Costa, Paulo Neves (1998). *Democracia nos Anos 50: Burguesia, Corporativismo e Parlamento*. São Paulo: Hucitec.

Cueva, Augustín (1977). La Cuestión del Fascismo. *Revista Mexicana de Sociología*, 39 (2): 469–480. Available (checked 30 January 2021) at: https://www.jstor.org/stable/3539774?seq=1.

Dalla Costa, Armando *et al.* (2012). *Desenvolvimento e Crise na América Latina. Estado, Empresas e Sociedade*. Curitiba: Editora CRV.

De Felice, Renzo. *Introduzione al fascismo e i partiti politici italiani*, Bologna: Cappelli. 1966.

Demier, Felipe (2013). *O Longo Bonapartismo Brasileiro (1930–1964)*. Rio de Janeiro: Mauad.

De Vito, Francesco (2020). La Repubblica di Salò: Gli Ultimi Giorni dell'Italia Fascista. Area51 Publishing. Kindle edition.

Dias, Rodolfo Palazzo (2012). *Organização e Posicionamento Político dos Bancos no Governo Lula*. Master's thesis. Universidade Estadual de Campinas. Available (checked 17 December 2020) at: http://repositorio.unicamp.br/jspui/handle/REPO SIP/281693.

Dimitrov, Georgi (1935). *Working Class Unity-Bulwark against Fascism*. Seventh World Congress of the Communist International. New York City: Workers Library Publishers.

Diniz, Eli (2006). Empresários e Governo Lula: Percepções e Ação Política entre 2002 e 2006. Workshop "Empresa, Empresários e Sociedade." Porto Alegre. Available (checked 29 August 2020) at: https://arquivofee.rs.gov.br/5workshop/pdf/mesa02_eli.pdf.

Diniz, Eli; Boschi, Renato (2004). *Empresários, Interesses e Mercado. Dilemas do Desenvolvimento no Brasil*. Belo Horizonte: Editora da UFMG: Rio de Janeiro: Iuperj.

Diniz, Eli; Boschi, Renato (2007). *A Difícil Rota do Desenvolvimento. Empresários e a Agenda Pós-Neoliberal*. Belo Horizonte: Editora da UFMG; Rio de Janeiro: Iuperj.

Duménil, Gérard; Lévy L, Dominique (2006). Une Théorie Marxiste du Néolibéralisme. *Actuel Marx. Fin du néoliberalisme?*, 40. Paris, PUF.

Elias, Denise (2003). *Globalização e Agricultura – A Região de Ribeirão Preto (SP)*. São Paulo: Edusp.

Farias, Francisco Pereira de (2009). Frações Burguesas e Bloco no poder. *Crítica Marxista*, 28: 81–98. Available (checked 22 August 2020) at: https://www.ifch.unic amp.br/criticamarxista/arquivos_biblioteca/sumario28.htm.

Farias, Francisco Pereira de (2017). *Estado Burguês e Classes Dominantes no Brasil 1930–1964*. Curitiba: CRV.

Fausto, Boris (1970). *A Revolução de 1930 – Historiografia e História*. São Paulo: Brasiliense, 1970.

Ferreira, Jorge (2001). O Nome e a Coisa: O Populismo na Política Brasileira. *In*: Ferreira, Jorge (org.) *O Populismo e sua História: Debate e Crítica*. Rio de Janeiro: Civilização Brasileira.

Filgueiras, Luiz; Gonçalves, Reinaldo (2007). *A economia Política do Governo Lula*. Rio de Janeiro: Contraponto, 2007.

Filgueiras, Luiz; Druck, Graça (2020). *O Brasil nas Trevas. (2013–2020). Do Golpe Neoliberal ao Fascismo*. São Paulo: Boitempo.

Figueiredo Filho, Carolina B. G.; Souza, Davisson C. C. (2012). O Sindicalismo e a Luta dos Desempregados na Década de 2000. *In*: Boito Jr., Armando; Galvão, Andréia (orgs.). *Política e Classes Sociais no Brasil dos Anos 2000*. São Paulo: Alameda,.

Forlini, Luana. (2020). *O Posicionamento dos Produtores de Soja no Contexto da Crise Política no Brasil – (2014–2019)*. Master's thesis, Universidade Estadual de Campinas.

Fortes, Alexandre, *et al.* (1999). *Na Luta por Direitos. Estudos Recentes em História Social do Trabalho*. Campinas: Editora da Unicamp.

Galvão, Andréia (2002). A CUT na Encruzilhada: Dilemas do Movimento Sindical Combativo. *Ideias* 9(1):105–154.

Galvão, Andréia (2006). Le Mouvement Syndical Face au Gouvernement Lula: Dilemmes, Défis et Paradoxes. *In*: Van Eeuwen, Daniel (org.). *Le nouveau Brésil de Lula*. Paris: Edition de l'Aube.

Galvão, Andréia (2012). A Reconfiguração do Movimento Sindical nos Governos Lula. *In*: BOITO Jr., Armando; GALVÃO, Andréia (orgs.). *Política e Classes Sociais no Brasil dos anos 2000*. São Paulo: Alameda.

Galvão, Andréia; Marcelino, Paula; Trópia, Patrícia (2011). As Bases Sociais da Conlutas. Unpublished research paper. Universidade Estadual de Campinas – Unicamp.

Galvão, Andréia; Marcelino, Paula; Trópia, Patr (2012). As bases sociais da Intersindical. Unpublished research paper. Universidade Estadual de Campinas – Unicamp.

Galvão, Andréia; Marcelino, Paula; Trópia, Patr (2013). A Reorganização da Esquerda Sindical nos Anos 2000: As Bases Sociais e o Perfil Político-Ideológico de CTB, Intersindical e Conlutas. Paper presented at the *IIe Conférence Internationale Grèves et Conflits Sociaux*. Dijon.

Galvão, Andréia; Marcelino, Paula; Trópia, Patr (2015). *As Bases Sociais das Novas Centrais Sindicais Brasileiras*. Curitiba: Appris.

Gentile, Emilio (2019). *Chi è Fascista*. Bari: Editori Laterza.

Gianotti, Vito; Lopez Neto, Sebastião (1992). *CUT ontem e hoje*. Petrópolis: Vozes.

Gomes, Julia (2015). Conteúdo Local e Neoliberalismo Neodesenvolvimentista: A Indústria da Construção Naval e a Política de Compras da Petrobras Durante os

Governos Lula. Paper presented at the VIII Colóquio Internacional Marx e Engels. Available (checked 8 December 2020) at: https://www.ifch.unicamp.br/formul ario_cemarx/selecao/2015/trabalhos2015/Julia%20gomes%20e%20Souza%2010 550.pdf.

Gonçalves, Reinaldo (2012). Governo Lula e o Nacional-Desenvolvimentismo às Avessas. *Revista da Sociedade Brasileira de Economia Política*, 31:5–30. Available (checked 26 September 2020) at: https://scholar.google.com.br/ citations?user= VR5A-pIAAAAJ&hl=pt-BR#d=gs_md_citad&u=%2Fcitations%3Fview_op%3D-view_citation%26hl%3Dpt-BR%26user%3DVR5A-pIAAAAJ%26citation_for _view%3DVR5A-pIAAAAJ%3Awbdj-CoPYUoC%26tzom%3D180.

Gorender, Jacob (1981). *A Burguesia Brasileira*. São Paulo: Brasiliense.

Gramsci, Antonio. 1978. *Sul Fascismo*. A cura de Enzo Santarelli. Editori Internazionali Riuniti.

Guérin, Daniel (1965 [1936]). *Fascisme et Grand Capital*. Paris: François Maspero.

Harvey, David (2005). *A Brief History of Neoliberalism*. Oxford: Oxford University Press.

Hirata, Francini; Oliveira, Nathalia Cr. (2012). Os Movimentos dos Sem-Teto em São Paulo no Contexto Neoliberal. *In*: BOITO Jr., Armando; GALVÃO, Andréia (orgs.). *Política e Classes Sociais no Brasil dos Anos 2000*. São Paulo: Alameda.

Ianni, Octavio (1972). *Estado e Planejamento Econômico no Brasil*. Rio de Janeiro: Paz e Terra.

Jaguaribe, Hélio (1954). O que é Adhemarismo? *Cadernos do Nosso Tempo* 2: 21–30.

Kalil, Isabela (2019). *Quem são e no que Acreditam os Eleitores de Jair Bolsonaro*. Available (checked 30 January 2021) at: https://www.fespsp.org.br/upload/usersfi les/2018/Relat%C3%B3rio%20para%20Site%20FESPSP.pdf.

Kowarick, Lúcio (1975). *Capitalismo e Marginalidade na América Latina*. Rio de Janeiro: Paz e Terra.

Krein, José Dari (2018). O Desmonte dos Direitos, as Novas Configurações do Trabalho e o Esvaziamento da Ação Coletiva. Consequências da Reforma Trabalhista. *Tempo Social* 30(1): 77–104. Available (checked 31 January 2021) at: https://www.scielo.br/ pdf/ts/v30n1/1809-4554-ts-30-01-0077.pdf.

Leão Rego, Walquiria ; Pinzani, Alessandro (2013). *Vozes do Bolsa Família. Autonomia, Dinheiro e Cidadania*. São Paulo: Editora Unesp.

Lenin, Vladimir (1975). *Para una Caracterización del Romanticismo Económico*. Moscú: Editorial Progreso.

Marcelino, Paula (2017). Sindicalismo e Neodesenvolvimentismo: Analisando as Greves entre 2003 e 2013 no Brasil. *Tempo Social*, 29 (3): 201–227. Available (checked 12 August 2020) at: http://www.revistas.usp.br/ts/article/view/125952.

Martuscelli, Danilo Enrico (2010). A Burguesia Mundial em Questão. *Crítica Marxista*, 30: 29–48. Available (checked 26 September 2020) at: https://www.ifch.unicamp.br/ criticamarxista/sumario.php?id_revista=30&numero_revista=30.

Martuscelli, Danilo Enrico (2012). A Transição para o Neoliberalismo e a Crise do Governo Collor. *In*: BOITO Jr., Armando; GALVÃO, Andréia (orgs). *Política e Classes Sociais no Brasil dos anos 2000*. São Paulo: Alameda.

Martuscelli, Danilo Enrico (2015). *Crises Políticas e Capitalismo Neoliberal no Brasil*. Curitiba: CRV.

Marx, Karl (1963). The Eighteenth Brumaire of Louis Bonaparte. New York City: International Publishers.

Meirelles, Antonio Carlos (1973). La Révolution de 1930: Une Révolution Passive. *Critique de l'Économie Politique*, 16–17.

Miglioli, Jorge (1998). Burguesia e Liberalismo: Política e Economia nos Anos Recentes. *Crítica Marxista* 6: 35–51. São Paulo. Available (checked 10 September 2020) at: https://www.ifch.unicamp.br/criticamarxista/sumario.php?id_revista=6&numero_revista=6.

Minella, Ary César (1994). O Discurso Empresarial no Brasil: Com a Palavra, os Senhores Banqueiros. *Ensaios, FEE*. 15 (2): 505–546.

Minella, Ary César (1997). Elites Financeiras, Sistemas Financeiros e Governo FHC. *In*: Rampinelli, Waldir José; Ouriques, Nildo Domingos (orgs.). *No Fio da Navalha. Crítica das Reformas Neoliberais de FHC*. São Paulo: Xamã.

Monteiro, Krishna Mendes (2006). *O Desencantamento da Razão: A Ideologia Política de Celso Furtado (1972–1992)*. Master's thesis, Universidade Estadual de Campinas. Available (checked 16 August 2020) at: http://repositorio.unicamp.br/jspui/handle/REPOSIP/279240.

Moraes, João Quartim de (1971). La Nature de Classe de l'État Brésilien. *Les Temps Modernes* 304.

Morais, Lecio; Saad-Filho, Alfredo (2011). Brazil Beyond Lula: Forging Ahead or Pausing for Breath? *Latin American Perspectives* 38(2): 31–44. Available (checked 22 August 2020) at: https://journals.sagepub.com/doi/10.1177/0094582X10395890.

Morais, Lecio; Saad-Filho, Alfredo (2012). Neo-Developmentalism and the Challenges of Economic Policy-Making under Dilma Rousseff. *Critical Sociology* 28(6): 789–798. Available (checked 22 August 2020) at: https://journals.sagepub.com/doi/10.1177/0896920512441635.

Mossé, Claude (1979). *Atenas: A História de uma Democracia*. Brasília: Editora UnB.

Nucci Júnior, Renato (2007). Possíveis Razões para a Oposição de Direita ao Governo Lula. *Sítio Portal Popular*. Available (checked 15 December 2020) at: https://resistir.info/brasil/a_oposicao_de_direita.html.

Nun, José (1978). Superpopulação Relativa, Exército Industrial de Reserva e Massa Marginal. *In*: Pereira, Luiz (org.). *Populações Marginais*. São Paulo: Duas Cidades.

Nun, José (2001). *Marginalidad y Exclusión Social*. México: Fondo de Cultura Económica.

Oliveira, Amâncio Jorge (2003). O Governo do PT e a Alca: Política Externa e Pragmatismo. *Estudos Avançados* 17(48): 311–329. Available (checked 16 October

2020) at: https://www.scielo.br/scielo.php?script=sci_arttext&pid=S0103-401420 03000200023.

Oliveira, Amâncio Jorge; Pfeifer, Alberto (2006). O Empresariado e a Política Exterior do Brasil. *In*: Altemani, Henrique; Lessa, Antônio Carlos (orgs.). *Relações Internacionais do Brasil: Temas e Agendas*. São Paulo: Saraiva.

Oliveira, Francisco de (2010). O avesso do Avesso. *In*: OLIVEIRA, Francisco de; BRAGA, Ruy; RIZEK, Cibele (orgs.). *Hegemonia às Avessas*. São Paulo: Boitempo.

Oliveira, Nathalia Cristina (2010). *Os movimentos dos Sem-Teto da Grande São Paulo (1995–2009)*. Master's thesis. Universidade Estadual de Campinas.

Patschiki, Lucas. 2012. *Os Litores da Nossa Burguesia – o Mídia sem Máscara em Atuação Partidária (2002–2011)*. Master's thesis. Universidade Estadual do Oeste do Paraná – Campus Marechal Cândido Rondon. Available (checked 31 January 2021) at: http://tede.unioeste.br/handle/tede/1789.

Paulani, Leda (2008). *Brasil Delivery: Servidão Financeira e Estado de Emergência Econômico*. São Paulo: Boitempo.

Paxton, Robert (2004). *The Anatomy of Fascism*. New York: Alfred A. Knopf.

Pereira, Luiz (1971). Populações 'Marginais'. *In: Estudos sobre o Brasil Contemporâneo*. São Paulo: Livraria Pioneira Editora.

Perissinotto, Renato M. (1994). *Classes Dominantes e Hegemonia na República Velha*. Campinas: Editora da Unicamp.

Pijl, Kees van der (1998). *Transnational Classes and International Relations*. London and New York: Routledge.

Pimentel Puga, Fernando (2006). Câmbio Afeta Exportadores de Forma Diferenciada. *In*: Torres Filho, Ernani Teixeira; Pimentel Puga, Fernando; Rocha Ferreira, Francisco Marcelo (orgs.). *Visão do Desenvolvimento*. Rio de Janeiro: BNDES.

Plessis, Alain (1973). *De la Fête Impériale au Mur des Fédérés – 1852–1871*. Paris: Seuil.

Pochmann, Marcio (2012). *Nova classe média?* São Paulo: Boitempo.

Pomar, Valter (2016). Um Programa Econômico Alternativo. *Le Monde Diplomatique Brasil* 104. Available (checked 8 December 2020) at: https://diplomatique.org.br/um-programa-economico-alternativo/.

Poulantzas, Nicos (1968). *Pouvoir Politique et Classes Sociales*. Paris: François Maspero.

Poulantzas, Nicos (1970). *Fascisme et Dictature*. Paris: François Maspero.

Poulantzas, Nicos (1974). *Les Classes Sociales dans le Capitalisme d'Aujourd'hui*. Paris: Seuil.

Poulantzas, Nicos (1975). *La Crise des Dictatures: Portugal, Grèce, Espagne*. Paris: François.

Poulantzas, Nicos (1976). *La Crise des Dictatures*. Paris: Seuil.

Poulantzas, Nicos (1978). *L'État, le Pouvoir, le Socialisme*. Paris: Presses Universitaires de France.

Prandi, Reginaldo (2019). Os 12% do Presidente – Em que Lugar da Sociedade Habita o Bolsonarista Convicto? São Paulo: *Jornal da USP*. Available (checked 30 January

2021) at: https://jornal.usp.br/artigos/os-12-do-presidente-em-que-lugar-da-socied ade-habita-o-bolsonarista-convicto/.

Puggina, Percival (2020). Vacina Chinesa, Não. *Mídia sem Máscara*. Available (checked 31 January 2021) at: https://midiasemmascara.net/vacina-chinesa-nao/.

Ridenti, Marcelo (2013). Que Juventude é Essa? *Folha de S.Paulo*, Jun 23 2013. Available (checked 9 December 2020) at: http://www1.folha.uol.com.br/opiniao/.

Saad-Filho, Alfredo; Morais, Lecio (2011). Brazil Beyond Lula: Forging Ahead or Pausing for Breath?" *Latin American Perspectives*, 38(2): 31–44. Available (checked 17 November 2020) at: https://journals.sagepub.com/doi/10.1177/0094582X10395890.

Saad-Filho, Alfredo; Boito Jr., Armando (2016). Brazil: The Failure of the PT and the Rise of the "New Right." *In*: Panitch, Leo; Albo, Greg (eds.). *Socialist Register* 52. Available (checked 30 November 2020) at: http://socialist register.com/index.php/ srv/article/view/25598#.VjPAt7erQdU.

Sabença, Mariana (2014). As Grandes Construtoras e a Política Econômica nos Governos Lula e Dilma. Paper presented at the 38o Encontro Anual da Anpocs. Available (checked 23 August 2020) at: https://bv.fapesp.br/pt/bolsas/136182/as -grandes-construtoras-e-a-politica-economica-nos-governos-lula-e-dilma/.

Sader, Emir (org.) (2013). *Lula e Dilma: 10 Anos de Governos Pós-Neoliberais no Brasil*. São Paulo: Boitempo; Rio de Janeiro: Flacso Brasil.

Saes, Décio (1979). *Classe Média e Sistema Político no Brasil*. São Paulo: T. A. Queiroz.

Saes, Décio (1994). A Reemergência do Populismo no Brasil e na América Latina. *In*: Dagnino, Evelina (org.). *Anos 90, Política e Sociedade no Brasil*. São Paulo: Brasiliense.

Saes, Décio (2001). *República do Capital*. São Paulo: Boitempo.

Santa Rosa, Virgínio (1976). *O Sentido do Tenentismo*. 3. ed. São Paulo: Alfa-Omega.

Santos, Theotônio (1977). Socialismo y Fascismo en America Latina Hoy. *Revista Mexicana de Sociología* 39(1): 173–190. Available (chacked 30 January 2021) at: http:// www.jstor.org/stable/3539794.

Silva, Luciana Henrique (2007). *Práticas Organizativas do MST e Relações de Poder em Acampamentos/Assentamentos do Estado de São Paulo*. PhD Dissertation. Universidade Federal de São Carlos. Available (consulted 26 September 2020) at: https://repositorio.ufscar.br/handle/ufscar/1414.

Silva, Luciana Henrique (2012). Acampados e Assentados: Pesquisa sobre a Base Social do MST. Unpublished manuscript. Universidade Estadual de Campinas – Unicamp.

Silva, Sérgio (1981). *Expansão Cafeeira e Origens da Indústria no Brasil*. 5. ed. São Paulo: Alfa-Omega,.

Silva, Suylan de Almeida (2008). *"Ganhamos a Batalha, Mas Não a Guerra": A Visão da Campanha Nacional contra a Alca sobre a não Assinatura do Acordo*. PhD Dissertation, Universidade de Brasília.

Singer, André (2012). *Os Sentidos do Lulismo*. São Paulo: Companhia das Letras.

Singer, André (2015). Cutucando Onças com Varas Curtas – O Ensaio Desenvolvimentista no Primeiro Mandato de Dilma Rousseff (2011–2014). *Novos Estudos Cebrap*

102: 39–67. Available (checked 12 December 2020) at: https://www.scielo.br/scielo .php?script=sci_abstract&pid=S0101330020150002000039&lng=pt&nrm=iso.

Sodré, Nelson Werneck (1979). *História Militar do Brasil*. 3. ed. Rio de Janeiro: Civilização Brasileira.

Telarolli, Rodolpho (1982). *Eleições e Fraudes Eleitorais na República Velha*. São Paulo: Brasiliense.

Thorstensen, Vera (2001). *O Brasil Frente a um Tríplice Desafio: As negociações Simultâneas da OMC, da Alca e do Acordo CE/Mercosul*. Lisboa: Ieei.

Togliatti, Palmiro (2019 [1970]). *Lezioni sul Fascismo*. Roma: Editori Riuniti.

Tomaz, Nathália Rocha Oliveira; Gouvêa, Lúcia Helena Martins (2017). Um Estudo do *Ethos* em Discursos do Ex-Presidente Lula. *Revista de Estudos da Linguagem*, 25(1): 441–471. Available (checked 12 August 2020) at: http://www.periodicos.letras. ufmg.br/index.php/relin/article/view/10954/9662.

Torre, Juan Carlo (1996). O Encaminhamento Político das Reformas Estruturais. *Lua Nova* 37: 57–76. Available (checked 12 December 2020) at: https://www.scielo.br/sci elo.php?pid=S0102644519960001000004&script=sci_abstract&tlng=pt.

Traverso, Enzo (2019a). Il "Post-Fascismo" in Europa: Un Processo di Trasformazione Politica di cui si Ignora l'Esito, intervista Enzo Traverso. *Communia Network* 12 November 2015. Available (checked 30 January 2021) at: http://www.communianet .org/polis/il-post-fascismo-europa-un-processo-di-trasformazione-politica-di-cui -si-ignora-lesito.

Traverso, Enzo (2019b). *Le Metamorfosi delle Destre Radicali nel XXI Secolo*. Milano: Fondazione Giangiacomo Feltrinelli.

Trindade, Helgio (1982). El Tema del Fascismo en America Latina. *Revista de Estudios Políticos* (Nueva Epoca) 30.

Trotsky, Leon (1968). *Revolução e Contrarrevolução na Alemanha*. Rio de Janeiro: Laemmert.

Vigevani, Tullo; Mariano, Marcelo Passini (2005). A Alca e a Política Externa Brasileira. *Cadernos Cedec* 74. Available (checked 17 October 2020) at: http://cedec.org.br/ cadernos/index/p/3.

Weber, Max (1946). Class, Status, and Party. *In*: Gerth, Hans Heinrich; Mills, Charles Wright (eds.). *From Max Weber: Essays in Sociology*. New York: Oxford University Press.

Weffort, Francisco (1978). *O Populismo na Política Brasileira*. Rio de Janeiro: Paz e Terra.

Primary Souces:

Agência Brasil (2012). Número de Moradias Entregues pelo Programa Minha Casa, Minha Vida chega a 934 mil. Available (checked 16 October 2020) at: http://memo ria.ebc.com.br/agenciabrasil/noticia/2012-11-19/numero-de-moradias-entregues -pelo-programa-minha-casa-minha-vida-chega-934-mil.

Agência IBGE Notícias (2012). Desocupação fica em 4,6% em dezembro e fecha 2012 com média de 5,5% Available (checked 5 October 2021) at: http: https://agenciaden oticias.ibge.gov.br/agencia-sala-de-imprensa/2013-agencia-de-noticias/releases/ 14354-asi-desocupacao-fica-em-46-em-dezembro-e-fecha-2012-com-media-de-55.

Cunha, Fernanda (2005). Rumo à Modernidade. *Revista da Indústria* 111. São Paulo: Fiesp.

Demarchi, Célia; Vieira, Maria Cândida (2006). Novo Comando, Novas Mudanças Possíveis. *Revista da Indústria* 117. São Paulo: Fiesp.

Dieese (1996). *Anuário dos Trabalhadores – 1996–1997*. São Paulo: Edição Dieese.

Dieese (2006). As Greves em 2005. *Estudos e Pesquisas*, 20. Available (checked 7 October 2020) at: https://www.dieese.org.br/balancodasgreves/2005/estpesq20 _greves2005.html.

Dieese (2007). Balanço de greves em 2007. *Estudos e Pesquisas*, no number. Available (checked 7 October 2020) at: http://www.dieese.org.br/esp/estPesq41Greves2 007.pdf.

Dieese (2009a). Balanço das Negociações dos Reajustes Salariais em 2008. *Estudos e Pesquisas* 43. Available (checked 7 October 2020) at: http://www.dieese.org.br/ 2009/estPesq43balanconegociacao2008.pdf.

Dieese (2009b). Balanço das Greves em 2008. *Estudos e Pesquisas* 45. Available at (checked 7 October 2020) at: <http://www.dieese.org.br/balancodasgreves/2008/ estPesq45balancoGreves2008.pdf.

Dieese (2010). Política de Valorização do Salário Mínimo. *Nota Técnica* 86. Available (checked 5 October 2021) at: https://www.google.com/url?sa=t&rct=j&q=&esrc= s&source=web&cd=&ved=2ahUKEwigr7n4tbTzAhXuqZUCHTomD1kQFnoECAI QAQ&url=https%3A%2F%2Fwww.dieese.org.br%2Fnotatecnica%2F2010%2Fnot atec86SALARIOMINIMO2010.pdf&usg=AOvVaw33iIYwo3a7p2aaoTXubryk.

Dieese (2012). Balanço das Greves em 2010 e 2011. *Estudos e Pesquisas* 63. Available (checked 7 October 2020) at: http://cspconlutas.org.br/wp-content/uploads/2012/ 11/DIEESE-EST-PESQ-63-bal-greves-2010-2011vf.pdf.

Dieese (2013a). Balanço das Negociações dos Reajustes Salariais em 2012. *Estudos e Pesquisas* 64. Available (checked 7 October 2020) at: http://www.dieese.org.br/bala ncodosreajustes/2012/estPesq64BalNegoc2012.pdf.

Dieese (2013b) Balanço das Greves em 2012. *Estudos e Pesquisas* 66. Available (checked 7 October 2020) at: http://www.dieese.org.br/balancodasgreves/2012/estPesq66ba lancogreves2012.pdf.

Dieese (2013c). Política de Valorização do Salário Mínimo. Available (checked 7 October 2020) at: http://www.dieese.org.br/notatecnica/2012/notaTec118salari oMinimo2013.pdf.

Fiesp, CUT; Força Sindical (2011). *Seminário – Brasil do Diálogo, da Produção e do Emprego*. CUT's website. Available (checked October 7 2020) at: https://sp.cut.org .br/noticias/seminario-brasil-do-dialogo-da-producao-e-do-emprego-13fe.

Folha de São Paulo (2004a). Lucro dos Bancos Cresce 52% no 10 Trimestre. June 4, B-9.

Folha de São Paulo (2004b) Fundos Rendem 4 Vezes Mais que Produção. June 11, *Caderno Dinheiro*, B-1, B-3 e B-4.

Folha de São Paulo (2004c) Lucros dos Bancos Sobem mais de 1.000%. *Folha de São Paulo*, June 21, B-3.

Folha de São Paulo (2004d) Múltis Usam País como Base Exportadora. October 17, B-1.

Folha de São Paulo (2005). Real Valorizado já Reduz Base Exportadora. May 27, B-1.

Fundação Dom Cabral (2012). Ranking FDC das Transnacionais Brasileiras 2012: Os Benefícios da Internacionalização. Available (checked 17 October 2020) at: https://www.fdc.org.br/en/research/publications/relatorio-de-pesquisa-27458.

Grabois, Ana Paula (2010). Lula e o Agronegócio: Interview with Luís Guilherme Zancaner. *Valor Econômico,* April 5. Available (checked 29 December 2010) at: https://psol5osp.org.br/2010/04/lula-e-o-agronegcio/.

Junot, Érica (2005). Ninguém Pode ser Contra. *Revista da Indústria* 111. São Paulo: Fiesp.

Kassai, Lúcia (2007). O Governo na Contramão. *Revista da Indústria* 130. São Paulo: Fiesp.

MDS (Ministério do Desenvolvimento Social) (2013). Bolsa Família. Available (Checked 5 May 2013) at: http://www.mds.gov.br/bolsafamilia.

MST (2009). Reforma agrária *X* agronegócio. Available (consulted 26 September 2020) at: http://www.mst.org.br/node/6713.

Moreira, Assis (2010). Coutinho Defende Dilma em Encontro de Banqueiros. *Valor Econômico*, June 11, A5.

O Grito da Indústria (2004). *Revista da Indústria* 102. São Paulo: Fiesp.

Report (2005). *Revista da Indústria* 103. São Paulo: Fiesp. 2013/06/1299690-marcelo-ridenti-que-juventude-e-essa.shtml.

Scarso, Aline (2012). E a Reforma Agrária, Presidenta Dilma? *Jornal Brasil de Fato*. Apr 4. Available (checked 26 September 2020) at: http://www.ihu.unisinos.br/noticias/508404-e-a-reforma-agraria-presidenta-dilma.

Skaf, Paulo (2004). Interview. *Revista da Indústria* 101. São Paulo: Fiesp.

Skaf, Paulo (2005). O Tempo Não Espera. Entrevista com Paulo Skaf. *Revista da Indústria* 110. São Paulo: Fiesp.

Soares, Jane. Nada Segura a Indústria (2005). *Revista da Indústria* 110. São Paulo: Fiesp.

Steinbruch, Benjamin (2004). *Revista da Indústria* 101. São Paulo: Fiesp.

Viveiros, Ricardo (2004). Fiesp Resgata Compromisso com o Desenvolvimento. *Revista da Indústria* 101. São Paulo: Fiesp.

Index

Temer, President Michel   xiii, 72, 155, 156,
157, 164, 174, 177, 179, 184, 197, 199

Unemployment reduction   78, 94, 103, 107,
112, 113, 183
Unified Workers' Central (CUT)   15, 35, 58,
59, 78, 100, 101, 108, 110, 111, 113, 115, 183
Union of South American Nations
(Unasur)   102
Union movement recovery   95, 107, 110, 113
United Socialist Workers' Party (PSTU)   46,
100, 101, 166

Vargas, President Getúlio   32, 56, 57, 58, 68,
69, 69n, 71, 72, 73, 74, 75, 79, 81, 161, 180,
181, 182, 183, 185

World Social Forum (WSF)   100
World Trade Organization (WTO)   15, 20, 98,
100, 102, 103

Working class   xix, 5, 15, 25, 26, 53, 58, 59,
62, 66, 69n, 71, 72, 73, 74, 82, 83, 89, 90,
94, 101, 105, 110, 115, 116, 127, 131, 141, 153,
156, 158, 159, 160, 164, 178, 180, 181, 183,
185, 190n
Workers' general union (UGT)   108
Workers' Party (PT)   ix, xi, xii, xiii, xiv, xv,
xvi, xvii, xviii, xix, xx, 15, 22, 30, 39, 40,
43, 46, 57, 59, 62, 64, 74, 75, 76, 77, 77n,
78, 79, 81, 82, 84, 85, 86, 87, 88, 89, 91,
93, 94, 95, 97, 100, 101, 104, 105, 107, 109,
111, 112, 113, 114, 115, 116, 117, 121, 122, 127,
130, 131, 135, 137, 138, 138n, 139 140, 141,
142, 143, 144, 145, 146, 147, 148, 149, 150,
151, 152, 156, 157, 157n, 158, 161, 162, 163,
163n, 164, 166, 167, 169, 170, 170n, 171, 172,
173, 174, 175, 176, 177, 178, 180, 181, 182,
194, 197

CPSIA information can be obtained
at www.ICGtesting.com
Printed in the USA
JSHW052147201222
35253JS00003B/5